BRIGHT SKIES AND DARK SHADOWS

REV. HENRY M. FIELD

BRIGHT SKIES AND DARK SHADOWS

By HENRY M. FIELD

𝔚ith 𝔐aps

 BOOKS FOR LIBRARIES PRESS
FREEPORT, NEW YORK

First Published 1890
Reprinted 1970

STANDARD BOOK NUMBER:
8369-5280-4

LIBRARY OF CONGRESS CATALOG CARD NUMBER:
77-114876

PRINTED IN THE UNITED STATES OF AMERICA

To Henry M. Flagler,

WHOSE INVITATION, COMING AT A MOMENT OF ILLNESS,
TOOK ME AWAY TO A PARADISE OF REST,
AND GAVE ME STRENGTH TO BEGIN THIS BOOK,
I NOW RETURN IT COMPLETE
IN ACKNOWLEDGMENT OF HIS GREAT KINDNESS,
AND IN TOKEN OF A FRIENDSHIP
THAT IS VERY DEAR TO ME.

PREFACE.

Migration to the South at the approach of Winter, has become almost as regular as the migration of birds. A journey that is so familiar needs little in the way of description; and if I linger here and there, or turn to some out-of-the-way place like Jupiter Inlet, it is not to magnify slight accessories, but to prepare a larger canvas for a principal figure, as these tropical surroundings furnish a background, the more effective by contrast, for the dark subject of my story. It is under these "bright skies" that the "shadows" creep on the scene. Out of the palms and the orange groves starts up a spectre, the ghost of something gone, that, though dead and buried, sleeps in an unquiet grave, and comes forth at midnight to haunt us in our dreams. The Race Problem is the gravest that ever touched a nation's life. The subject at once fascinates and repels by its tremendous import, its difficulty and its danger. I have been so oppressed by it that I could not keep from speaking, even if it were only to ask questions. That is the way to get light, by groping after it. Confession of ignorance is the first step towards knowledge. To one in perplexity of mind on a difficult question, it is a help to talk it over in a friendly way: to exchange suggestions with those who give as well as receive. Ideas which were extremely vague, crystallize in expression, and are useful if only to draw forth something better from others. With this frank statement, I give my thoughts for what they are worth, but do not

PREFACE.

assume for one moment to set myself up as an authority. I boast no superior wisdom : I only claim to have a few grains of common-sense, an earnest desire for the good of both races, and a boundless charity.

After this grave discussion of a question that has been the brooding mother of all our woes, last and greatest of which was the late civil war, it is not a violent transition to a stirring event in the war itself, the Battle of Franklin. As I went over the field with those who had a part in the scenes of that terrible day, I have tried to tell the story in a way to be just alike to friend and foe. Then, by way of contrast and relief, we turn to a quiet old mansion on the banks of the Cumberland, where one of our earlier heroes, Andrew Jackson, lived and died.

Returning home across the mountains, it came in my way to visit the graves of Lee and Stonewall Jackson, in writing of whom I have not sought to revive recollections that could stir up bitterness, but to contribute at once to the truth of history and to the cause of peace. These very sketches serve to show us "how near and yet how far" is the great drama in which these distinguished actors bore a part—so near as to be remembered vividly by the living generation, and yet so far as to have removed all irritation, so that we can write of these recent events with the calm, judicial temper of posterity. Can we make a better use of history than to learn from it this double lesson : to honor all the heroic dead, and to think kindly and generously of the living?

MARCH, 1890.

CONTENTS.

I. SENT AWAY. THE CONSOLATIONS OF EXILE............. 9
II. OVER THE MOUNTAINS: ASHEVILLE AND KNOXVILLE. A REMINISCENCE OF THE WAR 16
III. FROM CHATTANOOGA TO ATLANTA. ALONG THE TRACK OF SHERMAN'S MARCH................................ 27
IV. FLORIDA. ST. AUGUSTINE AND THE PONCE DE LEON... 36
V. SOUTH FLORIDA. WHERE THE PALMS WHISPER TO THE PINES. JUPITER INLET. ROBINSON CRUSOE LIFE ... 53
VI. NEW ENGLAND IN THE SOUTH. THE OLD HOME AND THE NEW HOME 76
VII. NORTHERN FLORIDA...... 89
VIII. "MARCHING THROUGH GEORGIA"........................ 97
IX. THE BLACK BELT AND THE RACE PROBLEM.............107
X. A NEW DEPARTURE. THE NEGRO VOTE................ 118
XI. CAPACITY OF THE NEGRO. HIS POSITION IN THE NORTH. THE COLOR LINE IN NEW ENGLAND....................131
XII. THE EXPATRIATION OF A WHOLE RACE 154
XIII. LOOKING FORWARD......................................165
XIV. OLD MASTERS CARING FOR THEIR OLD SLAVES.........179
XV. A CAMP-MEETING IN THE WOODS, WITH A FEW WORDS TO MY COLORED BRETHREN... 190
XVI. A STORY OF THE WAR: THE BATTLE OF FRANKLIN....209
XVII. THE HERMITAGE: THE HOME AND BURIAL-PLACE OF ANDREW JACKSON......................................257
XVIII. STONEWALL JACKSON AND THE VALLEY CAMPAIGN.....273
XIX. THE LAST DAYS OF GENERAL LEE..................... 295

BRIGHT SKIES AND DARK SHADOWS.

CHAPTER I.

SENT AWAY—THE CONSOLATIONS OF EXILE.

"Go! go! go!" said the doctor. "The sooner, the better!" This was sending me into exile at a moment's notice. I did not like it. There is no place like home, and though it may not be quite orthodox, I have always been of the opinion that the angel of the household was as good as an angel with wings. But the doctor was peremptory. He did not give advice, but command, and in such a case there is nothing to do but to obey. It would have lightened the matter a little if I could have had so much as a pleasant day to depart; but it was raining heavily as I crossed the Hudson, and one's spirits are apt to sink with the barometer. In such a mood, a ferry-boat is not the place of retirement that one would choose to indulge his sombre reflections; and the station at Jersey City, dark as a half-lighted tunnel, seemed almost like a cavern leading to the shades below. But even in the shades one may recognize some familiar faces, and as I stepped into the drawing-room car, whom should I see in the opposite seat but an old friend who had just been elected Vice-President of the United States! It is more than thirty years since I first knew Levi P. Morton: we recalled the very time and place at which our acquaintance began. He was then living in Fourteenth street, in a house twelve and a half feet wide ; but small as it was, it was full of brightness, and he was then the same gentle-spoken, quiet-mannered, and even-tempered man that he has been ever since, with a natural courtesy that makes all men his friends, and none his enemies. It is with a personal gratification that I see this true American gentleman elevated to the second position in the government of his country, and that he has at his side one who will do as much to grace the social life of Washington as any of her predecessors.

Pleasant company makes time pass quickly, and it was not long before the train rolled into the station at Philadelphia. The rain was still pouring, but there were bright lights and welcoming faces, and we were soon carried-off, willing captives, to taste the hospitality of the Quaker City.

When I am banished from feverish New York, I betake me to restful Philadelphia, the very sight of which, with its rectangular streets and slow-moving people, subdues me to a feeling of quietness and peace. If I were a doctor, and had a patient who was suffering from insomnia, I would prescribe for him a change to Philadelphia. It is a perfect anodyne. At once the heart beats more slowly, the pulse becomes more measured and regular, and the tired brain finds the welcome rest that brings life back again, and the weary pilgrim starts on his journey anew, with fresh courage and hope.

A Sunday in Philadelphia is next to walking the golden streets. The great city rests from its six days of labor. Men gather their families about them, and walk to the house of God in company. Angels are abroad, and we can almost hear the soft stirring of their wings.

In this city of churches I feel very much at home. If one is looking about for a sight that is at once unique and

A FAMOUS SUNDAY-SCHOOL.

inspiring, he may find it in the famous Bethany Sunday-school, the largest in America, founded by Mr. John Wanamaker, whose partner, Mr. Robert C. Ogden, not to be outdone in good works, has set up another, not in opposition, but in imitation. Mr. Wanamaker, at the head of his Bible-class, which includes many hundreds of mature age, who are still eager in their study of the Holy Book, is in his element. He loves to teach and to preach the Gospel, and he does a good deal in the way of practising it, too. When I saw him the next day in his place of business, which is such a centre of activity as would keep most men's heads in a whirl, he was as calm as a Summer's morning—not troubled in mind by the attacks upon him because of the part he took in the late election, nor carried off his feet by any political ambition. Indeed I believe he would rather be at the head of his Sunday-school than in the Cabinet of President Harrison, though he might be *both*. The fact that he has wrought so faithfully in the one, certainly does not unfit him for the other. I envy him, not for his wealth or worldly success, nor any political distinction which he may attain, but for the good that he has done among those for whom the rich generally care but little; so that at the last, when he comes into the heavenly kingdom, he will not come alone, but will have a great multitude of children, and of the poor and the lowly, to keep him company.

But Philadelphia is setting New York an example in other things than Sunday-schools, the last and greatest of which is a Tabernacle for Working-men, an immense structure, in which there is not only a church for religious services, but reception-rooms, a hall for popular lectures, and an infirmary for the treatment of diseases of the eye and ear, the throat and lungs—a treatment which, as it requires the skill of specialists, is on that account so costly as to be beyond the reach of working men, but which is here provided without cost. This part of the general plan has been in operation for two years, in which time, even with the limited accommodation, it has furnished relief to over seven thousand patients.

The planting of such a structure right against the walls of the sanctuary, with doors opening from one into the other, is a combination of the religious with the humane, which carries out the spirit of Him who went about doing good to the bodies as well as the souls of men. The church itself is so arranged as to invite the working classes. Instead of being patterned after the stiff and stately style of architecture, in which elaborate carving and florid decoration, and the general air of costliness, serve as a warning to all who may be "in vile raiment" to keep away, this "Beacon Church" is constructed for a popular assembly, its seats being ranged in the form of an amphitheatre, with great galleries into which crowds can pour, and in which a working-man would not hesitate to take his seat in his work-day clothes, if he had no other, with his wife and children, to hear anybody who has the art of speaking so as to touch his heart. And yet there is nothing about it cheap and mean-looking; on the contrary, it is quite grand from its size and massiveness. In short, it is a church good enough for the best, and not too good for the humblest, to which therefore both extremes of society may gravitate by a common impulse, so that "the rich and the poor may sit together, and feel that God is the Maker of them all."

But the design of course was chiefly for the workingmen, as is indicated by the location, in a distant part of Philadelphia—perhaps four miles from Chestnut street. It took us nearly an hour to drive there. But for all that, it is not beyond the reach of a dense population, as it is in the midst of large manufactories, that employ thousands of working-men and working-women, for whom this is intended to be a rallying centre, and a fountain of all good influences.

The carrying out of this grand idea is due to the unwearied labors of Dr. Francis L. Robbins, who has given his whole heart to it for several years, and who must have felt rewarded as he saw the great demonstration of Sunday evening. The church, which will hold three thousand people, was not only filled, but blockaded — floor and galleries and aisles, and every passage-way to the outer doors. On the platform sat Mr. Morton, who is the uncle of Mrs. Robbins, and who had come on from New York especially to be at this service; and beside him, Mr. Drexel and Mr. George W. Childs, Mr. Wanamaker, and others who are well known as men who put their hands to every good work. I have rarely looked in the face a more inspiring audience, and the tone of all the speeches was one of hope and congratulation. All felt that this was a step in the right direction; that it tended to solve the problem of reaching the masses with the Gospel; that it bridged the chasm between the rich and the poor, bringing them nearer together, and both under the influence of that Religion which is the only solid foundation of social harmony and national prosperity.

After the Sabbath was past, I lingered awhile in this goodly city to inhale the air of a place that is always restful to me. There are no ups and downs to cause unwary feet to stumble: all is plain and straight before my face. The city lieth four square, like the heavenly Jerusalem, and its surface is plain and smooth, as all the ways of life ought to be; and the streets run at right angles, and are so carefully named and numbered that "the wayfaring man need not err therein." There is a quaint harmony in the domestic architecture, there being some hundreds of thousands, more or less, of houses, all with the same brick fronts, the same doors and windows, and the same white doorsteps, the daily washing of which is the badge of respectability, if it be not indeed "the outward and visible sign of an inward and spiritual grace." It is a moral lesson to watch the people in the streets, who do not rush about with undue precipitation, but walk with measured steps, in which there is a kind of slow rhythm, that insensibly subdues the stranger to the same dignity and repose. All these things work in me a calm and equable frame of mind ; and when I have been up to the Presbyterian House, and talked with "all the holy brethren," and been assured that every department of our ecclesiastical machinery is in perfect order ; and to the editorial rooms of "The Presbyterian" and "The Journal," and meekly inquired as to the prospects of union between the Churches North and South, and have them both (though their views are exactly opposite) tell me confidentially that "it is all coming out right," I am greatly relieved in mind. Then I need only to ride down town, and look into the untroubled face of that model gentleman, George W. Childs ; and to sit with Mr. Drexel in his banking house—a man who is as simple as if he were not a king in the world of finance— and hear him speak hopefully of the prospects of the business world ; to be quite relieved of any fears for the country, under whatever administration it may be. It is thus that Philadelphia quiets my nerves and cools my blood, and leads me to think that the world is not going to the bad, after all. God bless the dear old city of Franklin and of William Penn, whose spirit of peace and of brotherhood abides upon her still—a city rich in its commerce and its accumulated wealth, but richer still in its noble men and women!

WASHINGTON AS A PLACE OF EXILE. 15

Washington is another city of refuge for me, when I am ordered away from home in search of a milder climate. There, hard by the Capitol, is a wide, roomy house, in which everything is, like its possessor, large and generous, with a great library, which is the very paradise of a scholar. Here the sunshine pours in all day long, and the weary pilgrim can enjoy the " sunshine cure," for there is sunshine without and within. The master of this hospitable mansion, when in college, bore the proud title of *Magnus Ager*, to distinguish him from a smaller edition of the same stock, who, being the very least, or littlest, of the tribe of Judah, had the diminutive appellation of *Parvus Ager*. These college names indicated the relations which existed between the two, and which continue still, for never am I " in any trouble of mind, body or estate," that I do not turn to him who is " older and wiser " ; and to this day, when I find myself in the arms of this big-brained, big-breasted, big-hearted brother, I feel that I am about as near "the realm where love abides " as I expect to be till I pass over the river.

The afternoon that I arrived the large house had been the scene of a reception at which there had been a brilliant array of Washington society, in which Mr. Blaine, who attracted all eyes, divided attention with the Chinese Ambassador. For all this I came too late, for which I was not sorry, as nothing fatigues me so much as a crowd, and there were over four hundred guests. So I was content to hear all about it, and to receive the report as one listening to the faint murmur of the outer world, when it is so soft and gentle as not to disturb the peace and happiness within. These are the consolations of exile. And so I find that to be banished is not a cruel punishment, if one may choose his place of exile, in which case I should certainly choose Washington.

CHAPTER II.

OVER THE MOUNTAINS—ASHEVILLE AND KNOXVILLE—
A REMINISCENCE OF THE WAR.

"On to Richmond" was the cry in the early days of the war: but it took our armies four years to make the distance which I now made in four hours. As I passed through it, I caught sight of a familiar face, that of the Hon. J. L. M. Curry, who had showed me so much kindness in Madrid, and now came to speed me on my way, only exacting a promise that I should pay him a visit on my return. With such friendly benedictions we glided away towards the going down of the sun, for though I had been ordered to the South, it was with full liberty as to the route I should take, so that I could "meander" hither and thither, towards the mountains or the sea.

From Richmond the direct route to Florida is by the Atlantic Coast line, passing through Charleston and Savannah, by which one who takes the Vestibule Train in New York, can be transported, with the greatest possible comfort, to Jacksonville, in thirty hours, and in two hours more to St. Augustine. But I was in no such pressing haste. My orders were only to keep moving southward, getting all the while into a milder climate. With this liberty, I followed my usual bent in turning aside, as the fancy took me, to places of interest, to reach my destination at last, though in a roundabout way. On the western border of Virginia is a chain of mountains, full of wild and beautiful scenery, to see which, instead of going directly South, I turned to the Southwest, and the next morning found myself at Asheville, in North Carolina, a place which has of late become one of the most famous resorts in the country. Its attractions are those of scenery and climate. It lies in the lap of mountains, being itself at an elevation of more than two thousand feet above the level of the sea. The air that sweeps through these pine forests is pure and bracing, while even the hill-tops are protected by ranges of mountains from the storms of the North. If a blizzard from Dakota, having lost its way, comes thundering down upon the Alleghanies, it is caught by these snowy peaks, some of which are six or seven thousand feet high, and tossed into the upper sky, while the air is kept untroubled below. To this position is due the remarkable evenness of temperature. Surrounded and protected by these guardian mountains, Asheville knows nothing of the extremes of climate. It is never very hot, nor very cold. For this reason it is a resort all the year round, in the Winter being taken possession of by Northerners, who at this moment throng the corridors of the Battery Park Hotel (one of the best hotels in all the South), but who at the approach of Summer return to their own beautiful country seats on the Hudson, or in New England, while their places here are filled by Southerners, who find this Hill Country a welcome retreat from the lowlands of the Carolinas or the Gulf States.

The region so healthful is equally remarkable for beauty, as one can see even from the hotel, which stands on a hilltop, with the ground sloping from it on every side, so that from my window I look down into a deep gorge that is shut in by the Eastern hills, over which comes the first gleam of the morning sun; and walking round the wide verandas, I can be in the sunshine all day long, from sunrise to sunset.

But for all this I should not have known how very beautiful the country was, and should have gone away with eyes but half opened, if a gentleman who lives in Asheville, and is a large landed proprietor, had not taken me to points of view which a stranger might not discover. This was Mr. Pierson, a brother-in-law of Dr. Curry, to whom the latter had entrusted me as his friend, and who therefore took me in charge as if I were an old acquaintance. Driving me out of town two or three miles, he led the way to a hill on which he is building a house for himself, a point of view from which the eye takes in a circuit of fifty miles, within which is included every variety of landscape. How many peaks there are on the horizon, I will not pretend to say. On the west are the Smoky Mountains of Tennessee, which figure so much in the stories of Charles Egbert Craddock, while northward and southward are the mountains of Virginia and the Carolinas. Nor is that other element of beauty in a landscape, water, wanting. At the very foot of the hill flows the "French Broad," a river worthy of its name, which in its volume and swiftness reminds one of the most famous river of Europe, as it "nobly foams and flows" with a majesty almost like that of the Rhine.

But this is not the only beautiful place near Asheville. On the other side of the town is another more finished, which by a curious coincidence belongs to another brother-in-law of Dr. Curry, Col. Connelly, a brave Confederate officer, who lost an arm at Gettysbury, but who "bates not a jot of heart or hope," and divides his time, with almost equal enthusiasm, between the care of his estate and the study of the Bible. The latter amounts to a holy passion with him. I found him with his dictionaries and reference books wide open on his table, and he told me that he devoted to this study six hours a day! From his library he has but to step out upon a broad balcony, to look round upon a scene as fair to the eye as that which Moses saw from the top of Pisgah. Indeed he has the advantage of Moses, in that he has already entered into his Promised Land, while Moses could only see *his* from a distance. Men who are devout lovers of both nature and the Bible, cannot help illustrating their ideas of one from what they see of the other, and I doubt not the gallant Colonel, as he looks across to the rich meadows on the other side of the river, has visions of " green fields beyond the swelling flood," and as the sun goes down in the west, and every mountain peak is tipped with fire, he may well think that he catches a glimpse of the heavenly towers and battlements.

In truth, it is an enchanting country, bringing forth in abundance all the fruits of the earth. Why do not the farmers of New England, who find their winters long and bitterly cold, and their soils hard and unproductive, seek new homes here in this milder climate, with this richer soil, instead of going off to the most distant territories? It would be a delightful change. Our good Presbyterians would find themselves at home, for Asheville has its Presbyterian church, with an excellent pastor. Many of them would live longer and make a living easier; for the soil is rich and productive, and they would not be so far away from the homes of their childhood, as if they had emigrated to Idaho or Montana.

When we left Asheville, we kept still westward, down the valley of the French Broad, which opened many a pretty vista as we wound along its banks, till we came to where the hills parted, and in the green intervale between, bubble up the Hot Springs, whose medicinal qualities have made it a great resort, both for invalids and for the fashionable world. Here is a hotel of such dimensions and so well appointed as to suggest that some Eastern capitalists have been putting their money into it; and inquiring, I learned that my old friends, George F. Baker (President of the First National Bank of New York) and Henry C. Fahnestock, whose long arms reach out in many directions, had found this lovely spot, and picked up a trifle of a few thousand acres among the mountains of North Carolina.

Soon after leaving the Hot Springs, we cross the border-line, and are in Tennessee. Like the other States which lie along the great Appalachian chain, it has a broad expanse, stretching from the mountains to the river, with its head lifted into the clouds, while its feet are dipped in the Father of Waters. It is almost an Alpine region through which we enter the State, winding upward till, a little after noon, we halt at Knoxville, the capital of East Tennessee. A long street leads up to the centre of the town, where, in the early settlement, were erected the Court House and other public buildings, as a nucleus for the gathering population. Knoxville is a place which has a history, being one of the first settlements west of the mountains. Of course I could not be in such a historic city even for a few hours without a desire to know all about it; but there was no one to tell me, for as I had not been quite sure of my own route, I had come without introductions. In this extremity, I did what I have sometimes done before—inquired for the nearest Presbyterian minister, and being directed to the parsonage, introduced myself to the pastor of the First Church, the Rev. Dr. Park. I found him a man of stalwart proportions, with a beard which gave him a patriarchal appearance, who, when he had looked me over, and concluded that I was "all right," invited me into his house, and gave me a seat before an open fire which warmed us both, and in the glow of which we soon got acquainted; and he ended by taking a buggy and driving me about the town, by which I learned more of its history in a few hours than I could have learned by myself in a week. Naturally the first object of interest was his own church, which is the mother of all the churches, in whose graveyard sleep many of Tennessee's illustrious dead, among them the Hon. Hugh L. White, once a candidate for the Presidency of the United States. Among the living relics of other days is Mrs. Ramsey, the widow of the historian of Tennessee, to whom I was glad to pay my respects.

And now for a stretch over the hills. Knoxville is a city of hills as much as Rome ever was, though I think there must be more than seven here. As we passed from one hilltop to another, my venerable guide was full of the information for which I was eager. We found that the city was growing on every side. New streets and avenues were being opened, and the sound of the hammer in many quarters told of the multiplication of dwellings to provide for the increase of inhabitants. Few cities in the United States have grown so rapidly in the last decade. "In 1880," said Dr. Park, "the population, according to the census, was 10,500. To-day it is 43,000. Thus within these nine years it has increased fourfold!" And very pleasant it was to see the homes that were provided for the incoming multitude; that, instead of the houses being crowded in blocks, plastered together like so many bricks in a wall, they stood apart, each in its little plot of ground, with a pretty yard in front, and room for flowers and vines, which not only gave a look of beauty as seen from without, but were suggestive of taste and refinement within. All this is a token of the general cultivation which becomes a city enthroned upon the hills. It would seem to be just the place for literary institutions; nor was I surprised to find one of its hills already crowned by the University of Tennessee.

But one thing more remained, and that was a visit to a point of great historical interest in the late war. The people of Tennessee were generally opposed to secession, but when the State Government cast in its lot with the South, many felt that it was the part of patriotism to share its fate. Others left their homes, and making their way across the mountains into Kentucky, joined the Union armies. Thus East Tennessee was between two fires, but no great event occurred till near the close of 1863, when Knoxville had a siege and a defence that were among the most notable in the war. That I might understand it better, Dr. Park drove me to Fort Sanders, on the outskirts of the city, which was the scene of the conflict. Here, as we stood on an angle of the old earthworks, he indicated to me the position of the two armies, till it was all spread out before me as on a map.

To know the momentous importance of what was here to take place, I must recall to my readers the situation at the moment, which was one of the most critical of the war. The year 1863 had seen great events. After the disasters of Fredericksburg and Chancellorsville, had come the invasion of Pennsylvania, that was beaten back by the battle of Gettysburg, a victory which elated the North as much as the previous defeats had depressed it. But now came another tremendous blow at Chickamauga—a battle of which I have always had a very vivid impression from the description given me by General Garfield. Again the country was in great anxiety. Grant was sent to Chattanooga to take command, and fresh troops from the Army of the Potomac were whirled with incredible speed over the mountains, across the Ohio, and down into Tennessee. Meanwhile Bragg held his position in front of Chattanooga, his army stretching for miles along Missionary Ridge. The two armies were in sight of each other ; they could see each other's camp fires, and both were preparing for the inevitable struggle. At this moment Bragg, with what seemed an infatuation, detached Longstreet, his best corps commander, to move to the North, and take Knoxville, which was an important point of communication between the western portion of the Confederacy and Richmond. Perhaps he thought it an easy matter, which could be done in a few days, and that Longstreet could return in time for the great battle that was approaching. But it was not so easy. Knoxville, with the country below it, was held by Burnside, not in great force, but with troops sufficient at least to check and harass the enemy. Grant watched the whole movement with the utmost satisfaction, for it suited his military plans to have this strong force out of his way, and he sent orders to Burnside to oppose Longstreet at every step, so as to delay his progress, and yet to fall back after every engagement, so as *to draw him on*, and as he expressed it, "toll him over the river," and then to hold Knoxville at all hazards.

Never were orders more faithfully carried out. Keeping on the defensive, Burnside pursued the policy of fighting and retreating, till his troops, worn out with marching and battle, dragged themselves over the hills and into Knoxville.

Of all this Dr. Park was himself an eye-witness. He said : "I was then pastor of a church ten miles south of Knoxville, and saw both armies as they marched by. First came the Federals : they passed my door, numbers of the officers were in my house, and spoke freely of the situation, anticipating defeat; and when the next day Longstreet appeared, and began to ask about the roads this side and that side of Knoxville, I said to him, 'You need only to march straight against the city, and send in a flag of truce, with a summons, to receive an immediate surrender!'" This was no doubt good sound Presbyterian doctrine, but perhaps the old soldier thought he was a better judge than even the most orthodox minister. However, the latter maintains to this day, that *if* his advice *had been* followed, the place would have fallen. Certainly it was in imminent peril, and every moment that the attack could be delayed was a gain to Burnside. No sooner had he entered the town, than his troops, though ready to drop with fatigue and cold and hunger, were set to work with spade and shovel; and the people of the place, white and black, were pressed into the service; and all together worked day and night, resting but two hours in the twenty-four; while a force of 700 cavalry, harassing the Confederates, delayed their advance, till their camps were pitched in sight of the town, when the place was in a state of defence that rendered it *possible* to hold it. For ten days the siege went on. Longstreet took it deliberately, perhaps thinking that he had a sure thing; that Burnside was caged where he could not escape, but as time became more pressing he determined to carry the place by assault. This is bloody business, but it is soon over. Dr. Park pointed out just where he planted his batteries, and the slope up which the attack must come. The garrison had cut away the trees so as to have free range for their guns, and strung telegraph-wires from stump to stump to trip the feet of the charging column. Longstreet had given express orders that the assault should be made *with a rush*, for he knew well that no troops could stand for many minutes the withering fire that would be opened upon them. Having thus issued the order of battle, he waited only for daybreak. Just as the sun rose the flag of the Fort soared to the peak, and the band saluted it with the Star Spangled Banner. On the instant from without the walls there rose a wild yell, as the troops that had crept up the slope under cover of a fog rushed to the assault. The same moment the earthworks were crested with flame, and shot and shell tore through the Confederates. Yet on they came, like the waves of the sea, dashed up by the tremendous force behind. Men rushed into the ditch and struggled up the embankment, but the fire was incessant; and to add to the destruction, hand-grenades were thrown by the hundred to explode in the mass below. Still the survivors climbed over the bodies of the fallen, and battle-flags were planted on the parapet, to be instantly torn down. An officer planting his hand on a gun, demanded surrender, and was blown into eternity. Such a fire no human endurance could stand long. In five minutes it was all over. Seven hundred men lay dead or dying in the trench below, and three hundred were taken prisoners. The siege of Knoxville was ended. The city remained in Union hands, but the assault was one in which the glory was divided: for never was greater courage shown in an assault, as never was a besieged place more bravely defended.

And now here were we, two ministers of the Gospel, standing on the top of the old earthworks, and talking it all over. My friend is an intense Southerner (for which I don't blame him), and I thought had a lingering regret that Longstreet had not followed his advice; but still, inasmuch as he is a good Presbyterian and a devout believer in Divine decrees, that "whatsoever is ordained surely cometh to pass," I think he is willing to submit to the decision of the Almighty.

26 A UNION MAN DURING THE WAR.

It was a thrilling story, which had tenfold interest when recalled on the very spot where the events took place, and I was extremely grateful to the best of guides who had brought me here, as well as for all his kindness and courtesy to "a pilgrim and a stranger."

But the hospitality of Knoxville did not end here. As we rode back into town, we met at a great warehouse in the main street a notable citizen, Mr. Perez Dickinson, a New Englander by birth, a native of Amherst, Mass., but who has lived here fifty-nine years, remaining through the war, though he was known as a Union man, and would never take the oath of allegiance to the Confederacy. As his carriage was at the door, he bade me "come up into the chariot," and took me off to his house, and kept me to tea and through the evening, during which, as we sat before the fire, I asked him innumerable questions, and learned more about East Tennessee, its early history, the character of its first settlers (who were in the main of Scotch-Irish descent), and of the late war, including the memorable siege, than I ever knew before, and now consider myself (at least among those who are as ignorant as I *was*) an authority on the subject. At nine o'clock the pastor of the Presbyterian church, which is connected with the Northern Assembly, called and accompanied me to the station, where I took the night train for Chattanooga.

CHAPTER III.

LOOKOUT MOUNTAIN—WAR MEMORIES—ATLANTA.

It was after midnight when we left Knoxville. In turning southward, we passed over the very route by which Longstreet had come up the valley of the Tennessee, to make the assault which I have briefly described; and as I was full of the history, it took such hold of my imagination that I seemed now and then to hear the tramp of armed men, and the rumbling of the artillery wagons as they moved forward to battle. But it was a relief to wake and find that such visions were only in my dreams, and that when I looked out through the curtains of my window, I could not see a single camp-fire, nor hear a sound but that of the wind whispering through the forest. When morning came, we were drawing into Chattanooga, and as a hungry traveller, I was looking round for a breakfast, when I was saluted by a familiar voice—that of Mr. S. A. Cunningham of the Nashville American, to whom I had telegraphed that I was to take this route, and who had come all the way from Nashville to meet me. It was a pleasant surprise, and of course I gave up at once the idea of going on directly to Atlanta, and accepted his suggestion to spend the forenoon upon Lookout Mountain. This is not at all difficult, as a street-car takes you to its foot, from which a railway, rising at a sharp angle, lifts you to the top. This is not the most romantic way of climbing a mountain. When I went over the Alps in my young days, I preferred to go on foot, with alpenstock in hand, and a trusty guide to lead the way, though of late I confess that when I come to the Rhigi, which is a pretty long pull, I am willing to take steam as a substitute for legs. It saves an immense amount of muscle, as it does here, and there is a pleasant sensation in being carried up, as in the chariot of Elijah, and alighting on a mountain peak. The car stops at the extreme end of the ridge, where stands a hotel, planted on a ledge of rock, far above the "sea of pines" that waves below. Here, as you walk round the broad veranda, you look down into forest depths on every side, while you seem to be on a level with the eagles that are soaring into the blue vault of heaven.

At this point you "change carriages," taking another track, which runs along the very crest of the mountain. You are now in the *rear* of Lookout (calling the side toward Chattanooga the front), and as you pass slowly along the edge of the cliff, you take in the exact scene of "the battle above the clouds." My ideas of it had been somewhat vague, and indeed I had heard some would-be critics (who, however, had never smelt gunpowder) intimate with a sneer that this boasted engagement "was not what it was cracked up to be." Far be it from me to argue with such learned authorities; but without pretending to any military knowledge, I must say that my impression of what the battle must have been was greatly increased by what I saw, for the mountain is higher, and the ascent more precipitous. All round the top, it is so escarped by nature as to present a succession of crags, so high and bold as to constitute a natural fortress, easy of defence, which the bravest soldiers would not wish to attack in the face of an enemy. Scanning the position more closely, we could see why Hooker threw his troops round the mountain, and took it in the rear, for here are points more accessible, and the ascent was through a forest which was itself some protection. As the advance had to be made through thick woods, it could not be in close formation, where a well-aimed shot, tearing through a solid column, would strike down numbers. The companies and regiments had to be broken up as in a skirmish line, by which they were less exposed, and were partly screened by rocks and trees. Then, too, as they came under the cliffs, their very steepness was an advantage, for the guns above could not be depressed low enough to do execution. For this reason the mountain batteries were almost useless, and the combat was chiefly with musketry, men fighting hand to hand. All these concessions we make willingly, and yet, when all is said and done, it was a daring attempt to storm that mountain height, and the literal truth of history can take nothing from the glory of "the battle above the clouds."

Alighting from the car, we walked perhaps a mile across the plateau of the mountain. I was surprised at its extent. It is covered by a grove, under the shade of which a large body of troops might pitch their tents. As we come to the other side, we are again on the brow of a cliff, from which we take in the whole wide valley below. Yonder is Chattanooga, round which, as a centre, was encamped the army of Grant, stretching northward as far as the eye could reach, while the army of Bragg lay in full sight of it, and hardly out of cannon range. My friend, *who was in the battle*, was able to point out the positions of the two armies, and as he spoke of the movements of that terrible day, it seemed as if the roar of the guns was still in his ears. Of the battle itself the story has been told so often, and by the best of all witnesses, the Commanders on both sides, that it does not need to be repeated here. It was one of the great events of American history, which I can understand far better now from the hours spent that day on Lookout Mountain.

When on that mountain top, we were in the very centre of a theatre of great events. Only a few miles distant is the field of Chickamauga, where the battle was fought in September, 1863, two months before that at Chattanooga, which followed in November. A few months since there was a gathering of old soldiers at Chickamauga, in which Federals and Confederates united, (with Gen. Rosecrans, the leader of the Union Army, on one side, and Gen. John B. Gordon on the other,) at which it was proposed that this historic field be set apart by the Government, as Gettysburg had been, to be kept forever sacred as the scene of a martial prowess such as has rarely been recorded in the annals of war. If the best proof of courage be the number of losses in proportion to the number of combatants, few battles of modern times can be compared with Chickamauga. The late Franco-German War is often quoted as having furnished an exhibition, not only of strategic skill unequalled since the time of Napoleon, but of an impetuous valor that took no account of human life. Of this the most signal display was at Mars la Tour, where, a movement of the French army impending for which the German army was not prepared, in order to gain a few hours, a picked corps of cavalry was ordered to dash itself against the ranks of the enemy. Officers, who saw that such an attack meant the destruction of those who made it, protested against the sacrifice; but the imperturbable Moltke calmly replied, "It is not a question of men: it is a question of necessity!" As the order to charge was an order to die, the regiments drew lots to determine which should die first, and then one after the other rode madly against the foe. It was Balaklava over again, only on a larger scale. When the remnants of the squadrons that had passed through the fire, came back again, one-half of that splendid corps was left upon the plain! But a recent report, made upon exact returns obtained from the War Department, shows that many *regiments* in our war lost in a single battle more than half of the men who went into it! Much as we deplore the fact that this was in a civil war, we should not be worthy of the name of Americans if we could forget such splendid courage.

The battle of Chattanooga virtually ended the campaign of 1863. Bragg withdrew his army forty miles farther south to Dalton, where the narrow valley broadens into a space sufficient for a large camping-ground. He was soon relieved by General Johnston, who spent the Winter in repairing the losses of the last campaign, and preparing for the next. It came in the Spring with the advance of General Sherman, and for two months there was a battle, large or small, almost every day. The line of march was along the Western and Atlantic Railroad, without which indeed it is doubtful if the campaign could have been made at all : for the mere provisioning of the army required a hundred and forty-five car-loads a day!

As I passed over this road, of course I was in the route of the great "Mountain Campaign," and every few minutes the conductor called my attention to some historic spot. Here was Resaca, at which General Harrison, then in command of an Indiana regiment, is said to have distinguished himself. And yonder by the track stood an old frame building, weather-beaten and ugly, but which took on a strange interest as I heard that this was the veritable "Big Shanty," which gave name to a battle. It has a gaunt and spectral appearance ; but it once shook with the roar of artillery that thundered through the valley, and its floors were covered with wounded and dying men.

But the most picturesque scene of battle was Kenesaw Mountain, a noble height, which, overlooking the country round for many miles, formed a sort of Gibraltar for the Confederate Army, by which it was occupied as the centre of its position, with batteries on its very summit and along its sides, while the right and left wings of the army reached out for miles on either side. To carry such a position required both generalship and courage of the highest order. Every point was defended with the utmost obstinacy, while the assailants charged in front and on the flank day by day, meeting with terrible losses, but continually bringing up new forces, and pushing forward with irresistible power. When at last Johnston was obliged to fall back, the mountain was immediately occupied by the Union troops, but with no such advantage as before, as the Confederates did not propose to attack it. It answered the purpose, however, of a point of observation, and it was from its summit that, later in the campaign, was signalled the message to a post in the rear that had been suddenly attacked by the enemy, "Hold the fort, for I am coming," which furnished the motto for the famous hymn—a result quite unexpected by the grim old soldier who sent it. He is said not to be always quite "devotional" in his habits of thought or modes of speech, and must have been surprised that his message from the top of Kenesaw Mountain should be caught up as a battle-cry to be used in spiritual conflicts, and to be heralded far and wide, over land and sea.

But it is hardly possible to count all the fields of battle and of death that lie between Chattanooga and Atlanta. Every valley and every mountain side is hallowed by soldiers' graves, which lie thicker as we get farther South. Of the terrible combats that raged round Atlanta, I saw a sad memorial the next day, as I drove out two or three miles to a solitary place in the woods, where a heavy cannon, set upright, stands as a monument to the gallant General McPherson on the very spot where he fell.

It was a little after dark when we rolled into the station, and found shelter in that spacious *caravanserai*, the Kimball House, where with bath and bed the fatigues of travel were soon forgotten.

Atlanta is a place in which I feel very much at home. Not that I have been here often, only two or three times; but we have a representative of Atlanta in Stockbridge, in the person of Mr. John H. Inman, who has his Summer home on our hill-top. There I have become acquainted with his relatives, who came to visit him, so that when I come here, they receive me almost as one of the family— a relation in which I am very glad to be recognized. This cordial welcome, with perhaps something in this Southern climate, soon warms even my cold Northern blood.

Atlanta has another attraction for me in Henry W. Grady, whom I place alongside of another Summer neighbor of mine in the Berkshire Hills, Joseph H. Choate, as two of the most delightful men that ever charmed an audience, moving them at will to laughter or to tears. Mr. Grady is not a man you would make a hero of at first sight. He has not the tall figure of Mr. Choate (he is short and thick-set), nor the keen eye that looks through and through an ugly witness, and by a kind of fascination draws the truth out of him in spite of himself. I found him in his *den* (for being an editor myself, I know what dens they inhabit) amid piles of newspaper rubbish, which have such an ancient look that they might be mummy cloths unwrapped from the bodies of Egyptians that have been dead thousands of years. He was sitting in one of those convenient office chairs, which are mounted on springs, so that the sitter can turn in any direction (for an editor has sometimes to shift his position very quickly), leaning back, with his feet on the table in front, and hugging to his breast a pad on which he was writing a letter. Thus doubled up, he dashes off letters or newspaper articles right and left. The versatility of the man amazes me; no amount of work disconcerts him; he sees everybody, talks with chance visitors, while he keeps on writing; and then can jump up at a minute's notice, and go to any sort of gathering, and make a speech on any subject! He has in him the elements of a successful politician: for he is as nimble as a cat, and like a cat, always falls on his feet. I do believe, if you should toss him into the air or throw him out of the fourth-story window, he would light on the ground all right, and be ready to start off on the instant to speak at any public gathering, political or religious, whether it were to address a camp-meeting, or make a rousing speech at a Democratic Convention.

Though he has been for some years known at the South, he was little known at the North until two years ago, when he appeared at the New England dinner in New York. I was at that time abroad; but one day in Palermo, in Sicily, a lady just from Naples handed me an American paper which contained his speech, and I read it, not once but many times, and each time with a new appreciation of its wonderful pathos and power. That speech made his reputation at the North. When I came home I got the pamphlet that contained the proceedings of the New England Society, in which it was reported in full, and it is often read in my family, though I confess to a little spite against it, for there is a person whom I cannot bear to see shed a tear, who, when she tries to read it, always finds something in her throat.

Busy as he was, Mr. Grady must needs have me to dinner, and, to tell the truth, "Barkis was willin'," for, like Mr. Choate, he is nowhere so delightful as in his own home, where all preoccupation is gone, and he can give himself up to his friends. Here his wit and humor are infinite. Few men can tell a story so well. To hear him give the outlines of a recent work of fiction, as he did of "The Two Little Confederates," was next to reading the story. Out of respect to my clerical character, he invited three of the city pastors to meet me, a Presbyterian, a Methodist, and a Baptist, of whom I can only say that, if they are fair representatives of their respective denominations, the pulpit of Atlanta will rank with the pulpit of New York.

[The above was written some months ago—in May, 1889—and now as these pages are going to press, it is with inexpressible pain that I have to add, that he who was the life of that happy home, the centre of all that brightness, has gone to the grave. Mr. Grady was of a compact frame, capable of any amount of labor and endurance. Subject to no disease, he had the promise of a long life, with ever growing influence and power. But late in the Autumn he took a cold, which, though severe, would have yielded to treatment, if he could have remained under his own roof. But he was continually pressed to go away, to speak on public occasions. Yielding to this importunity, he had accepted an invitation to address the Merchants Club of Boston, for which he had prepared himself, and as the time approached, though unfit to leave home, he could not bear to disappoint his friends. He went and made a speech on the Race Problem, which was considered by those who heard both, as even more able, if not more eloquent, than that at the New England dinner. But it was at his peril that he came out of that crowded and heated room into the wintry air. The exposure was increased by an excursion to Plymouth Rock: so that he returned to New York, not better but worse. But still those about him were not alarmed: and as he was with a party of friends, he yielded to his urgent desire to return home. At Atlanta a crowd was waiting for him to cheer him for his success at the North, but he was too weak to receive their congratulations, and was driven directly to his home, where all that medical skill could do, with the fondest love and care, was done for him, but without avail, and on the 23d of December, in the early morning, his brave heart ceased to beat. So passed away, at the age of thirty-eight years, in the very prime of life, the most brilliant young man of the South. One of the last things he said, was, "If I die, I die serving the South, the land I love so well. My father died fighting for it: I am proud to die speaking for it," words that might well be graven on his tomb.]

CHAPTER IV.

FLORIDA—ST. AUGUSTINE—THE PONCE DE LEON.

It was a long night-ride from Atlanta across Georgia. The State is imperial in extent, and like a good many other grand things, if you have too much of it, becomes a trifle wearisome. "Jordan is a hard road to travel," and in this respect, if in no other, Georgia is like Jordan, as indeed any other State would be, if you had to travel over it in the dark, seeing nothing, and with every bone in your body in pain from fatigue. I do not find much poetry in travelling at night, though sometimes, as I listen to the incessant rolling in the long dark watches, I try to comfort myself with the inspiring negro melody, "Roll, Jordan, roll!" and to imagine that these ever-rolling wheels and fire-drawn cars are the mighty chariots of civilization. But all this poetry and philosophy I would give for a good sound sleep. The real necessity for these night-journeyings is that the days are not long enough, the distances are so great. Thus it was Georgia when we went to bed, and when we rose it was Georgia still, and it was full noon before we crossed the border into Florida.

At last we are in the Peninsula State, and stop at Jacksonville, which but a few months ago was desolated by the yellow fever. But of this not a trace remains, either of the fever or the panic it inspired. It was hard to realize, as we walked along the quiet streets, that this was the place from which, even so late as the Autumn, the inhabitants were fleeing in terror. Now every precaution has been taken against its recurrence, and there is once more a feeling of perfect security; and the broad and beautiful river that sweeps past the town does not flow more tranquilly than the lives of the easy-going population.

A couple of hours more brought us to St. Augustine. It was dark when we arrived, but a few minutes took us from the station into such a centre of stately halls and blazing lights and music and gay society, that we might have been in the very heart of Paris.

St. Augustine is the oldest town in the United States, having been settled by the Spaniards in 1565, forty-two years before Captain John Smith landed at Jamestown, fifty-five years before the Pilgrims set foot on Plymouth Rock, and only seventy-three years after Columbus first saw the shores of the New World! Hardily was it settled before it was fortified, for even in those early days enemies were abroad. The story of the riches of Mexico and Peru had filled all Europe, and the ships that bore the treasure to Spain tempted the sea-rovers of all nations, and the Buccaneers—another name for pirates—kept watch along this coast for the gold that was being carried across the sea to fill the treasuries of the successors of Ferdinand and Isabella. This kind of robbery, pleasantly disguised under the name of war, was continued for the better part of a century, and even distinguished English navigators did not disdain to enrich themselves with the treasure of Spanish galleons. Sir Francis Drake, sailing up the coast, and descrying across the low sandy shore some sign of human habitation, landed here and burnt the town. This disaster compelled the Spaniards to still greater efforts for protection, and in place of the old stockade rose a formidable Fort, which remains to this day, the best specimen this side the Atlantic of the style of fortification common in Europe in the Middle Ages. It covers perhaps an acre of ground, with walls of stone twelve feet thick, intended to mount a hundred guns, with projecting bastions, and round towers at each corner of the quadrangle, from which sentinels kept watch over land and sea, the whole surrounded by a moat, that could be filled with water. Connected with this was a canal extending across the peninsula, so that entrance to the city could only be through massive gates, that were strongly guarded. The Fort, when fully garrisoned, would hold a thousand men. Thus St. Augustine was secure against any attack that was likely to be made upon it.

Of course these defences would not be of much use in our day. A ship of war, or even a gunboat, carrying the heavy modern ordnance, would knock the old Fort to pieces in half an hour. No attempt is made to keep it in condition. The guns are not even mounted, but lying on the grass, or in the moat, with pyramids of balls beside them.

The interest of the old Fort therefore is not as a fortification, but as a relic of the past. As such, it has indeed a strange and curious interest, mingled with suggestions of the barbaric warfare of those old times. For here are not only embrasures for guns and casemates, but dungeons dark as the tomb, in which prisoners were confined. Even the chapel has a melancholy suggestion in the side rooms, where the condemned sat to listen to mass before they were led to execution. In one of the dark underground rooms two skeletons were found suspended to the wall, where perhaps the living had been hung in chains till they

A SPANISH MASSACRE. 39

should expire. Outside the Fort, in the moat, is a projecting wall riddled with balls, which, before being buried in the stone, had passed through the quivering bodies of the condemned who were "stood up" against this wall to receive the fatal shot.

These surroundings affected me as did the old quarters of the Inquisition in Seville. Of course those who perished here may have been murderers and deserved their fate. But they may have been helpless Indians, or merely Huguenot emigrants who landed on this inhospitable coast. There is nothing in the history of Spanish persecutions or massacres on the other side of the ocean, more cold-blooded and cruel than the massacre of some hundreds of French Huguenots, who, fleeing from persecution at home, sought a refuge in Florida. Shipwrecked a few miles south of St. Augustine, they were overpowered by the garrison, and were deliberately led out and butchered, their captors telling them, with the exultation of fiends, that it was not because they were Frenchmen, but because they were heretics! That was the freedom to worship God which the exiles found on the shores of the New World! It was a terrible crime, and brought a terrible retribution: for years after, a Frenchman, filled with indignation at the horrible atrocity, fitted out an expedition, which safely crossed the sea, and landed a few miles above St. Augustine; and coming suddenly upon a detached post, captured the garrison, who were made to pay for the cruelties of their leaders a few years before. The sentence was deliberate, and they understood it well. As they were marched to execution, it was announced to them that they suffered death, not because they were Spaniards, nor yet because they were Catholics, but because they were robbers and murderers!

Remembering all these things, and what cruelties had

been perpetrated by the Spaniards in Mexico and Peru, I could but think it not at all improbable that the deadly shots fired in this ditch of the old Fort at St. Augustine, may have struck down the innocent as often as the guilty.

These are dark shadows on the tropical beauty and loveliness around, though partly hidden in the far-off twilight of three centuries ago. It makes one shiver even now to think such deeds were ever possible in this New World. But again there comes a reaction, and this Spanish massacre is a landmark from which we can measure the progress made since that bloody time, and thank God that such crimes can no more be committed in His name!

And now the old Fort is only a picturesque ruin; and very picturesque it is to me, as I walk along the sea-wall at sunset, just as the evening gun from the barracks in another part of the town signals the close of day, and look up to the little round towers, out of which the Spanish sentinels looked, to keep watch for the terrible English rovers who were sweeping the seas!

St. Augustine is a thoroughly Spanish town, so that now and then, as I wander about its narrow streets, I feel as if I had gone astray, and were back again in some out-of-the-way place of Old Castile. The original settlers were largely from the island of Minorca, and my friend, Dr. Anderson, who last year made a visit to Spain, crossed over to Port Mahon, where, from the names on the shops in the streets, he seemed to be among his neighbors in St. Augustine. These associations give a singular charm to this quaint old town, which is full of nooks and corners, about which those who are beginning to be in "the sere and yellow leaf" (shall I count myself among them?) can wander all day long, and dream dreams and see visions.

But after all is said and done—after we have walked round and round as many times as the pilgrims to Mecca walk round the holy Kaaba, in which is the black stone that fell down from heaven — what remains? I have been about the world a good deal within the last fifteen years, and my rule has been to see everything as rapidly and as thoroughly as possible, and then "move on." And now, after seeing Europe, Asia, and Africa, what is there that should detain me, or detain any man, very long in St. Augustine, or in Florida? I confess there is not a great deal, if we come merely to see sights. The country is not picturesque; no mountains rear their summits to the sky; nor has it even the full beauty of the sea, for though almost surrounded by it, its long shore-line lies too near the level of the water. As you sail past it, you see no Dover cliffs, which look down into "the confined deep"; you miss the rugged grandeur of a wild and stormy coast; in fact, there is hardly coast enough for the waves to dash against, so that the mighty ocean, unless stirred by a tempest, lies as flat and tame as the land beside it. Indeed it is not long ago that the mainland *was* the sea-bed, with the Gulf of Mexico flowing over it; and it still has a drowned appearance, as if it could hardly keep its head out of water.

If you turn back into the interior, the country has a dreary monotony. For a hundred leagues you ride through an endless succession of pine barrens, and as you look listlessly through your car window, you ask, "Why do our Northern people come to Florida?" And yet for thousands of them this desolate country has a strange fascination. What can it be?

It is all expressed in one word — *climate*. Though the land be flat, the sky is blue, and bends over the earth with a warm and loving embrace, and the soft and balmy air seems to have dropped down from heaven itself, as if it were the very atmosphere that angels breathe.

Such a climate I have found indeed elsewhere, but far from home. If one could choose absolute perfection, I should say that the *perfect* Winter climate of the world is that of Egypt, where there are no swamps and no jungle, but every particle of miasma is absorbed by the hot air of the surrounding deserts. I speak from my own observation, as I have been twice in Egypt, and some years since spent several weeks on the Nile, where I seemed to be floating in Paradise. But that is very far away : I suppose a man who should take the fastest steamer, and rush through England and across France and Italy day and night, and catch the steamer from Brindisi for Alexandria, might reach Egypt in fifteen days ; but he can reach Florida in thirty hours, without the fatigue and discomfort of a sea voyage, and all this wear and tear of his mortal frame. And when he gets here, he has found, not Egypt indeed, but a country that holds about the same place on the earth's surface. Florida is in the same latitude, and has very much the same climate. To be specific, the Great Pyramid stands exactly on the 30th parallel. St. Augustine differs from it by less than one-quarter of a degree, its latitude being 29 degrees, 48 minutes, and 30 seconds! Owing to the deserts, the climate of Egypt is drier ; while the Gulf Stream, flowing near to the Florida coast, makes its atmosphere moist as well as warm.

Many who come to Florida feel as if, for the first time in their lives, they knew what it was to *breathe*. When I was in Madrid, I observed that the Spaniards always went about wrapped in cloaks, the right skirt of which they tossed over the left shoulder in a way to cover the mouth, the reason of which is given in the Spanish proverb, that the air of Madrid, "while it might not blow out a candle, could put out a life." In our Northern cities many have to take similar precautions, going about muffled up to the chin, and even covering their faces, lest they should inhale the keen and frosty air.

Such chronic invalids, who have been all their lives taking care of their health, come to Florida and find that it takes care of itself. The consumptive and the asthmatic throw off their wrappings, and have a new sense of freedom, since they are not afraid of nature's best medicine, the pure air of heaven. They do not have to "catch their breath"; to gasp for it; but take a long, deep inhalation, which causes their lungs to expand as never before. Such breathing is a luxury that makes life worth living. I find the atmosphere so exhilarating, that I can never get enough of it. When I am walking along the bay, or riding through the woods, in some lonely spot where I shall not be observed, I "open my mouth wide," according to the Bible direction, to drink in the heavenly air.

But to get the benefit of all this, one must have a habitation. When I was on the desert, on the way to Mount Sinai, I lived in tents, like Abraham, Isaac, and Jacob; but you can hardly live in a tent in Florida. Even in the pine woods you must have a roof over your head, if it be only a log cabin. The old-fashioned Southern houses were roomy and comfortable, and their long and wide verandas furnished a cool retreat in the heat of the day. In still hotter climates, as in India, this is the chief thing to be regarded. In the Indian bungalow, it may almost be said that the main idea is to have a veranda *with a house thrown in,* the domestic arrangements and the sleeping apartments being mere attachments to the great lounging place, where men sit all day long, and far into the night, smoking and talking, and where the real life of the people goes on.

The first hotels in the South were merely enlargements of the old houses on the plantations. Some of those in St. Augustine were modelled on this plan, and answered the purpose of the travelling public very well, until they were succeeded by one so unique and so magnificent, as to deserve a detailed description.

Connoisseurs of fine architecture are not apt to look for models in hotels, but in churches and cathedrals; in palaces and stately mansions. The city of New York abounds in hotels, but it has not one that is worth looking at for its architecture. "The Windsor," if it stood out in the country, beside a stream of water, would be taken for a paper mill or a cotton factory. Or it might be some public institution, whose needs required that which was useful rather than ornamental; as its stories are all just alike, with just so many windows, of just the same size, as if they opened into the small rooms intended for the wards of an asylum. There is some excuse for this in a crowded city, where the largest buildings must be put on a line with the street, to utilize every foot of space, for there is not room to have a great central court. This must be reserved for a situation less crowded, where there is more elbow-room. It is also more suited to a climate warmer than that of the North—conditions which seem to meet in this old Spanish town of St. Augustine. And so it came to pass quite naturally that a gentleman of New York, who had been here often enough to appreciate the place, and see its possibilities, should have a mind to build a Hotel after his own fancy, that should meet all requirements, and be a welcome retreat for those who, fleeing from the severe Winters of the North, should seek a place of health and of rest. He saw that the Spanish style of architecture was best adapted to a warm climate: and having the good fortune to engage an architect who entered with spirit into the design, despatched him to Spain, to study the best specimens of Spanish architecture in Toledo, Cordova, Seville, and Granada. The result has been a structure quite unique in this country, and the like of which I have not seen anywhere.

Having ample space, there was no need to crowd anything; so that the building, instead of being one huge mass, could be thrown into pavilions, grouped round a great court, with its fountain and flowers; with projecting balconies (which, if not crowded with Spanish senoritas, are none the less charming with American ladies); and belfry-like towers, rising at the angles, with open arches, from which one can overlook the town, and look far out to sea; and that are hung at night with many-colored lights, which shed their varied rays upon the enchanted scene.

Such is the general plan. But of course, in a building of such extent, there is no end of details, which have to be worked out with the utmost care. Now I do not profess to know much about architecture; but, like a good many others, I know *just enough to find fault.* Without technical knowledge, I have an instinct of proportion and of harmony, which detects what is not in accord with them, even when it may be difficult to point out just where the fault lies. If I go into a new church, and it be too long for its width, or the ceiling be too high or too low, I "feel it in my bones." So in the decoration of a room, or the furnishing of it, if there be a want of harmony of color, *my flesh begins to creep* before I can tell precisely what is the matter. In this way I have gone about the Ponce de Leon, not with a measuring line in my hand, but trusting solely to my eye, and I have not been able to detect a single fault. "The height and the length and the breadth of it," are not "equal," but they are in perfect proportion. As an editor, true to his calling, I have been a little disappointed that I could not find something to criticize; but I give it up. Nor have I found any glaring color which offends my taste. On the walls and ceilings and even in the furnishing, in carpets and curtains and upholstery, everything is subdued to that soft and quiet tone which is most pleasing and grateful to the eye.

Nor is there in the whole structure a single piece of *cheap work*, where unsound places are covered up with lath and plaster. This is a great deal to say in these days (when huge buildings tumble down with their own weight, and others show cracks in the walls), that here is a structure of immense size and cost, every cubic foot of which is solid from the foundation to the capstone.

The erection of such a building is not only a notable event in the way of art, but reflects the greatest credit upon those who designed it, and the powerful friend who stood behind them, and furnished the munitions of war. It shows genius as well as skill in the young architects who wrought upon it for three years, and who by this work alone must take rank with the most promising of the architects of our country. I am proud to say that one of them is the son of my friend for more than thirty years, the Rev. Dr. Hastings, President of the Union Theological Seminary of New York.

But with all their genius, they could have produced nothing so perfect if they had been hampered or restricted by the desire for economy on the part of the owner. There are many who begin with great designs, but, like the man in the Gospel, " are not able to finish," or they get frightened at the magnitude of their own undertakings, and suddenly begin to take in sail, to cut down the estimates, and to cheapen everything. If he who undertook to build the Ponce de Leon had been of that temper, it would have soon come to grief, for when money is going out at a fearful rate, most men who have put their hand to the plough not only "look *back*," but look very *black* also. Not so with its projector. On the contrary, I hear that during the progress of the work, if he ever made a criticism, it was to express a fear that this or that was not good enough, or rich enough, or handsome enough. Instead of holding in the architects, he gave them free rein, and spurred them on to do their very best.

And who is he that has stood behind this great undertaking from the first, never flinching even when the cost mounted up into the millions? It is a gentleman who writes a part of his name as I write mine (though unfortunately I cannot complete the signature), Mr. Henry M. Flagler of New York, who, having conceived the project, had the nerve to carry it through; and who, instead of taking the honor to himself, rates his part very lightly, giving all the credit to the architects, saying modestly that he "only signed the checks!" This was a mere trifle. Only somehow we find that, however elaborate may be the design, and however vast the preparations, but for this little matter of "signing the checks," the wheels will not move. But indeed in this statement he does not do justice to himself. For if he did not draw the plans, he had the taste to know a good thing when he saw it, and, having faith in his architects, to give them *carte blanche* to carry out the magnificent design. Out of this combination of means, genius, and will, came the structure which fitly bears the name of the old Spanish navigator who first set foot upon these shores.

But a single building is by no means the limit of this benefaction. The Ponce de Leon has two large *annexes*, in two massive piles, with Spanish names—the Cordova and the Alcazar. In the rear of the latter rises a dome which might be the roof of a mosque, and which has under it what may be found in the outer courts of St. Sophia, and of all the great mosques of the Moslem world, viz: plentiful means of ablution, for here is arranged a system of Baths the most complete that I have seen anywhere on this side the Atlantic or the other. The Russian baths are as complete as the most luxurious in St. Petersburg, and the Turkish equal to any in Constantinople. In both of them the stranger will find stalwart creatures, speaking a foreign tongue, but who seem to understand their business; who will take him in hand, and steam him till it seems as if every drop of perspiration were oozing from his body, and plunge him into the depths, and bring him up again (still alive!), and "douche" him, and at last, after he has been a long time, as it seems, in the hands of the tormentors, will have mercy upon him, and bring him to gently, and rub him with soft warm towels, till there comes over him a delicious feeling, as if he were, though still in the body, a being of another sphere, purified and glorified, freed from the stains of sin, and indeed rather too good for this world. If after this there should reappear a trace of original sin, it may be necessary, on the second or third day, to repeat the ablution!

But the great feature of the Baths is a Pool, a hundred and fifty feet long, continually supplied with water from an artesian well, which is the largest in the world. As this is tinctured with sulphur, the stream is carried *over the roof* of an adjoining building, where it is exposed to the air, and is so thoroughly aerated that it is as fresh and pure as if it were from a mountain spring. This supply of water from above instead of below, has a pretty effect, as it falls into the Pool in a cascade, which keeps it always stirring, as if the angel of healing were descending into the waters. In this ample space swimmers at all hours are plunging and splashing, while the band discourses inspiring music, and the galleries are crowded with spectators looking down upon the animated scene.

Here is health united with pleasure—a combination

A BUILDER OF CHURCHES.

which ought to make us forever grateful to him who has furnished both. The Koran pronounces a blessing upon the man who opens a fountain in the desert, or plants a tree that the pilgrim may rest under its shade! What blessing ought to be his who has opened a Pool of Bethesda, that will continue to flow long after he is gone, to be for the comfort and the healing of many generations!

But Mr. Flagler's efforts for the public good are not confined to the physical purification of his fellow-creatures. He has built two churches. The Methodist came first, as they are pioneers in almost everything; and now he has built us Presbyterians such a "cathedral" that we are persuaded that we have the apostolic succession, and are the true, if not the *only* true, Church. A man who has supplied such physical and spiritual purification, has certainly done his part both for "cleanliness and godliness."

And now is it not time for him to stop? After these years of labor, the work he has undertaken for St. Augustine must be nearing completion, so that it can all, to use a common phrase, be "fenced in and painted." "Done?" It will never be done as long as he lives. Indeed it is all the time extending; even now he is opening new avenues, paving new streets, building a railway station here, and an iron bridge across the St. John's at Jacksonville, just to keep his hand in; so that if he lives ten years longer, (as he ought, for he is only in his sixtieth year,) he will be recognized, not only as the constructor of a beautiful building, but as the founder of a city.

Of course this marvellous creation, that has sprung up in Florida, like Tadmor in the wilderness, is the wonder of everybody who comes here, and it is amusing to observe the look of surprise of new comers, and hear their expressions of astonishment. And yet the American feeling will crop out, and after they have exhausted their admiration, one is sure to hear the subdued question, *"Does it pay?"* as if nothing great could ever be done except as a speculation ; and there are many mysterious inquiries as to what could be the motive of this lavish expenditure so far away from the commercial centres of the country. There is no mystery about the matter. A man who has for many years made his annual visits to this portion of the South, till it has become as attractive to him as it was to Ponce de Leon, (when, enraptured by its perpetual bloom, he named it Florida, the Land of Flowers,) takes it into his mind to create a paradise of beauty somewhat in keeping with the gorgeous tropical vegetation. Fond of grand architecture, and having the means to gratify his taste, he conceives the idea of a building unique in its structure and in its surroundings, which shall be " a thing of beauty " and " a joy forever." Whether it will pay in the common sense, does not enter into his calculations, any more than it does into the mind of one who gives himself a costly library or gallery of paintings. He does it, as an artist paints a picture, for the pleasure of doing it. Is there anything more natural or more reasonable than this ? It is indeed something to be proud of, in this commonplace and prosaic age, that there should be one man bold enough to form a design, and to carry it out without flinching, which is simply to put into stone " a beautiful dream."

Whether it may not in the end pay even pecuniarily, is a question. When St. Augustine becomes, as we believe it will, the great Winter resort of the United States, and a city grows up around these marvellous buildings, standing in the midst of open squares, as a centre, it is not at all improbable that the money "sunk" so many years before, may yield a full and even ample return. But whether it does or not, is a matter which does not disturb their builder at all. If it does not pay in money, it pays in another and better way; and we can assure any anxious inquirer that the creator of all this luxury gets a return *every day* in the sight of the pleasure that it gives.

The best of it all is that his beautiful creation is for the public good. Palaces abroad are for kings and princes. This American palace is open to all—a place of rest and health, as well as of luxury and enjoyment: and he who has placed it within reach of his countrymen, is a public benefactor.

In this delightful retreat I settled down for a Winter vacation. Some may think it a strange place to seek for quiet, in the midst of so much gayety. But the Ponce de Leon is a perfect Liberty Hall. Every man does what is right in his own eyes. He can have as much of society, or as little, as he pleases. As it was not for this that I came, I did not seek it, though entertained by the sight of what passed before my eyes. But to me the charm of the place was its perfect rest, the sweet oblivion of care. Not that I was idle. I could not stand that. I do not find rest in idleness and vacancy, but in change of scene and of occupation. A portion of every day I spent in writing; but it was very different from writing in an office in New York. Here my desk was at an open window, through which came, not only the soft and balmy air, but the music of the band playing in the court below. This did not disturb me, but rather gave an inspiration to my thoughts. With such an accompaniment, I found a pleasure in keeping up communication with the world. If after four or five hours I felt a little weary, I started out on a tramp; or a ride through the woods, or a sail on the water, made a pleasant close to the happy day.

But the place was not without its excitements, though these were of such a mild character as not to be dangerous. Strangers were constantly coming and going, so that the

Rotunda of the Ponce de Leon was a kind of Exchange, where you met people from every city of the North, finding old acquaintances and making new ones. Among the habitués were some who had been in different parts of the world, with whom an old traveller like myself could have many a pleasant hour; while young men and maidens strolled in the grounds in the moonlight, or took their pleasure in the ways they most delight in.

In this country, which embraced first and last a good many notable people, I was most attracted to the creator of all this beauty and luxury, of whom I am restrained from saying all that is in my heart lest I should offend his modesty, for he is one of the most unassuming of men. Seldom is so much strength united with so much sweetness. A man who can do a kindness with such delicacy that he makes you feel as if you were conferring a favor upon him in accepting it, is a master in the fine art of courtesy. Nor was it to me only. So far as I could see, he was the same, though in a more general way, to every one. For weeks we were constantly together, always sitting at the same table, and in all that time I never saw him in the least excited; never heard him speak a work of impatience to anybody or of anybody. I felt this daily association to be a pleasure constantly renewed, and I count it the chief satisfaction of my visit to St. Augustine, that it gave me the opportunity of knowing somewhat intimately one whom I am proud to call my friend.

CHAPTER V.

SOUTH FLORIDA—JUPITER INLET.

"You don't know Jupiter Inlet?" Neither did I a week ago: for aught I knew, it might be some newly discovered point in the planet Jupiter; but now that I do know it, how can I help being lifted up with the vanity of superior knowledge, and looking down upon those who do not know it, as showing ignorance of American geography? Perhaps you will think a place not worth knowing where (aside from the Light-house, the Signal Station, and the Life-Saving Station) there is but one house, and travellers have to find lodging in an old steamboat that is moored to the wharf! But I will not raise the curtain too soon. First of all, where is it?

If you will take a map and run your eye down the Atlantic Coast, you will find its lower portion protected by an almost continuous reef, broken here and there into long and low-lying islands, which form a natural breakwater against the ocean. Between this and the mainland is a succession of lagunes, which, with trifling interruptions, furnish a complete inland navigation for hundreds of miles. At long distances there are openings or "Inlets" in this ocean barrier, through which light boats, and in some cases large ships, can pass, if they see a storm approaching, and take refuge in these sheltered waters. One of these "Inlets" far down on the coast, bears the mighty name of "Jupiter." To this distant point two gentlemen connected with one of the great railroad systems of Florida —Mr. Mason Young, a name well known in New York, and Mr. Alfred Bishop Mason, a name equally well known in Chicago—were about to make a visit, and invited me to keep them company. As the journey was partly by rail and partly by boat, it gave opportunity to see both the interior and the river and coast scenery.

At Palatka we crossed the St. John's, a river which, contrary to what we are accustomed to consider the natural course of rivers, runs north, so that, as far as we followed it, we were going up stream, though down south. Travelling in a private car, we were a little company by ourselves, and I was happy to find that there was a lady in the party, whose society gave all that was wanting to make it complete. As the car was attached to the train at the end, and had plate-glass windows on both sides and in the rear, we had an unobstructed view of the country as we rolled swiftly by. New settlements were sprinkled here and there: sometimes houses would be standing alone in the pine woods, and at others half a dozen would be clustered together so as to form the nucleus of a village. In the latter case there was sure to be a New England air about the place, indicated in the fenced grounds and framed houses, neatly boarded and painted, with a pretty church and school-house in the centre—which showed where the first settlers came from. This part of Florida is largely settled by people from the North, and I am told, that while there is no conflict between them and the poor whites known as the "Crackers," yet that the latter, finding themselves unable to compete with the more industrious habits of the new comers, are generally quite willing to sell out their plantations, which have been run down by long neglect, and move off into the less settled parts of the South, to begin life anew. Their successors here have tried other methods of cultivation, the result of which is seen in the orange groves, richly laden with the golden fruit, that extend for miles along the road.

Look at this pretty village of Seville, that in spite of its Spanish name, might have been transplanted from Massachusetts, since we see in it, what is very rare in Florida, a well-kept *lawn*, which shows that with proper care it is possible to have the green turf of New England. Here several friends joined us, and added to the gayety of our little party. One gentleman, an old army officer, gave me his experience of life in his new home. He had come here broken in health, almost seeking a place to die; but after awhile concluded that it was better to live; and took his section, of a hundred and sixty acres, to which he was entitled by his soldier's warrant, on which he planted, not his "vineyard and olive-yard," like the ancient Jew in Palestine, but his orange grove; and in due time found himself not only reëstablished in health, but prospering in his worldly affairs. Lest, however, anybody should jump to the conclusion that he has but to move to Florida and plant an orange grove, to be rich, it should be added that from the time of *planting* to the time of *bearing* will take eight or ten years; so that none need try it who have not some little capital to start upon, and above all a large stock of New England thrift, patience, and perseverance. I could not but listen with wonder to his report of the productiveness of Florida, which reminded me of the marvellous tales that I had heard in Southern California. At first I was a little incredulous: for the country looked very barren, and I thought it must be poor and unproductive. But he explained that, while this soil would not produce much at the North, it would here, owing to the greater warmth, combined with the greater moisture. The elements which enter into vegetation come not from the soil alone, but from the air, the vapor, and the dew, the rain and the sunshine, all of which are supplied from the resources of nature; so that if man will but help a little, giving very moderate cultivation, the earth will bring forth abundantly.

Nor is this prodigality of nature confined to the sub-tropical fruits, but extends equally to all the produce of the garden (Irish potatoes growing as well as sweet potatoes), to peas and tomatoes and cauliflowers, from which it seems probable that with the increased production from year to year, and sufficient transportation (for already it is said that the railroads are not able to carry the crops), Florida will soon be able to supply the markets of Washington, Baltimore, Philadelphia, and New York, with green peas and early potatoes, and all the produce of vegetable gardens, a month or six weeks before they can be obtained from Charleston and Savannah.

The road that we had been following continues to Tampa Bay, where it connects with a line of steamers to Cuba, which will land the traveller in Havana in thirty hours, or in three and a half days from New York, instead of the week now taken by steamer. This will furnish also the quickest route to South American ports. As we however were bound to a point on the Atlantic coast, we left the main line at Enterprise, and turned eastward, and in an hour were at Titusville, where the train ran down to the wharf beside the steamer, and at three o'clock we were afloat on the Indian river—a name hitherto known to us only by its delicious oranges, but now to be known by its beautiful scenery. But first of all, it is not a river at all, but simply an arm of the sea, a long lagune, which in some places is three or four, or even five and six, miles broad. The beauty of it is on its western bank, where the low, flat country rising a few feet above the water, is dignified with the name of a *bluff*. Its apparent elevation is heightened by its being densely wooded with palms! Not indeed the stately date-palms of Egypt, but only with the "cabbage palm," so named from its cabbage-like head, but which still, with its tall trunk and tufted crown, forms a striking figure in the landscape, giving it more of a tropical character than anything I had seen before, and as I sat on the deck in the gloaming, and watched the shores growing dim, memory went back to the old days when I floated past groves of palms on the banks of the Nile.

All along this bank there are plantations, the houses peering out from under the trees, and every few miles a little village, from which a projecting wharf gives facilities for the conveyance of travellers and the shipment of freight. The most considerable of these river-towns is Rock Ledge, to which they brought President Cleveland and his wife on their visit to Florida last year, to show them the beauty of the country—where we landed and walked a mile along the bank, past a succession of pretty Winter retreats, embowered in palms.

Back of the palms were the orange groves in all their luxuriance: but the orange region ends soon after, oranges giving place to fruits of a more tropical character. The guava is cultivated for the jelly made from it, of which there is a manufactory on Merritt's Island, the product of which is shipped largely to Northern cities; and at Eden, a few miles farther south, is a very extensive plantation of pineapples, which are grown here with entire success.

The morning found us still floating southward, which soon brought us into the narrows of the Indian river, where for some miles it is not wider than the Housatonic at Stockbridge, while the dense vegetation on either hand was delightfully suggestive of the willows that bend over our beautiful stream. Here the palms give place to mangroves, the tree that lives in water, in swamps, and on the banks of streams. This amphibious character is almost a necessity, for as the country itself is so largely under water, if trees could only find a foothold on dry land, there would be no vegetation at all. And yet, to complete the contradictions, these trees, which live in water, have half their roots *above* water as well as above ground, so that they seem to be standing on stilts. They are like the blue herons that we see in these waters, putting their long skinny legs without fear into the ooze and slime of the river bed, while they carry their brilliant plumage high in air. I have been watching these birds with admiration to see how, while the flocks of ducks go " scooting " by, the herons stand with quiet dignity, stepping slowly with eye cast downward till they spy the looked-for fish, which is snapped up in an instant, when they spread their wings and soar majestically away. What the herons and the cranes are among birds, the mangroves are among trees, standing on long legs, that are naked as bones, and yet, carrying crowns of verdure on their heads. As their foliage is a vivid green, the two banks form a beautiful fringe to the waters, so calm and still, that flow between.

The navigation through this mass of vegetation is very intricate. The river has so many twists and turns, that it seems as if it could only be threaded by a rowboat. The mazes would be quite impenetrable for a steamer, except one of the lightest draft. Our boat, the St. Lucie, draws but nineteen inches of water, and is propelled by a wheel at the stern. Yet even with this light build, she finds it difficult to work her way through, and has to be handled with the greatest care. At such times the captain, whose name of "Bravo" indicates his Spanish origin, and who is very proud of his new boat (this was her second trip), not trusting to any one but himself, throws off his coat, that he may have free use for his strong arms, and takes his place at the wheel. In some places a channel has been marked by stakes just wide enough for her to squeeze through. Sometimes she swings with the current, or with the tide (for we are nearing the sea), and as she is 122 feet long, she touches the bank on both sides, and the negroes have to push her off with their poles at one end and the other. Then the captain is in his element, shouting right and left *"All clare thar?"* till after a tug of a few minutes the boat eases up, and swings into her place, and as she moves forward, the boatmen, relieved of their strain, break out in some negro melody, that makes a pleasant accompaniment to the motion of the boat as she glides gently through the water. And thus at noon of the second day, we reached Jupiter Inlet on the coast, nearly three hundred miles south of St. Augustine.

Having reached this remote quarter of the world, we look round to see if there be anything worth coming for. It does not look very promising. There is but one house, and that I have not been into. Yet here I have spent three days on an old steamboat, with about as many resources as Robinson Crusoe had on his desolate island. No! that is "putting it rather strong": for Robinson Crusoe, with all his handicraft and skill in using pieces of wreck to make his island castle, never had anything so habitable as the good old Chattahoochee; and for company he had to content himself with his man Friday, while here I have three charming companions. Still, stranded on this Florida coast, which has been strown with hundreds of wrecks, it does not take much imagination to fancy ourselves cast away on a desolate island. But if the experience be new, it is not unpleasant ; on the contrary, it is delightful now and then to come into this close contact with nature, and to be living for a few days like babes in the woods.

The old steamer which is our home, has itself a history. Its very name tells the place of its birth, on the Chattahoochee river, which in the times before the flood—that is, before the war—was a great highway of commerce, bringing the product of the cotton fields of Georgia and Alabama to Apalachicola, then the third cotton port of the United States, but which is now all overgrown with weeds, since the opening of railroads has diverted its trade to other commercial centres. In those days she was a famous steamboat, and even still, if her fires were lighted, would show her heels to many a boat that has not seen half her years ; but she is now honorably retired, and moored in a quiet haven, and being fitted up for her present use, serves as a kind of wayside, or rather seaside, inn, and is a truly delightful place of rest for wanderers like ourselves.

We arrived Saturday noon. Hardly had we sat down to dinner, before one of the party invited me to take a drive with him in the afternoon to Lake Worth, and we were soon mounted in a rough country wagon, drawn by a pair of mules, with which we went jolting over the road. Once out of the border of trees that skirt the water side, and on what might be called the open prairie, our course was straight as an arrow, for it was along the track of a railroad which has just been laid out, and is only waiting for the rails, so that we had not to turn to the right or left, but only to " plough ahead " through the deep sand. "And what does this ride across country remind you of ? " " Why, of dear old Nantucket." Sure enough, it was the ride to Sconset over again. The rough plain was like a Scottish moor, bleak and bare, though instead of the gorse and heather, it was covered with the coarse palmetto grass, which, though now mere useless stubble, is said to furnish the finest possible material for paper, if it were within reach of a port, from which it could be shipped to the Northern markets. The country was not so dismally flat as much of that we had passed over, but slightly rolling. These swells of ground are really sand-dunes cast up by the waves, and rising over them one after another, we came at last in full view of the ocean.

A mile or two farther brought us to Lake Worth, or rather to one end of it—the smaller of the twin lakes—which in New England we should call a pond. It is a lonely spot, on which stands a solitary house, with the master of which Mr. Young had some business, and whose name, to my surprise, was the same as my own. While they were engaged in conversation, I turned to the young wife and learned that her husband was the son of my old friend Richard Field, of Bound Brook, New Jersey, who more than forty years ago was a trustee of the church in St. Louis of which I was the youthful pastor. The husband added, on learning my name, that I had baptized him! This was indeed finding a lost sheep in the wilderness. I could but hope that the grace communicated in baptism, whatever that might be, had not wholly departed from him.

The place is quite out of the world, but it will not always be so, for it lies in the pathway of progress. If it had not been Saturday afternoon, and we could have continued our excursion a little farther, we should have seen more of its possibilities; for, taking a boat and rounding yonder point, we should have come into the larger part of Lake Worth, where is the promise of one of the most beautiful Winter resorts in Florida. On a ridge of land between the lake and the ocean, are already several gentlemen's places, with extensive grounds laid out as if by a landscape gardener. The air is deliciously soft because of the nearness of the Gulf Stream, which, coming up from the Gulf of Mexico, is here so wedged in between the main land and the Bahamas (only eighty miles distant) that it almost touches the coast. The vegetation of the country also takes another step, for these plantations are not of oranges, nor pineapples, nor bananas, but cocoanut palms, which shows that we are advancing towards the tropics. Indeed, it is only by taking such a stretch through the interior and along the coast of Florida, that we realize how many degrees of latitude are traversed by this mighty Peninsula, in which we pass from one climate to another.

On how grand a scale is everything here, we may see by another measurement of distances. Not only is the State immense in territory, but it has counties that are larger than some of our Northern States. For example, the county in which we now are, begins far up on the Indian river, and yet the county-seat is sixty miles (a whole degree of latitude) to the south of us, to reach which one must pass through a country so destitute of inhabitants that the mail has to be carried on foot! There is not a wagon road, nor even a mule path! The carrier has to tramp the whole distance, taking two days for the journey there, and two days for the return. Sometimes (as a resident informed me) he carries one letter, and sometimes his mail-pouch is empty! But it has to go!

This lonely journey, as might be supposed, is attended with a good deal of difficulty, and with some danger. There are rivers to be crossed, for which a boat must be always ready. Last year a postman came to the bank, and found that some tramp had taken his skiff and rowed himself to the other side, and left it there. Full of patriotic zeal to do his duty, the faithful messenger,

"Accoutred as he was, plunged in";

but before he could reach the other side, a man-eating shark had seized him, and with no respect for a government officer, made a meal of him! I hope it was a consolation to him that he died in the performance of his duty. His country could ask no more. Some years since President Wayland published a book on "The Limitations of Responsibility." It is a nice question in many cases where responsibility ends; but I think the most severe moralist would agree that a man who had been eaten up by a shark, could not be expected to appear at roll-call the next morning!

But these dangers will not always attend this service, since this state of isolation will not continue, for it is proposed to bring the local government sixty miles nearer by transferring the county-seat to the north side of Lake Worth, indeed planting it on the farm-land of my namesake, who offers to give the ground for the court-house. If he should also give a site for a religious purpose, and in time there should spring up a little church in the wilderness, I should think that the water of baptism which I had poured upon his childish head, had not been sprinkled in vain.

It was late in the afternoon when we turned homeward. By this time the air had changed. In coming over, it was so warm (though it was the 2d of February) that I had to raise my umbrella to protect me from the sun, and should have been glad of a straw hat. But now it was the cool of the day, and we drew our overcoats about us. Yet the ride was more beautiful than before, for as the twilight fell on the landscape, its bareness was softened, and as it were clothed with a mantle, by the gathering shades of evening, and we saw before us only the dim outline of a wide sweep of country rolling like the sea, as if it were keeping measure with "Old Ocean's gray and melancholy waste," while the silence was broken only by the dashing of the waves. On our left a new moon hung its crescent in the sky, and above it shone the evening star. One by one the stars came out, till the firmament was all aglow with the celestial fires. I was a little confused not to find the constellations in their accustomed places. The change of fourteen degrees of latitude, from New York to Jupiter Inlet, had upset things, and it was not till I was on the deck of the steamer that I could take my bearings. I found the Dipper, though with the handle turned downward, but the last two stars still pointed faithfully to the north. It was a relief to find that "all things continued as they were from the beginning," and that suns and systems still revolved around "the steady pole."

As I woke the next morning, I missed the dear faces and the dear voices that make a part of the Sabbath at home; but it was not all silent and vacancy. There were friends who made a little home circle even so far away; and there was another presence, as on the gentle air of morning came the Angel of Peace. It is not necessary that the Sabbath should be ushered in by the ringing of bells: it can come to us in the solitary place where no man is. Some of the sweetest that I have ever known, have been in almost absolute solitude. Years ago I spent a Sabbath in the Wilderness, on the way to Mount Sinai, when we camped where Moses camped, in the Wady Feiran, a deep valley surrounded by mountains; and at sunset climbed the very peak on which he prayed while Israel fought with Amalek, and Aaron and Hur held up his hands till the going down of the sun. Here we are not among rocks and mountains, but amid woods and waters; but here, as there, is the same stillness and rest, the same absence of all intrusion from the world, and the same sense of being brought nearer to God.

THE SIGNAL STATION.

Across the water, hardly a stone's throw from us, stood the Lighthouse and the Signal Station, and they had such a solitary look, and the keepers must lead such a lonely life, that it seemed the part of humanity to go over and give them a little of our company. Accordingly towards evening the Captain of the Chattahoochee rowed me across. At the Signal Station I found a young man who had received his training at Washington, and was then assigned to this post of observation. Twice a day—at eight in the morning and eight in the evening—he climbs his signal-tower, and takes the figures recorded by the barometer and other instruments, showing the pressure of the atmosphere, and the direction and velocity of the wind, and transmits them to the Signal Bureau at Washington, where, from these and the like observations made on Mount Washington and Pike's Peak, and at fifty, or perhaps a hundred, other stations reaching from the Atlantic to the Pacific, and from Canada to the Gulf of Mexico, is made up the general report of the weather throughout the country, with the probabilities of coming storms, which are given to the public the next morning. The work is very interesting in a scientific point of view, and yet it is a hard life as well as a solitary one. It is one in which there is no let-up: for as day and night, Summer and Winter, do not cease, so the observations must not be intermitted for a single day. In the blackest night, or the most terrific storm of thunder and lightning, the observer must climb his watch-tower, and take the record of the storms and the gales. And what a lonely existence! To be sure, he has an assistant, a man Friday; but even two must find this Robinson Crusoe life very wearisome. The only reflection that can make one endure it, is the military one: that he is a soldier on duty, a sentinel keeping watch over the public safety; and that a brave man must not desert his post.

From the Signal Station I turned to the taller tower near by, and climbed the iron stairway that winds round and round to the top of the Lighthouse. Here is another post of duty that must be trying to the nerves. The tower is, I think, a hundred and forty feet high, and though solidly built, with massive walls, yet at that height, when the wind howls, even this mighty column must seem to rock. It must be a fearful place when the tempest is abroad. But no matter what the danger may be, that light must never go out. It is at such times that it is most needed, for it is when the Atlantic gales are sweeping in all their fury, and ships are struggling in fear of wreck on the dangerous coast, that the mariner watches most eagerly for this light, on which his safety may depend.

My sympathies had been so much enlisted for the men leading this lonely life, that it was a relief to hear that the keeper of the Lighthouse, who had been here some twenty years, was proud of his profession, and so far from regarding himself as an object of pity, was in love with his calling. He has indeed (besides his two assistants) his family with him, and that makes all the difference in the world. It was very pleasant as we came down to the boat to meet a motherly face leading a flock of children. It is true these did not happen to be *his* children: but so much the better, for it showed that there were other children also in the woods about here; and children, even more than the old folks, give a look of home to the solitude. On the bank of the river behold a little thatch-covered schoolhouse, nestled at the foot of a cocoanut palm, which leaned over it as if to give it protection! But protection sometimes involves danger, for if one of those cocoanuts that hang so high, should fall upon the head of one of the children, it is altogether probable that

"The subsequent proceedings would interest him no more."

So real is the danger that last year an athletic young fellow climbed to the top of the tree and cut off every cocoanut, lest a premature or unexpected descent upon some tender brain not yet sufficiently "armored," should interfere sadly with the cause of education at Jupiter Inlet.

Returning to the Chattahoochee, I found all on deck, watching the sunset. The day had been perfect. Light, fleecy clouds had softly veiled the deep blue of the sky, and now they lay along the west, receiving and reflecting the last rays of the sun, which, as the country is low and flat, swept all round the horizon. Slowly the light faded out, but only to be followed by another illumination, for in the distance were the prairies on fire! This is done by the cattle owners, who every year burn them over, so that out of the stubble may spring a fresh, succulent growth for the food of their flocks and herds. The practice provokes much opposition, and may yet be done away with. But for those who are mere spectators, it is a brilliant spectacle. At last, however, in spite of fire and sunset, and the kindling stars, the night covered the earth, and then it was that we perceived the full power of the great reflector in the Lighthouse that towered above us. It is a revolving light, that is, one that is constantly turning, now growing fainter and fainter till it is almost extinguished, and then suddenly blazing out with such intensity that it is seen twenty miles at sea. At such moments it is like the full moon coming out of a cloud, its long trail of light quivering on the water. There was something fascinating and yet startling in these sudden transitions from light to dark, and dark to light, and as I looked up at that great orb as it burst upon us in its fullest splendor, it seemed as if it were the awful eye of God, looking down from the height of heaven upon the darkness of this world, and discovering all the crimes and wickedness of men.

SPORTSMEN AND FISHERMEN.

Life is full of surprises, bitter and sweet. Our experience here has been of the latter kind. I feared that our "boat-house" might be very dull (quiet, to be sure, but rather too much of a good thing), and was ready to cry out

> "O Solitude, where are the charms
> That sages have seen in thy face?"

But, in truth, it is not so very solitary. If there be not much life upon the land, there is upon the water. The Inlet is a great resort of sportsmen and fishermen: for there is abundance of game in the woods, and of fish in the sea. Yachts from the North put in here for a few days' sport, and naphtha launches skim the water like birds. As I sit on the deck, I see here and there a rowboat putting off from under the mangroves that line the river, the oars in the hands of some old sea-dog, while a landsman sits in the bow, with his gun across his knees, as they approach softly a flock of ducks that are floating on the water. Every few minutes I hear the crack of the rifle. The spoils of the sea are still greater. The fish caught daily are counted by the hundred. It seemed like a waste of the bounties of Providence, that the greater part of them should be thrown away for want of any man to eat them. What a pity when there are so many hungry mouths in the world! Here are some lovely monsters of the deep—a saw-fish (not a sword-fish), a veritable "Jack the Ripper," with a projecting saw three feet long, set with teeth like spikes, with which to cut and tear on every side; and a shark that is only a baby, four or five feet long, but as he is hauled up on the dock, and turned over on his back, and the little darkies pry his mouth open, they start back at seeing half a dozen rows of teeth that would make mince-meat of one of the aforesaid pickaninnies, if the scene of operations were transferred from the land to the water.

ALONG THE SEASHORE.

Monday morning gave promise of another perfect day, and as on Saturday we had taken a ride inland, it was proposed that now we should take a walk by the sea. Along the Inlet, as along the bank of the river at Rock Ledge, the palm trees make a pleasant shade. In this thicket or jungle I did not find, as indeed I have not found anywhere in this country, trees of great size, that show in their prodigious girth and altitude centuries of growth—nothing to compare in majesty with the oaks of Old England, or the elms of New England.

In the interior, in the swamps and lowlands, the live oaks and cypresses hung with moss, true gray-beards of the forest, give a funereal aspect to the vast, interminable wastes, which remind one of

> . . . "The forest primeval,
> The murmuring pines and the hemlocks,"

of Longfellow's poem, but in general there is a depressing monotony. One exception, however, we found this morning in a tree that has a strange name, gumbo-limbo, and whose appearance is as grotesque as its name, which indeed had something almost human in its aspect, as its exposed roots and arms were like the naked limbs of savages bronzed by exposure to the elements. It was so gnarled and twisted, that it seemed to writhe in pain, as if it were a living creature that had committed some fearful crime, whose hands were stained with blood—a deed which it was to expiate by centuries of torture.

But here is something which has puzzled the learned more than any vegetable growth—a shell mound, composed wholly of oyster shells, and yet it must be of a great age, as it is covered thick with earth, and overgrown with vegetation. It is so large and so regular, rising on the shore of the Inlet, like the earthwork of some ancient fortification, that it must have been the work of men's hands.

THE OYSTER MOUNDS.

But whose hands? Civilized or barbarian? And how many ages have passed away since they were piled upon this shore? These are questions more easily asked than answered. Commodore Douglas of the Yacht Club, who has visited Florida for many years, and devoted much of his time to the opening of these mounds, is of the opinion that they are the remains of Indian feasts. The records of the early Spanish explorers tell us that on its discovery Florida had a dense population. The natives lived in the interior, on plantations which are now grown up with pine woods, but once in the year, after they had planted their fields— between the planting and the reaping—they migrated to the seashore for the food which the sea afforded in abundance. Here they pitched their wigwams and fished in the sea, and dug oysters out of their beds, and gathering on the shore, had their pow-wows and barbecues, the remains of which are now disinterred to be the wonder and the riddle of modern explorers. It is an ingenious theory, and yet I am a little staggered by the extent of these mounds, as fifty miles below St. Augustine, at Ormond, there is a mound eight miles long! Truly there must have been Indians in those days. The woods must have been full of them. If these are the remains of Indian feasts, I have a horrible suspicion that they were scenes of cannibalism, or were attended with human sacrifices! And perhaps some old savage chief, who delighted in blood, has been punished for his cruelty by being turned into that gumbo-limbo tree, where he now writhes in pain, like Laocoon and his sons, wrapped in the coils of the python, to be crushed in its mighty folds.

Thus observing and philosophizing by the way as we strolled along the shore, we came to the mouth of the Inlet through which the tides ebb and flow, making it a part of the sea, where we stretch ourselves like so many children.

THE SANDS AND THE SHELLS. 71

Is there a more delicious sensation than that of lying down on the soft warm sand on the shore of the sea? How clean it is, washed by a thousand waves! I do not wonder that the ancient Fathers of the Church allowed the use of sand in baptism where, as on the desert, water could not be obtained, for there is no more perfect emblem of purity. And how soft it is, yielding under us like a bed of down, while the waves come rolling in, not roughly and angrily, but softly, gently rippling up the beach. And the air! was there ever anything so pure inhaled by human lungs? There seems a waste in nature, that the water and the air that might revive so many, are thus spent in vain. If they could only be carried into our cities, into the tenement houses, where tens of thousands swelter in the Summer heat, and gasp for a breath of air, how many poor suffering creatures might be brought back to life. As I lie here, looking up into the light clouds sailing by in this heavenly atmosphere, I feel like repeating the prayer of the old prophet: "Come from the four winds, O breath, and breathe upon these slain [the sick and the dying] that they may live"!

The sea shore is a grand school for the study of natural history. The beach is strown with shells, miracles of beauty of color and exquisite in design. Here is the little nautilus with its tiny sail. How fragile it seems! as if a breath of air, or the toss of a wave, would dash it to atoms. And yet He without whom not a sparrow falls to the ground, guides its little bark over the troubled sea. The shells scattered on this beach, in the hand of a master like Agassiz, would furnish a powerful argument for that Creative Mind which he saw behind all the forms of nature, a beautiful illustration of the wisdom and goodness of God.

As it is a bright morning and the sea is smooth, passing ships come in quite near to the land. Yonder is a great steamer bound to Havana. Off the Inlet the Gulf Stream does not come so close to the coast as at Lake Worth, and South-bound ships pass inside of it, so as not to have to breast the mighty current which flows north at the rate of three miles an hour, while ships bound in the opposite direction, strike out boldly into the middle of the Stream, so as to be swept along all the more swiftly by it. We are now in the track of a great commerce, to all the shores of the Gulf, and to the northern and western coast of South America. Through the narrow passage between the mainland and the Bahamas, the Spanish galleons once carried the gold and silver of Mexico and Peru, and here the Buccaneers lay in wait for them. There is no part of the American coast more full of legends of wild adventure, or that has witnessed more scenes of battle and of blood.

Nor did the adventures end with the Spaniards and the Buccaneers. The peculiar formation of the coast of Florida, and of all of the northern shore of the Gulf of Mexico, studded with innumerable islands, afforded secret passages for those embarked in unlawful enterprises, and so became the hiding-places of pirates, who were for a time the terror of the Western Continent, as the Barbary pirates were of the Mediterranean. From this concealment the famous Capt. Kidd made his raids upon the commerce of his day,

> Till his career was ended
> By his being suspended.

But he did not mean that the world should forget him, for by burying his treasure in the sand, he kept curiosity alive, and set treasure-hunters to digging to the present day.

The execution of a few such bold leaders as Kidd was of course a great damper to "the business," yet as late as the beginning of the present century, the pirates of the Gulf were still a terror to all who sailed along the Southern coast; one of the sad tales of which was that the only daughter of Aaron Burr, returning from Charleston, was taken by pirates, and made to walk the plank! Still later, a remnant of them had their lair at the Belize near the mouth of the Mississippi, to watch for ships coming to New Orleans. But all these nests of piracy were finally broken up as the country became more thickly settled. The "good old times" were gone, and with them

> . . . "the good old plan
> That he should take who had the power,
> And he should keep who can."

Pursued in their hiding-places, and cut to pieces, the last of them finally surrendered and made their peace with the Government, by taking service with Gen. Jackson, and fighting bravely at the battle of New Orleans. Since then, we have heard no more of the pirates of the Gulf.

But all dangers of the coast are not over. The sea is not always so smooth as it is this morning. Storms come out of the Gulf of Mexico, as well as the Stream which bears its name, and sometimes sweep along the coast with tremendous power. Now and then the Weather Bureau at Washington gives warning of the approach of a cyclone, that is coming up from the South, which may not expend itself till it has cast up wrecks all along the seaboard to Maine. Its first destruction is felt on the coast of Florida, where along the border of the Gulf Stream there are eddies and currents that drive a ship, that has become helpless in the fury of a gale, upon the rocks and reefs. Hence this coast has had a bad reputation for the number of its shipwrecks, and out of this has grown another ugly business: that of "wreckers"—a rough set of men, who lived along the shores, keeping a lookout for ships that might be caught in gales and storms. It is to be feared that they were not always so full of sympathy as they might have been for the sufferings of their fellow-creatures; for it is said that they even set decoy lights to mislead seamen in dark nights, and draw them on to destruction. No sooner did they see a ship in the breakers going to pieces, than they pounced on the helpless crew as vultures sweep down upon a camel that has fallen on the desert.

There was a time when this "business" was lively and flourishing, but the "profits" are not what they were. Do you see that little building on a point that overlooks the sea? That is the Life-saving Station, manned by trusty seamen, who keep watch for any accident, great or small. Only yesterday, as some of our party were walking on the seashore, they observed a yacht trying to enter the Inlet. There was no heavy sea, but as the passage is narrow, she fell off to one side, and was soon fast in the sand. There was no danger so long as the sea was smooth, but a strong wind might soon put her in peril. But hardly had the accident occurred before half a dozen stalwart seamen came at full speed from the Station, and lending their stout arms to those of the men on board, soon got her off into deep water again.

But this was a trifling incident compared with some which they have to face, when great ships are utterly wrecked. To meet this appalling danger, the Stations are furnished with life-boats and every appliance for extending immediate relief to those in the utmost peril. If a ship gets on the rocks half a mile at sea, and the waves are running so high that no boat can reach her, there is another resource. In a corner of the Station stands a short but big-throated howitzer, like a huge St. Bernard dog on the top of the Alps, waiting for the moment of greatest peril, when the storm is wildest and the snows are deepest, to show what he can do. Into its capacious mouth the seamen thrust a ball, to which is attached a long line, and then the gun is pointed high in air and fired, the ball streaming away like a rocket ; and as it falls into the sea, it drops its line across the deck of the foundering bark, by which those on board can pull in a heavier rope and make it fast, and then lashing themselves to it one by one, can all at last escape safe to land!

Of course the old wreckers look very sullenly at this interference of the Government with their "legitimate business." What with lighthouses that are seen twenty miles at sea, and life-saving stations all along the coast, there does not seem to be much chance for them to pick up a living in the old way. All that is left for them is to do a little smuggling. Cuba is conveniently near to the Florida Coast, and it is easy to fill a boat with a cargo of Havana cigars, and running in among the "Keys" (as the little islands on the coast are called), secrete their treasure in some hidden nook. But here again they are pursued by evil fortune. Hardly have they got on shore, and are sitting round their camp-fire, when the "myrmidons of the law" swoop down upon them, and "gobble up" the cigars, and "hale" the daring boatmen to prison. These things are trying to the greatest courage and endurance, and we can hardly wonder that they sometimes ask the question, which is asked by tramps and idlers and thieves all over the world, "How is a fellow going to live?" That we leave them to settle among themselves. We feel the same sort of sympathy for them that we do for so many old wharf-rats that have been burrowing under and into a staunch ship, and that are suddenly routed out; and as we see them flying in all directions, we turn with renewed satisfaction to the lighthouses along the coast that have let in daylight upon them, and to the vigilant men who have broken up these old haunts of crime, and say, Blessed be civilization!

CHAPTER VI.

NEW ENGLAND IN THE SOUTH—THE OLD HOME AND THE NEW HOME.

Florida is not a part of the country in which we should look for New Englanders, any more than for Southerners in the forests of Maine. But the irrepressible Yankee is everywhere, from the Tropics to the Pole. The war sent the men of Massachusetts and other New England States, to the South by tens of thousands, and many found it a goodly land to stay in when the war was over. Of those who marched with their comrades to the North, where the troops were disbanded, some made their way back again, finding the fertile lands and mild climate of the South more attractive than the rocks and snows of New England. But they did not come in great numbers, nor in armed battalions, but at most in small "squads." The greater part indeed came singly. Here and there an old officer, broken in health by his hard campaigns, had come to Florida to die; but after the experience of a few months, concluded to postpone his departure, and still abides in the land, enjoying health and prosperity. More often those who had served in the camp as common soldiers, leaving behind them their knapsacks and their guns, and with nothing in the world but their strong arms, sought out lonely places in the wilderness where land was cheap, and with their axes made clearings in the forest, and there built them cabins and planted a few acres. Thus coming one by one, in the course of a few years there came to be "quite a sprinkling" of New Englanders through the pine woods of the South; and as they were a hardy tribe, in whom industry and economy took the place of the old shiftlessness, they began to thrive in the land.

Now the Yankees are a clannish race, and when a few of them find themselves within reaching distance, they flock together, using any public occasion—an Agricultural Fair or a Sub-tropical Exposition—to gather round some board, where, as at the cherished Thanksgivings, old memories are revived and old customs recalled. The day which New Englanders have a right to consider as peculiarly their own, is the 22d of December—the day on which the Pilgrims landed on Plymouth Rock. But such a celebration is a Movable Feast, the particular day for which may be made to suit the convenience of the celebrators. In Florida the New Englanders who have been North during the Summer and Winter, often return late, and are not all back even in December; so that it was thought better to fix a later day, and for this year they chose the 22d of *February*, not thinking it a misappropriation of the birthday of the Father of his Country, to devote it to remembering the Pilgrim Fathers.

Accordingly on that day there was a gathering of the clans at Jacksonville—a notable company of typical New Englanders, sturdy in frame, and carrying big heads on their broad shoulders—who had come from all parts of Florida to do honor to their common mother. Of course, as is usual on such occasions, there had to be a good deal of talking, in which many took part, I among the rest.

Though what I said was of no great importance, it seemed to please "the boys." That was not difficult: for when a company are in a mood to be pleased, it is easy to please them. As we were all "of the family," it was natural that they should respond to allusions to the Old Home. There was another tender chord, in the experience of Jacksonville the previous Summer, which responded to whatever recalled that terrible calamity. For the sake of the kindly associations of the hour, and in the hope that it may touch a chord in the hearts of other "old boys," I reprint a part of what I said to those at Jacksonville: for I am sure that the sons of New England, wherever they may be, in whatever new homes they have found in the South or West, will always welcome that which reminds them of the dear old hills and valleys among which they were born. And after this manner I spake:

This is a gathering of the sons of New England, who, though they have removed far away from it, yet do not forget the place of their birth, and come together once a year to revive the recollections of the Old Home. We are met to keep an old-fashioned Thanksgiving, and now that we have partaken of the feast, we may imagine ourselves gathered round one of those huge fireplaces that some of us remember; piled high with hickory logs, and as the flames roar up the chimney, and the firelight shines in the familiar faces, we talk of old times and old friends, the living and the dead.

It is not that New England is better than any other place on the face of the earth (though about that we have our private opinion), but she is Our Mother: she rocked us in our cradles; she formed in us the principles and the habits to which we owe whatever of success we have had in life; and we should be unworthy of her, if we did not remember her with filial affection, reverence, and honor.

The country itself is not attractive, at least not at this season of the year, in the depth of Winter. If we could transport ourselves there to-night, what should we see? Not the orange groves of Florida, but only naked trees, with branches all stripped and bare, while hills and valleys are buried in snow. And yet a New England Winter is not without its attractions. Even in the storm-blast there is something which rouses the manhood in our breasts, and causes the blood to course quicker in our veins. Who of us cannot say with Burns :

> " E'en Winter bleak has charms to me,
> When winds rave through the naked tree,
> And frosts on hills of Ochiltree
> Are hoary gray ;
> Or blinding drifts wild furious flee
> Darkening the day."

The pleasures of Winter are not to be despised. How I wish I could hear at this moment the jingle of the sleigh-bells, and the merry laugh and song of the boys and girls as they ride home in the moonlight!

But it is in the Spring-time that New England puts on her robe of beauty : when, after the long sleep of Winter, the life of nature returns, as our little friends the robins come back ; the tender grass begins to appear, and the trees put forth their leaves ; the apple blossoms fill the air with fragrance ; and the verdure from the meadows along the river's banks creeps up the hillsides, till the foliage of the oaks and the birches and the chestnuts, mingled with the evergreen of the pines and the hemlocks, makes the full glory of the forest, and the mountains shake like Lebanon.

In these green valleys and under the shadow of these mountains, have sprung up villages of a peculiar type— not centering in some lordly pile, as an English village gathers round a nobleman's castle—with no great mansions, but a general air of comfort and modest beauty. If I were to take one village as a sample of many, it would be the one I know best, that in which I was born, in Western Massachusetts, in the Berkshire Hills—Stockbridge—a village not laid out in the English style, nor the French style, nor in any other "style," except the good old-fashioned New England style; having one broad street lined with elms, whose giant branches, reaching high in air and drooping towards each other, form an arch like that of a cathedral, which, when lighted up by the setting sun, is more glorious than the nave of Westminster Abbey.

Along this street, under these elms, are scattered homes, not pretentious in any way, but each with its smooth-shaven lawn, its grass and its flowers without, and its books and pictures within, which show it to be the home of taste and refinement.

If there were time to dwell on these home pictures, I might take you over the town, to the farm-houses, with capacious barns, and other signs of abundance, in front of which the spacious foreground is overhung by trees, and graced by

"The moss-covered bucket that hangs in the well."

Next to the homes of the New England village are its institutions, around which its life gathers. Of these there are two, the church and the school. You see the little schoolhouse at the foot of the hill, or it may be under the shade of an elm: how modest it looks! But in many a New England village that was the only "institution of learning." Yet out of that humble door have gone the men that have led your armies, that have fought your battles and ruled your Government. The schoolhouses of New England have made its people the equal in intelligence of any other on the face of the globe.

THE OLD MEETING-HOUSE. 81

Yet the schoolhouse would not have amounted to so much, if it had not been for the motherly old "Meeting-house," that stood on the village green, which was the educator of the people in moral and religious truth, as the school taught them the rudiments of knowledge. What an awe fell upon my childish heart as I looked up at the steeple from which the bell called us to the place of prayer! As a boy I often wandered about the old graveyard, where

"The rude forefathers of the hamlet sleep";

and if at that moment the old sexton struck the bell for some approaching funeral, that solemn toll struck upon my heart as if it were a warning sound from eternity itself.

Within the old meeting-house our associations are of a mingled character: grave and solemn, with observations of manners and customs that were quaint and curious, some of which may even provoke a smile. The high pulpit was at one end of the church, and the gallery at the other, in which the choir stood facing the minister, as if determined to keep up their end of the house, and do their full part in public worship. In those days we did not have a fashionable quartette, but pure home talent, in which the "spruce" young men of the village showed themselves beside the comely maidens. In our village church, in the centre of the choir stood a man six feet high (I say six; it might have been seven or eight—to my childish imagination he seemed to be ten or twelve), whose "front view" was made still more striking by a tremendous nose. As he rose in his full proportions, he lifted up with him a bass viol as big as himself, out of which he ground unearthly music. The sight was so awe-inspiring, that I had to turn aside my eyes to rest them on the gentle Priscillas at his side. The Lord will forgive me in the circumstances. In truth, I did not look upon those faces as I might if I had seen them on the street, lighted up with smiles. I regarded them only with what President Edwards calls "the love of complacency," which he approves and commends as "a very sweet affection" (he is certainly right in that), and also very pure and holy, if it be not indeed the essence of all virtue!

But if anybody imagines that the Sabbath worship was merely an occasion for mutual observation, he is greatly mistaken; the old meeting-house was truly a solemn place, as the house of God ought to be : where all that was evil in us was rebuked, and all that was best was awakened to a new life; where heads were bent low, and tears fell from weeping eyes; and as we mourned over all that was wrong in the past, we resolved to live better in the future, and our solemn vows were mingled with humble prayers.

Then as we raised our bended heads and down-cast eyes to the pulpit, we listened to him who spoke as a messenger from above. I have stood upon the top of Mount Sinai, where God gave the law to men; but God never came so near to me as when He spoke, not by the lips of Moses, but of one to whom I looked up with far more reverence than I did to Moses, because he spoke not only with authority, but with that love which gives to authority its highest power. How can I ever speak, or think as I ought, of that white haired patriarch who taught me the way of life, and of whom, as he went up out of our sight, I could only exclaim, "My Father! My Father! The chariot of Israel and the horsemen thereof!" We shall see him no more, and yet we mourn not, since we think of him now as having passed into the highest heavens, where he is without fault before the throne of God!

Nor was the religion of New England merely inculcated in public; it entered into the families of the people, and was a part of their daily life. How well do I remember the morning and evening prayers! In my father's family we read the Bible through in course, beginning with Genesis, and going straight through to Revelation. We knew all the generations from Adam. We had as clear an idea of the geography of the Garden of Eden, as we had of our own village. Did we not have a map of it in the old Family Bible, with the four rivers running out of it at right angles! About that household worship linger sweet and blessed memories. I had a sister with a gentle voice, who at our morning prayers often sang:

> Early, my God, without delay,
> I haste to seek Thy face;

and at evening,

> Glory to Thee, my God, this night,
> For all the blessings of the light;
> Keep me, O keep me, King of kings,
> Beneath the shadow of Thy wings.

Her voice thrills me even now, though I hear it only dying away in the distance, as she long since passed within the heavenly gates.

Pardon these personal allusions. But in the associations that are brought back to-night, thoughts of the living are mingled with memories of the dead, memories which it is good to recall, as they will help us to live and to die. That morning and evening worship was repeated in ten thousand homes, as the Cotter's Saturday Night was repeated in the homes of Scotland; and if

> " From scenes like these old Scotia's grandeur springs,
> That makes her loved at home, revered abroad,"

not less is it true of our dear New England.

Of what that North country has been and has done in our national history, I will not speak. As Mr. Webster once said on a memorable occasion of Massachusetts: "There she is; behold her, and judge for yourselves! The bones of her sons, fallen in the great struggle for independence, lie mingled with the soil of every State, from Maine to Georgia, and there they will lie forever."

Such is New England, and such the inheritance which she has left to her children.

Having thus spoken of the Old Home, may I say a few words of the New One? Though we meet to-night as sons of New England, we are not in New England, but a thousand miles away. Yet we do not feel that we are strangers here, who must, like the captives in Babylon, hang our harps upon the willows, saying "How can we sing the Lord's song in a strange land?" We are still at home, in the same country, under the same flag, and among those who are our countrymen and brothers.

I have no wish to revive painful recollections: indeed they cease to be painful when we come to recognize the hand of God in a bitter experience, leading us on to an end better than we knew. The great Civil War, which covered our land with mourning and woe, accomplished for us in four years what could not have been accomplished in a hundred years of peace. It removed the one great bar to a perfect union, and made us know each other as never before. Hatred between nations, as between individuals, is often born of ignorance. The Germans and the French hate each other, because they are rival powers and have had many wars, but this hatred would die out, were it not that they live in different countries and speak different languages, so that they cannot have that free communion with each other, that would exist between those of the same race and speech, passing to and fro, from city to city. So in this country—the North and the South were long separated by great distances as well as by different institutions. Now, it may seem strange for a minister of the Gospel to say it, but it is the sober truth of history, that nothing promotes acquaintance so much as war. Soldiers who meet face to face do not need any formal introduction: they do not stand on ceremony, but at once present their salutations, and in an hour they are better acquainted than they would be in years standing aloof and indulging in mutual recriminations. Still further, men who have fought each other generally have an immense respect for each other. And while respect is not love, yet it is an essential element in an attachment that is to be strong and permanent. And so it is that good often comes out of evil, and peace is established by war : " Out of the lion cometh forth meat, and out of the strong cometh forth sweetness."

The truth of this was never more fully illustrated than in the result of our late war, by which we have not only kept the old union, but established a still better one—one that I believe will last forever. This is the third time that I have come South within a few years, and it has been with increasing satisfaction that I have observed how old prejudices were dying out, and those long divided by ignorance of each other, were coming to know each other better, and to feel a genuine mutual respect.

In addition to this general reflow of fraternal feeling, the people of this city, more than of almost any other in our country, have been drawn together during the past year by common trials and common sufferings. For months there was no place which was the object of such constant and painful interest. I see across the table a gentleman who stood at his post here through all that dreadful time (I am proud to say that he is a brother-editor), and sent daily messages to the North of the ravages of the destroyer. He can hardly realize what min-

THE YELLOW FEVER IN JACKSONVILLE.

gled feelings of terror and pity and sympathy those tidings created. Jacksonville seemed to us like a besieged city, in which your people were fighting with sickness and death. Nothing tries human courage and endurance so much as this daily hand-to-hand fight with an enemy, not without but within your gates—an enemy all the more terrible because it is invisible; because it walketh in darkness and wasteth at noonday.

You have read the story of the siege of Lucknow: and remember how it dragged on for months, the enemy all the while coming nearer and nearer, and the defenders growing fewer and fewer. Still they only closed up their ranks, and stood at their posts—men, and women too, all involved in one common suffering, some dying every day, but with their last breath animating their survivors.

You in Jacksonville have been through somewhat the same experience. Month after month the pestilence was never for a single moment out of your thoughts. Day after day those whom you had seen in robust health were carried to their long home, and the mourners went about the streets. The strain of such prolonged anxiety must have been terrible. How bravely it was borne, you best know. Some of your foremost citizens—those who could least be spared—sacrificed their lives to save yours. In an address delivered here only day before yesterday, at the reopening of your Sub-Tropical Exposition, I find the following allusion to one who at the first opening introduced the President of the United States: "You all remember that the Chief Magistrate was introduced by a man the memory of whose unselfish life is a heritage beyond price—God's nobleman and our martyr—James Jacquelin Daniel." As I read this, my thoughts went back to Lucknow and to one who perished there. Sir Henry Lawrence, the commander, exposing himself too bravely, was struck by a shell, and covering his uniform that the soldiers might not know their terrible loss, was carried away to die. Like Havelock, he was a Christian soldier, and partook of the communion, and asked that no eulogy should be inscribed upon his tomb, but simply these words : " Here lies Henry Lawrence, who tried to do his duty : may God have mercy on his soul ! " With equal truth might these words (which, simple as they are, comprehend everything) be written over the grave of your martyr : " Here lies one who tried to do his duty ! "

These sacrifices have not been in vain, if they teach a lesson to those who survive. They should not be forgotten, for the memory will be an inspiration to you and to those that come after you, to meet whatever trials may be in store for you in the future. Those trials may not come in the form of pestilence ; they may come in flames, which may lay a part of your city in ashes. But no matter what may be, nor how it may come, it will never be irretrievable if you stand together, thinking only of the common safety, and meet danger with that presence of mind, that calmness and resolution, of which men of your own city have given such splendid examples.

But while we recall this great calamity, it is gratifying to see how quickly and completely you have recovered from it. If we had not had such full details in our Northern papers in the daily despatches from Jacksonville, we could not believe that it had passed through such a bitter experience. But already trade has revived, and business goes on as before, giving signs to the stranger of what I hear from many quarters, that this is to be the great commercial city of the South Atlantic coast, taking the place formerly held by Charleston and Savannah.

If you would allow me, as an outsider, to express an opinion, it would be that this prosperity has been greatly promoted by the complete fusion of the North and the South. I see here on every side the signs that Northern capital and Northern enterprise have come among you, and come to stay. But I should be sorry to think that this was to be a Northern city in any exclusive sense. It is Southern by latitude, by climate, and by population, and such it must remain, only deriving additional strength from the infusion of another element, the mingling of Northern and Southern blood.

In this beautiful city of the South, you, sons of New England, have fixed your home. You are not aliens here, but fellow-citizens with your Southern brethren of this goodly Commonwealth. You will be none the less so for remembering where you were born, and cherishing the principles and the habits which you learned from your fathers: industry, integrity, fidelity; and that fear of Almighty God which becomes the descendants of the Puritans. Brothers! you who have come from Maine and Massachusetts; from the Green Mountains of Vermont and the White Hills of New Hampshire; from the valleys of Connecticut and the rocky shores of Rhode Island: you are heirs to a great inheritance—the inheritance of two hundred and fifty years of honor and glory. Keep that honor unstained! Wherever your lot may be cast, in the North or in the South, or in the mighty West, let the sons of New England show that they are not unworthy of their glorious Mother.

CHAPTER VII.

NORTHERN FLORIDA.

I felt a real sinking of the heart when it came to saying good-bye to St. Augustine. For seven weeks (except the interval of the excursion to Jupiter Inlet, and a longer visit to Havana) it had been my home. Never have I been in a more restful spot. Coming from the incessant roar of city streets, the change was as great as if I had been transported to some mountain top, or to some deep valley in the Alps, where the sounds of the busy world could not reach me, and I could quietly gather strength for the opening year.

But all its pleasures come to an end as the stalwart porter—a man of mighty physique and stentorian voice—comes up into the Rotunda, and cries in a tone that rings through the halls, "All on board for Jacksonville!" Reluctantly we vanish from the scene, and as we roll under the arches and over the smooth road to the new Union Depot, we keep looking back to the Spanish towers of the Ponce de Leon, under the shadow of which we have passed so many weeks of rest and of happiness.

It softened a little the pain of departure, that I could make the first stage of my homeward journey a short one, and stop at Jacksonville, and spend an evening with the friends who had invited me to make the trip with them to Jupiter Inlet. We met as brave companions-in-arms, and as we sat round the table, we recalled our thrilling experiences by flood and field, and fought our battles over again in the most approved style of old soldiers.

When I first saw Jacksonville, it was only to pass through it from one end of the main street to the other, which I supposed to be the whole town; and I thought that, though it might be called in Western or Southern phrase, "a right smart chance of a place," it was not very picturesque nor attractive in any way. It was not till I came again for the New England dinner, and spent a day, that I got any idea either of its extent or its beauty. But when it came to a drive of several hours, I found the place expanding in every direction; and that the business portion, instead of being confined to one street, overflowed into many, in which the shops and stores and markets, the railway stations and landing places, had an air of busy, bustling activity, not common in a Southern town. A stately ship, just coming up the river, reminded us that this was a seaport, and had connection with all the cities on the Atlantic Coast. Miss Thursby, whom I met at St. Augustine, told me that she had never had a more delightful voyage than that from New York to Jacksonville. The Sub-tropical Exposition, inaugurated last year by President Cleveland, but broken up by the yellow fever, had been recently reopened—an event which was welcomed by the people as a good omen, it being interpreted as a sign of the revival of general prosperity.

The city is well laid out, having as a centre a square, on which are two fine hotels; and the wide streets, along which they have begun to plant trees, are adorned with many beautiful residences. The ground already built over, must be two or three square miles in extent. Nor is this all that is available for a city. Behind it is a large plateau, elevated above the river sufficiently to furnish perfect drainage, now covered with pine woods, but where in the future I see in imagination hundreds and thousands of suburban homes, such as now line all the roads radiating from that most beautiful city of the west, Cleveland, Ohio. In truth, Jacksonville reminds me of what Cleveland was when I first saw it, forty years ago; and suggests the pleasant anticipation that what Cleveland is to-day, Jacksonville may be in forty years to come: her own enthusiastic people would probably say, in half that time.

Returning from this plateau, we drove for a couple of miles along the bank of the St. John's, where at intervals are spacious dwellings, half hidden from view by the shade of trees, and that on the other side look out upon the broad surface of this noble river, the sight of " a busy city far away" only adding to the sense of perfect seclusion. I did not wonder that Mrs. Stowe had pitched her tent a few miles to the south of this, at Mandarin, where under the overhanging boughs, she could enjoy to the full the solemn stillness, the whispering winds, and all the majesty and inspiration of a forest home.

When I left Jacksonville the next morning, it was not to take a course directly north, but west, which took me through Northern Florida, a portion of the State that has a character of its own. Southern Florida, all of which is in the peninsula, is as flat as if it had but just risen from the ocean bed, but here the country rises in gentle undulations, like the rolling prairies of the West. The vegetation also changes: instead of endless pine barrens, the trees are at once larger and more varied, reminding one of the oak openings of Michigan. There are also signs of activity along the road, more frequent than in the farther South. Villages are sprinkled in the woods, and now and then the welcome sound of a saw-mill mingles with the rushing of a stream. I was not looking out for streams, for I was not making a study of geography; and perhaps my readers will smile when I tell them that the only one which I asked to have pointed out to me, was the Suwanee river. It is not much of a river, and as it glides away under the trees along its banks, it seems to be hiding from sight. But even the glimpse of it as the train rushed over the bridge, set me to humming to myself:

> " 'Way down on de S'wanee river,
> Far, far away—
> Dere's where my heart is turning ebber;
> Dere's where de old folks stay."

This is one of the most popular songs in the world. Years ago it was said that half a million copies of it had been sold. It is the echo of the old plantation melodies, though the words and the music were by a Northern composer. Yet he must have made a study of the native songs, till he caught their peculiar rhythm and was infused with their spirit. What a pity that these old melodies, that charmed a past generation, are dying out! It may be said that they are "slave songs," which were born of a state of servitude, and that now the negroes are free, we cannot expect them any longer to sing the songs of their captivity. This may be one reason, and yet I cannot help thinking that there is another still more potent, viz : that they are ashamed of them, as if they were reminders of their old state of bondage.

The evening before I left St. Augustine, there was a gathering of the colored people in the Opera House, which was chosen as the only building in the town large enough to hold them. As I sat on the platform, between the principal speaker and Dr. Paxton of New York, and looked over the assembled multitude, it was a stirring scene. The choir, composed wholly of colored singers, sang a number of pieces, and sang well, as such singers always do, for they have an instinct of melody; and yet I felt a disappointment, and said to the leader, "Why did you not sing some of the old plantation melodies?" "Because," he answered, "I thought I would educate my people to something higher!" That tells the whole story. It is in the effort to rise to "something higher," that they have lost what gave their songs such a wonderful pathos and power. The feeling may be a natural one, but the result is to be lamented, for so perishes what we would not willingly let die. These songs have still a place in a world that is full of breaking hearts. Slavery is dead, but sorrow is not dead, and the time has not yet come, and perhaps never will come, when mourning hearts will not need to sing

"Nobody knows the sorrows I've seen,
  Nobody knows but Jesus,"
and
"Keep me from sinking down,"

At two o'clock we came to a city set on a hill. Not a very high hill, to be sure, but one that it was refreshing to see after so long dwelling on the plains. This was Tallahassee, the capital of Florida, a city which, compared with the new towns that have sprung up here and there, is quite venerable, and was in the former days a home of the Southern aristocracy, and that still has many old families, which, though reduced in wealth, retain that dignity and courtesy of manners, which was the most attractive feature of the olden time. It is still one of the most charming towns in the South.

Riding over the hills, through long streets, past the Capitol (in which the Legislature meets for a few months of the year, when the town is filled with the atmosphere of politics), we come to the Leon Hotel—so named from the county in which it is, that received *its* name at the first settlement of the country, when it was christened from the province of Spain that was united with Castile hundreds of years ago.

There is another reminder of the Old World in the graveyard, where, beneath a modest stone, lies the body of Achille Murat. What a story is told in the name graven on that monument! He who lies here was born in a palace, the son of that fiery soldier whose deeds were known on every battlefield of Europe, and of Caroline, sister of the great Napoleon. Nephew of the master of France, he seemed born to great destinies. His father was made King of Naples, where, possessed of an independent sovereignty, he thought to manage his little kingdom in his own way, and chafed at receiving orders from Paris, to the indignation of his Imperial creator; but restraining his own impatience for a time, it broke out after the triumph of the Allies in 1814, when he turned against his former master, who was so angered by this treachery that when he returned from Elba, he would not receive his former lieutenant—a degree of displeasure which cost him dear, for with Murat (as he thought) he might have won the battle of Waterloo. "It needed only," he said, "to break a few English squares, and Murat would undoubtedly have effected that." Meanwhile the latter had lost his throne, which he endeavored to recover by a revolution that was immediately suppressed, and he was shot.

Then the several branches of the Napoleon dynasty sought a refuge in different parts of the world. Joseph Bonaparte, the eldest brother of Napoleon and former King of Spain, came to the United States, and for some years lived in retirement at Bordentown, New Jersey;

while the son of Murat, as yet hardly grown to manhood, came to Florida and married an American wife, and no doubt was happier in his quiet home than if he had inherited the throne of the two Sicilies.

After the restoration of the Empire under Louis Napoleon, the representatives of different branches of the family were recalled to Paris, and shone as the stars of the Imperial Court. But Achille Murat was in his grave. The old residents of Tallahassee still remember him as the quiet French gentleman, who won their respect and their good will by his courtesy; and they point out to strangers the mansion on yonder hill where he lived with his true-hearted American wife, who wrote the touching inscription on his tomb, where she now sleeps beside him.

But I had come to Tallahassee chiefly to see an old friend, Prof. E. Warren Clark, who many years ago wrote Letters from Japan, when that country was less known than it is now. I did not see him in Japan, nor become acquainted with him till after his return to America; nor even since had I seen him often. But I felt such genuine respect for him as one of the pluckiest men I had ever known, that, although it was nearly two hundred miles out of my way, I would not leave the South without seeing him. Inquiring for him I found that he was living on a plantation five miles from the city. Asking for a carriage to take me there, the proprietor of the Leon kindly offered to drive me himself; so that I had not only his spirited horses, but an excellent companion and guide. It was a pleasant afternoon, and the new-plowed furrows in the fields lay open to the sun, and as they melted under the increasing warmth, gave promise of an early Spring. My friend, coming South a few years since for his health, had taken an old plantation, which had run to waste after the war, but which he had set to work with his usual energy to restore, and bring into cultivation. The place was a large one, comprising several hundred acres of upland, dotted over with grand old oaks, and looking down upon a beautiful lake, across which the hills on the opposite side cast their evening shadows.

But he had no end of troubles to encounter. He was attacked with chills, which would have shaken the life out of a less resolute man ; while he daily groaned over the easy-going and slow-moving blacks, who would wear out the patience of a saint. In hearing his story, I could not but think that his "fight of afflictions" was greater in some respects than Paul's : for while the Apostle had to fight with beasts at Ephesus, he never had to fight with the fever and ague ; and though his patience was tried in dealing with all sorts of "unreasonable men," he had not to deal with the Sambos and Topsys of an old plantation. However, my brave friend did not ask pity from anybody, and while he told of his manifold experiences, laughed heartily over them. Fortunately he stays here but a part of the year. His family are settled in a delightful home in Columbia, Tennessee, to which I hope he will be able to remove, to engage in that varied work, as teacher and preacher and lecturer, for which he is admirably fitted.

As he was alone except with his workmen, I immediately laid hold upon him, and carried him off captive to Tallahassee for the night. A pleasant evening it was in the spacious parlors of the Leon Hotel, before the blazing fire, where were many visitors from the North, among whom we found, as usual, the three Cs—Cincinnati, Cleveland, and Chicago—well represented ; while in our private talks we went back in memory and imagination to the happy days that we passed in the Land of the Rising Sun.

CHAPTER VIII.

"MARCHING THROUGH GEORGIA."

When Sherman made his famous March to the Sea, the Boys in Blue enlivened their "tramp, tramp," with many a song as well as story—songs that were sung, not only on the march, but by the camp-fire, and echoed far and wide through the dim aisles of the Southern forest. Of these, no one was more popular than "Marching through Georgia." I do not remember ever to have heard it; if I have I did not know it at the time, as I could not even now tell it from "Dixie." But as any verse of the Bible may serve for a text, so the title of this old war-song is a good enough heading for the wayside observations of one who has been lately "marching through Georgia," from one end to the other, though he did not capture anybody, but on the contrary, must admit (if he had to confess the truth) that the people captured him.

I "invaded" the State from the south. It is less than thirty miles from Tallahassee, the capital of Florida, to Thomasville, which (to keep up the military phrase) was my first "strategic point." This is one of the new creations of the New South, that has sprung up in the pine woods. Dr. Metcalfe, the eminent physician of New York, "discovered" it a few years since, and finding that it combined many of the features which he desired, recommended it to his patients as a sanitarium for invalids, from which (as is often the case) it became a fashionable resort for a great many besides, chiefly well-to-do people from Northern cities, who, not being kept at home by business, sought a pleasant retreat from the severity of their own climate. It has no great attractions of scenery, but is in a rolling and well wooded country, far enough away from the sea to escape the damp air, so trying to weak lungs. Here a number of fine hotels have been built in the woods, where one sitting on a broad verandah, may not only breathe an atmosphere that is dry and pure, but inhale the balmy odors of the forest. I am not surprised to find these pleasant camping grounds taken possession of by large colonies of Northerners, who swoop down on them "like the wolf on the fold "—a class of "invaders," however, more welcome than the soldiers of Sherman, since, instead of coming with guns in their hands, they bring no other weapon than the gold which they scatter lavishly in a region where it is greatly needed.

One has hardly an idea of the dimensions of Georgia, until he makes a journey across its whole length or breadth, as it stretches one way nearly five degrees of latitude, and the other as many of longitude. It is called the Empire State of the South, as New York is the Empire State of the North; but this does it injustice as to its magnitude, for it is larger in territory than New York by more than ten thousand square miles, the figures being for New York 47,000 square miles, and for Georgia 58,000! The latter has not indeed some features of our Northern "Empire," such as the Great Lakes on one border, and the mighty Port, which receives the commerce of all parts of the world, on the other; yet it has beauties of its own. If it has no Alpine heights covered with eternal snow, like Mount Hood, or other peaks on the Pacific Coast, it has sufficient variety in a surface which stretches from the mountains to the sea. On the north, the great Appalachian chain (which, coming down from Virginia, forms the boundary between the States on its eastern and its western slope, having the Carolinas on the one hand, and Kentucky and Tennessee on the other) at last looks down upon Georgia. From this mountain chain the Savannah river, running to the sea, divides Georgia from South Carolina, while the Chattahoochee, turning southward to the Gulf of Mexico, divides it from Alabama. Within these boundaries of nature lies the broad imperial domain of a State, in which there are no less than one hundred and thirty-seven counties, and which has three millions of inhabitants.

Central Georgia has not in its appearance much to attract the eye of a stranger. It has not even the interest of war, for Sherman's march from Atlanta was to the southeast, in the general direction of the Savannah river, though often at a long distance from it. The country is flat, and the towns have a rough frontier look, like the new settlements in the Territories of the West. Nowhere does one see the finished beauty of our New England villages. But my curiosity is always piqued to observe the mixed population. Some travellers note peculiarities of Southern dialect, but I do not see that they are greater than those at the North, or that the New Englander who "guesses," has much to boast over the Southerner who "reckons." The negroes are a source of infinite amusement, as they swarm around every railway station, as if they had nothing to do but to enjoy this idleness—always happy, as they are easily pleased, any poor joke being enough to set them grinning from ear to ear.

In the crowds that fill the trains—it is a great mystery to me where they all come from and go to—there are many strongly marked faces of men whom it would be a pleasure to know. Whenever I see a man enter the car who has lost an arm or a leg, I set him down as an old soldier, and have a great desire to take a seat by him, and hear him fight his battles over again, for, strange to say, instead of being full of bitterness, and cherishing old animosities, no class are so free from them as these war-worn veterans.

Among these was a man of fine presence, with an air half military, half ministerial, with whom, as he took a seat beside me, I fell in conversation. He proved to be, as I had thought, an old soldier, who, when he laid down his arms, took to preaching the Gospel. Having served in the army of the Confederacy, did not unfit him at all for serving in the army of the Lord. On the contrary, it rather fitted him for his special duty, inasmuch as he is now a presiding elder in the Methodist Church—a position in which he has at once to command and to obey. I have often thought that a little of this military discipline would not be a bad thing for any of us, ministers or laymen. We talked about the war with as much freedom as about politics or churches. As a soldier he had fought for the cause which he thought to be right, and I have no doubt fought bravely. Perhaps some of my Northern friends may think I failed in my duty that I did not seize the opportunity to give him "a piece of my mind" on "the sin of rebellion," with an exhortation to repentance; but, as that might have been followed by a piece of *his* mind on the wickedness (as he would look upon it) of invading his State, I do not think the conversation would have been profitable to either. He talked very frankly, yet without a particle of bitterness, nor did the fact that he had left an arm on the field of battle make him feel that he had a right to hate every man who hailed from the North. So the conversation ran on for an hour, till he reached his home, when I was truly sorry to part from him; since I had found in him one who was certainly not an enemy, and "no more a stranger," but "a brother in the household of faith," whom, if I do not meet again this side of the river, I trust I shall meet when we both have "passed over the river, and rest under the trees."

It was evening when we reached Macon, and I saw it only as we passed round it, getting glimpses here and there into the lighted streets. I was sorry not to see it in the broad light of day, for it is reputed to be one of the most beautiful cities in the South, on high ground, and laid out in broad streets, lined with trees, with two or three colleges and other public institutions.

But another hundred miles remained of our long journey before we should finish our "marching through Georgia," and it was after ten o'clock when we rolled into the station at Atlanta, where the first face to greet me was that of Mr. Samuel M. Inman, who was waiting for me with his carriage, in which he "took me to his own home." Delightful it was, after a long day's journey, to be once more in that sweet atmosphere, to look in kindly faces, and receive the greeting of kindly voices. In such a home I spent the three or four days of my stay in Atlanta.

Of all the cities in the South this attracts me most—perhaps because I know it best—but apart from any personal associations, it has attractions of its own. It is a new city, risen from the ashes in which it was consumed a quarter of a century ago. And often it is with cities as with men, a resurrection is not only a rising to a new life but a better life than that it had before. I believe the people of Chicago look back upon the great fire that laid a large part of their city in ashes, as in the end a blessing —a hard discipline, it is true, but one in which good came out of evil. So with Atlanta; it seems not only to have sprung to a new life, but a far more vigorous life than it had before. Now it is not altogether a Southern city, but as in the old days it was sometimes said of a conservative politician, that he was "a Northern man with Southern principles," so reversing the pithy epigram, we may say of Atlanta that it is a Southern city with Northern energy and enterprise. More than any other city I know, it has shaken off the incubus of old habits, the result of old institutions, and sprung forward like a giant to run a race. In the old slavery days there was a sort of slipshod air about everything and everybody; planters were head over heels in debt, falling behind from year to year; trying in vain to extricate themselves; now selling their slaves one after another, even to the family servants; and not unfrequently the old plantation had to be mortgaged, till in cases not a few, the proud possessors of old estates, and the inheritors of honored names, had to go forth at last from the mansions which they had received from their fathers to eat the bitter bread of poverty.

At last by the hard discipline of war, this downward tendency has been checked, and now the movement is the other way. The power to endure hardship, which was developed in war, has been turned to the arts of peace. Poverty begets industry, and industry begets prosperity. When people are not ashamed to work, nor to economize, they soon grow rich; and so it is that Atlanta has become the prosperous city that it is to-day.

But it is not merely a money-making town, where nothing is thought of but the almighty dollar: it is honorably distinguished for the attention paid to education, as shown in its schools and higher institutions, the latest of

CHURCHES AND MINISTERS. 103

which, an Institute of Technology, is modelled after that of Boston.

Well provided also is it with churches, which are both numerous and strong. One cannot spend a Sunday here without feeling that it is eminently a church-going city. All denominations flourish. The two largest bodies in the South are the Baptists and the Methodists. The former are well represented, as everywhere in Georgia; while the Methodists, if they will pardon the expression, "keep up steam" at a tremendous rate. This is not meant as a flippant remark—for I could not speak lightly of a body which I greatly love and honor. From the day that Wesley preached in the American colonies, and laid the foundations of Methodism this side the Atlantic, his followers have been pioneers in carrying the Gospel into waste places. All honor to them for the courage and self-sacrifice with which they have gone before to prepare the way of the Lord!

Nor have the Presbyterians any reason to be ashamed, for their churches also are both numerous and strong. Dr. Barnett is now absent on a pilgrimage to the Holy Land, sent by the generous kindness of a people who know how to appreciate one of the best of ministers. Dr. Strickler, like many others of the leading preachers of the South, had had his military discipline and experience. When the war broke out he was in College at Lexington, Virginia; and about the time that Stonewall Jackson left the Military Institute to enter on his memorable career, a number of the students formed a company, of which young Strickler was chosen captain, and fought in a number of battles, until at Gettysburg he was wounded and taken prisoner. It was, if I remember rightly, more than a year that he was confined at the North—a time that would be wearisome to most, but which he did not pass in idleness, for in it he applied himself to study, under the instruction of a learned fellow-prisoner, and it is said, made himself master of two languages! When at last he was exchanged and returned to Richmond, he and his fellow-prisoners expected to be received with a joyous welcome; but as they steamed up the James river and came to the familiar landing, they were surprised at the absence not only of enthusiasm, but of people. The streets were almost deserted, ominous token of an impending flight. He slept there that night, paying (as he told me) seventy-five dollars for his lodging! (so worthless had the Confederate money become), and got out of the city by the first train the next morning, fortunately for himself, for in less than a week the crash came, and all the means of transportation were choked up by the mass of those fleeing from the city. This is the man, who, having endured hardness as a soldier, is now a soldier of Jesus Christ, with a manner so kindly and gentle that it is hard to realize that he ever led a charge on the field of battle! As a pastor he is greatly beloved by the large congregation to which he ministers, and respected by the whole community.

Georgia has vast natural resources, the materials in herself of great prosperity. In mineral wealth, in coal and iron, she is perhaps not the equal of her sister State, Alabama; but in products of the soil far richer: first of all in the fruits of the earth needed for man's subsistence: in a rice crop second only to that of South Carolina; and sweet potatoes, the food of the South, second only to that of North Carolina; while her cotton crop, second only to that of Mississippi, furnishes the staple of foreign commerce, that brings to her planters the money of the manufacturers of both New England and Old England.

With such elements of wealth, the credit of the State, if not quite so high as that of New York or Massachusetts, is higher than was that of any one of the States, or even of the National Government itself, before the war.

Apart from this, the government of the State is a good government—it is in good and honest hands, by which the laws are faithfully administered. The present Governor, General John B. Gordon, is the most popular man in the State, if not in the South—a popularity which he owes undoubtedly to his services in the war. The man who followed the fortunes of the Confederacy till the last hour, and stood by the side of General Lee when he surrendered at Appomattox, will never be forgotten by his soldiers. Nor does he forget them. If there be any class for which he feels most, it is Confederate soldiers, who are left penniless and destitute. The Union soldiers are provided for munificently by a government that is rich, and that scatters among the veterans nearly a hundred millions a year. But the soldiers of a Lost Cause have no National Government to look to—nothing but State authority, and the charity of their old comrades, many of whom are as poor as they. Georgia gives a hundred dollars a year to each of her own soldiers who has lost a leg or an arm. But that is a pittance for those who have families dependent on them. Sitting in the Governor's room one day, he told of the destitution of old soldiers, scarred with wounds, unable to work, yet who had wives and children in absolute want. Almost every day they came to him with the same pitiful story. Only last week, he said, came in an old man, who began: "Governor, I have not seen you since the war," and after telling the story of his life, said: "Now I am an old man, with seven daughters, and not money enough to buy a loaf of bread!" With this, said the Governor, "he sat down in that chair, and wept like a child." No wonder that the hero who has led these very men to battle, should be touched to the heart by the sorrows of his old companions-in-arms, and that it should be the dream of his life to establish a Confederate Soldiers Home, where these wrecks of the war should be saved from any further "going to pieces." He would not have them separated from their families, and put as pensioners in a kind of public almshouse, but be gathered in a number of homes, under a general management, where there should be some simple industries, by which they could do a little towards their own support. Thus they would be shielded from want, and be able to pass the evening of their days in quietness and peace.

Of such a governor Georgia may well be proud, and not less of his heroic wife, who for four years followed the camp, never being out of the sound of battle, when there was need for her womanly courage and devotion. Atlanta has many old soldiers, whom the South counts among her bravest and her best, and who, after being foremost in war, are now foremost in peace. The city and all the country round are full of stirring associations; and as we walk through these bustling streets, there seems almost a disaccord between this business activity and the mighty memories that gather, like dark clouds, on the surrounding hills. But so it is that the Dead Past is merged in the Living Present. As the centre of such a mingled life, where the Old South and the New South come together, Atlanta sets one thinking of the war, and of the terrible problem that it has left behind it; and so it is a good place to linger, while we consider the great question of Race which now confronts our American civilization.

CHAPTER IX.

THE BLACK BELT—THE DEAD LION—SPEAK GENTLY OF THE DEAD!

As I came up from the Gulf States, I had crossed the Black Belt—the portion of the South most densely populated by the black race. It is not a fixed zone, running between two parallels of latitude, but surges back and forth, like an ocean current where two seas meet, now rising and rolling on, and now falling back, as if sinking away into fathomless depths below; but covering all together a vast surface, reaching half way across the continent. In this enormous Belt there are places where the blacks form fifty, sixty, and even seventy and eighty, per cent. of the population. Along this line of deep shadows lies the great problem of American politics and American history.

So rapid has been the march of events that it is hard to realize that, within the memory of men still in their early prime, this was a population of slaves; that they were bondmen in the land of Egypt, out of which the Lord brought them, though not by the way of the Red Sea! What had seemed impossible was accomplished, not by insurrections, not by massacre, but by a struggle in which they took no share, but of which they were to receive the benefit. To-day, as we look back at the change, there is something appalling in the stillness of death that has come over a Power that but lately held the land in awe!

But there is an old saying, honored for thousands of years, that we should speak kindly of the dead. It may seem indeed a strange moment to preach a funeral oration when the *corpus vile* is lying, like a dead lion, in the streets, for every ass to kick at. But it is the chivalrous custom of soldiers, not to bear even an enemy to the grave, without some remembrance of the brave deeds that he has done, that may redeem his evil career. In this spirit let us say a good word, if we can, for the old African lion that fought so hard for its life, but to which none is now " so poor as to do it reverence."

The system of slavery that has now passed into history, is known to us of the present day chiefly through "Uncle Tom's Cabin"—that marvellous story, so vivid, so dramatic, so intense in interest, written with a degree of womanly feeling and pathos that at once caught the ear of the world, till it was translated into all languages, and made the circuit of the globe, filling all civilized nations with horror at the cruelties and crimes of American slavery. The book was true—that is to say, it was a *possible* truth; it depicted what might have been a fearful reality. All that it tells *might* have taken place on a plantation in Louisiana; but whether it *did* take place (except in rare instances), is another question. Its Southern critics say that it gave but one side to the picture; while there was another that was kept in the background, which needed to be brought forward in clear relief, to see the whole surroundings of the system of slavery.

This criticism is not strictly accurate: for no fair-mind-ed reader can say that Uncle Tom's Cabin gives but one side of slavery—the dark side—as it contains some exquisite pictures of plantation life in the old days of Louisiana, that furnish a relief to the blackness that follows; but it is true that, while there are these vivid contrasts in the picture, yet the story is so told that the dominant impression is one of unmingled horror, and this it is of which Southern men complain as unjust to the truth of history.

Certainly the pictures of slavery that were drawn with such power, and took such hold of the imagination that they even haunted us in our dreams, were very different from the milder form of servitude known to most of the Southern people, to whom it was a part of their domestic life. The relations of the two races were the closest. The negroes were not only a part of every community, but members of every household. Though they stood in the relation of servants to their white masters, yet they "belonged to the family," and were the objects of a degree of family affection. White children, almost as soon as they were born, were placed in the arms of black nurses, who cared for them in babyhood and childhood. This constant intimacy naturally led to the warmest attachments, which often continued when the children had grown to be men and women. Whoever has known the Southern people must have been struck with the way in which not only women, but strong men, not given to sentiment, speak of the old "aunties" and "mammies" who cared for them in the years of their childhood.

As to life on the plantations, those who remember it tell us that they were conducted on a rather easy-going system. The masters were not cruel men, nor even hard men, who overworked the negroes, or subjected them to undue severity. Indeed they were proverbially indulgent, rather slipshod in business matters, and disposed to let things run along pretty much as they might. The planter's house, with its wide porches and broad verandas, was the centre of a little settlement, in the background of which were rows of cabins neatly whitewashed. During the day the men were in the fields, where the labor was not hard, except perhaps at the time of the cotton-picking or getting in the sugar-cane. While they were thus occupied, the women were out of doors in the sun, doing their various kinds of work, singing some plantation melody; while the pickaninnies were scattered about in costumes which, if not very neat and trim, were at least free and easy. Pass along these cottages at the close of a Summer's day, and you might see pictures indicative of anything but oppression or unhappiness. The negroes are a mirth-loving race, and the thrumming of a banjo, to the tune of some poor ditty, was enough to gather a group of these children of nature, as merry as nature intended them to be.

This is a very picturesque scene. But it was sometimes rudely interrupted. The master was very apt to find, after some experience, that the old plantation, run in this easy-going way, was run at a loss; and that at the end of the year he was in debt, and going from bad to worse; so that, to save himself, he was obliged to get an overseer, who would not lie abed quite so late in the morning, but would be up at daybreak, riding over the plantation, seeing that every hand was at work, and keeping them at it till the sun went down. It was these overseers, who were generally Northern men, to whom should be ascribed the use of the lash, and most of the severities and brutalities, on the old plantations.

In this family—comprising perhaps, in men, women, and children, hundreds of souls—the one on whom came the heaviest burden, was not the negro, nor the planter, but the planter's wife, who was at the head of the large household, and supervised it all, laying out the work for the women, often cutting their dresses with her own hands, thus making herself the slave of her slaves! Nor should it be forgotten how she made her round among the cabins, looking after the sick, and not seldom kneeling by the side of some old mammy or aunty, to pray with her, and support her with the consolations of religion.

This affectionate care was repaid with gratitude and devotion. The negro race has its weaknesses and infirmities; but whatever these may be, it is at least capable of a degree of affection that sometimes leads them to forget their own interests. Of this the most conspicuous example was given in the late war, when in many cases the whole male portion of the family, all at least capable of bearing arms, marched to the field, leaving their wives and children wholly to the care of the blacks. Then was their opportunity to break away and strike for freedom, at the same time striking terror into the defenceless households. But not once, even in the darkest hours of the war, did they harm those left to their care, nor leave them to shift for themselves. Instead of violence, they gave protection; instead of neglect, they worked the fields, and raised the crops, and fed the families of their absent masters, who were engaged in a war, the result of which would be, if successful, to keep these very laborers in perpetual bondage.

But this was not all. In many cases masters sent their most trusted servants to the war, to look after the safety and comfort of their own sons who were in the army. My friend, Major Baxter of Nashville, tells me of a case within his knowledge, where a young man—a mere boy—seized as boys at that day were apt to be (whether they lived at the North or South), with a desire to see the war, was at last permitted by his father to go, but only because he could send him with a trusted family servant to look after him, who of course felt that he had the authority of an old uncle. As it happened, in some petty affair the boy received a trifling wound, a mere scratch, that caused the blood to trickle, which no sooner caught the eye of the old darky, than he took the youngster in hand in the most vigorous manner, calling him to account in this fashion: "What shall I say to my ole massa, who sent me to look arter you, when here you've been done gone and got hurt?"

Thus did the blacks follow their masters in camp and field, as faithfully as they had worked for them on the old plantations. Never in the history of the world was there greater devotion of one race to another, for which the white people of the South owe to their former slaves a debt of gratitude which they can never repay.

Looking back to these happy scenes, which he dimly remembers, Mr. Grady has several times expressed to me his earnest wish that some one of the young writers of the South, who show such genius and give such promise, should write a tale of Southern life in the old days, that should be an offset to Uncle Tom's Cabin, bringing into clearer light the softer aspects of the patriarchal institution. I doubt if he will ever find his man or his story: for if the writer would avoid the partisanship which is ascribed to Mrs. Stowe, he must tell the truth, and the whole truth; and he knows the awful possibility that lurked, as a shadow, behind all that gayety and happiness. He knows how a turn of fortune would have sent all those happy creatures to the block. A friend who spent a Winter on a plantation at the South, in a family of the highest culture and Christian character, tells us that there existed the greatest affection towards the servants, which showed itself in many ways: as, for instance, a marriage among the latter was the occasion of a rural fête as pretty as if for a son or daughter of the family. Here surely slavery appeared in its least repulsive form. And yet, on the very next plantation, the cruelty to the slaves was a scandal that was the talk of all the country round; and on a still night one might hear the baying of the bloodhounds, that told how the hunters were pursuing the fugitives in the forest! These are things which cannot be covered up by flowers of rhetoric; that cannot be turned into poetry. For these slavery has received the condemnation of the civilized world, and it is too late to ask for a reversal of the decree. No young author could afford to risk his reputation by writing a book to apologize for slavery: it would be howled down as soon as it was born. No man is strong enough to fight against the sympathies of the age. There are some things which are as impossible in literature as in actual life, and one of these is to resuscitate what is dead and buried, or to clothe with dignity what men have pronounced accursed. For these things it "behooved the Lord" that the system should come to an end—and it came!

But all was not joy when it came. Liberty has its hardships as well as slavery. The master's hand might be heavy, but it carried with it protection and support, shelter and food and raiment—substantial realities to be set in the balance against freedom. Miriam sang the deliverance of her people on the shore of the Red Sea, but it was not long before they sighed for the banks of the Nile. So slavery, with all its harshness, took care of numbers who could not take care of themselves, and who but for their kind masters would have been utterly destitute; but who, under this rule, were not cast off in the time of sickness or old age, but had at least a place to die.

All this is now over. When the Day of Jubilee was

come, the negroes received as their legacy from the war the priceless boon of freedom. But with all the exultation of their new-found liberty, many of the poor creatures must have felt their heartstrings pull as they turned their backs on the old plantations, with the world all before them where to choose. It was a very big world, but to many of them it must have been a very cold world; and we cannot blame them if, like lost children, they sometimes sighed for the shelter of their old homes. The negro is a very domestic creature; he loves familiar scenes; and he clung to old Massa and Missus, to whom he had been accustomed to look for protection. But they too are gone. The two races are parted forever: parted in their homes—the cabins stand no longer in the shadow of the planter's house, but far away in the lonely forest—parted in their domestic life; parted in every interest; parted even in the worship of God. There is something very pathetic in this rupture of old ties, cleaving not only through households, but through churches. Not only do the two races stand apart in all domestic relations, but they cannot even go to the house of God in company. In the old days the colored people were a part of every congregation, and a very numerous and picturesque part. In the great churches of Charleston and Savannah the galleries were black with Africans, among whom were many bouncing matrons, resplendent in a blaze of highly colored dresses, with their heads wrapped in gorgeous turbans of red bandannas, in which they shone in a glory quite equal to that of their masters and mistresses whom they looked down upon. Now all that has departed. Now and then a solitary, woebegone darky may come back to the old church, and creep into a corner and think of other days, but the poetry and the picturesqueness are gone forever.

Since then twenty-five years have passed, and what is

the result of the experiment of freedom? We find that the emancipation of the blacks has wrought no change in their industrial position; that they are still hewers of wood and drawers of water to their old masters, though they are no longer bondmen, but freedmen, receiving wages for their labor. In this readiness to work under the new conditions, they have disproved the confident declaration of their enemies, that black labor must always be forced labor; that the negro was such an idle creature that he must be compelled to work by some legal power; that if he were not driven to the field by the lash, he must be subject to some more or less gentle compulsion. Some prophets of evil at the close of the war, went so far as to predict that society would go to pieces; that four millions of slaves, set free, would refuse to work; that they would become idlers and vagabonds, and finally thieves, robbers, and murderers; till life would become absolutely intolerable, and the whites would have to flee for refuge to some part of the earth which still retained a trace of order and civilization.

This fear has been entirely dispelled. The negroes were perhaps a little frisky at their first experience of freedom, and may have taken a good spell of idleness just to know "how it felt." But the result proved that the poet wrote truly:

"O nebber you fear
If nebber you hear
De driver blow his horn!"

After "lying off" for a few days or weeks, they slowly came back to the old plantations, resuming their places in the fields, only receiving wages, like other hired laborers. The result has been satisfactory. I know it is said that they are lazy and shiftless, and this is true to some extent, particularly in towns, where they idle about the streets. But generally the habit of obedience to their old masters, and the pleasant feeling they have when at the close of the day or the week, they have dropped into their hands the bright silver dollars, has brought them back to habits of industry. The prediction that they would not work, has been answered by themselves in the fact that they *do* work, of which this very year (1889) furnishes magnificent proof in the largest cotton crop ever known, exceeding that in the year before the war by over two millions of bales! True, this enormous production is ascribed in part to white labor. So much the better, as it proves that those who once disdained the hard work of the field, have now put their strong arms to the task of Southern regeneration. Yet, with all that they have done, the heaviest part of the burden has been borne on the stalwart African shoulders.

But the most notable fact which this quarter of a century has demonstrated, is the prodigious physical vitality of the black race. When slavery was abolished, some shrewd observers predicted that it would result in their complete extinction. This was gravely expressed in the most opposite quarters, as an illustration of which I give the opinions of two distinguished men, representing the extreme wings— Dr. Palmer of New Orleans and Theodore Parker. The former, in a sermon preached before the war, affirmed of the negro in so many words, "*His freedom is his destruction*"; and Theodore Parker, champion as he was of the colored people, thought they were such a weak race—so helpless and dependent, and so utterly incapable of taking care of themselves—that, if set free, they would dwindle and disappear. He said, "When slavery is abolished, the African population will decline in the United States, and die out of the South as out of Northampton and Lexington!" Naturally we look upon these strange predictions as relics of a prehistoric age, and yet within a few weeks I have received a speech by an Alabama Senator, in which he argues at great length that "the African cannot survive in America," and that "freedom has sealed the fate of the colored man!" Well! if he is going to die out in the land, he takes a long time about it, and enters on the task of self-extinction in a strange way. Whether it be according to any law by which races living in poverty, with scant clothing and hard fare—or, as some philosophers would say, living nearer to nature—multiply more rapidly than those living in comparative luxury, the fact is apparent that the black race, instead of diminishing, has increased; some say much faster than the whites; that while the whites have also increased, the blacks have *swarmed!* The relative proportion can only be decided by the next census. But, even admitting the increase of the two races to be equal, that alone shows in the black race a physical vitality which will give it strength to live for many generations.

In 1865, when the war closed, there were four millions of colored people in the Southern States; to-day there are seven millions—an increase of three millions in twenty-five years, or over a hundred thousand a year! Thus, instead of dying out, the race increases with great rapidity; the Black Belt grows denser and blacker, till it lies like a dark thundercloud along the Southern horizon.

CHAPTER X.

A NEW DEPARTURE—THE NEGRO VOTE.

The fidelity of the blacks to the whites during the war, we should suppose, would have awakened in the latter a feeling of gratitude to those to whom they owed so much, and made their relations closer than ever. So it might have been if these had remained unchanged. So long as the two races lived together as masters and servants, there was no friction between them, as the one was subject to the other, and its attitude was that of submission and obedience. But when the war was over, and the sky had cleared, "old things had passed away, and all things had become new." There had been an upheaval and dislocation of the former strata of society; so that those who had been accustomed to look down upon their inferiors, suddenly found themselves standing on the same level and in close proximity. There were no longer masters and slaves, but simply white and black "fellow-citizens."* From that

---

* This is the order of events, which shows the several stages of progress:

In the early part of the war Mr. Lincoln had been urged by the more pronounced anti-slavery men to issue a Proclamation of Emancipation; but with his usual caution, he hesitated and

moment jealousies arose which did not exist before, and a process of alienation began, which has continued to widen till the two races now stand apart in complete separation.

The climax was reached when, in addition to the fullest

delayed from month to month, hoping that the ending of the war would render such an extreme measure unnecessary. But as it still went on with increasing bitterness and doubtful issue, he began to perceive that in the last resort he might be compelled to take this step; and on the 22d of September, 1862, (within a week after the battle of Antietam, when perhaps he thought the South might be more disposed to listen to reason) he sounded the first note of warning: that if it persisted in rebellion, in just one hundred days from that date—viz: on the 1st of January, 1863—he would issue a Proclamation declaring that "all persons held as slaves within any State, the people whereof should be in rebellion against the United-States, should be then, thenceforward, and forever FREE." The warning was not heeded. The war went on, and on the appointed day the thunderbolt fell in that great Proclamation of Emancipation, which was to mark the beginning of a new era in American history. It closed with these memorable words: "And upon this act, sincerely believed to be an act of justice, warranted by the Constitution upon military necessity, I invoke the considerate judgment of mankind and the gracious favor of Almighty God."

In the very year that the war ended, 1865, slavery was forever abolished by the Thirteenth Amendment to the Constitution, which declares that "neither slavery, nor involuntary servitude, except as a punishment for crime, whereof the party shall have been duly convicted, shall exist within the United States, or any place subject to their jurisdiction." Three years later, in 1868, was added the Fourteenth Amendment, securing, not only the liberty of the blacks, but their *citizenship*, as it declared that "all persons born or naturalized in the United States are CITIZENS," and that of their privileges as such they cannot be deprived by any State; and in 1870 came the Fifteenth, and last, Amendment, that "the right of the citizens of the United States to vote, shall not be denied or abridged by the United States, or by any State, on account of race, color, or previous condition of servitude."

personal liberty, the blacks were raised still higher, and invested with political power. This is not included in freedom. Alexander II. emancipated twenty millions of serfs in Russia, but that did not give them the right to vote. Neither did it give the right to the freed slaves of America. It is important to keep these two things distinct. Personal liberty may be a natural right, but the privilege of voting certainly is not. We have heard a great deal of late of "manhood suffrage" (which has a brave sound, that fits it to be a political war-cry), as if suffrage were a right which attached to every man, of woman born, however ignorant, though he were a fool or an idiot, for this did not destroy the fact that he was still a man! In all the countries of Europe that have free institutions, even in aristocratic England, there has been a tendency towards this feature of a pure democracy. Every few years there has been an extension of the suffrage, making the qualifications less rigid, till now the voting class includes almost the whole population of England. These changes Americans are wont to hail as movements in the direction of liberty. But whether they are in the direction of good government, is another question. That depends on whether those to whom the vote is given are fit to use it. If not, every extension of the suffrage, so far from being a step in the way of progress, is a step backward towards barbarism. It is this absurd notion of natural rights, carried to the utmost extreme, that lies at the bottom of all the false and destructive theories of socialism and communism, which threaten society in the Old World. It is in political philosophy what "original sin" is in theology—the "primeval curse," the "Adam's fall, in which we sinned all."

From that entailed curse no nation has suffered more than our own. The first downward plunge was made when the suffrage was given to the immigrants just landed on our shores. History could not furnish a better argument against the suicidal folly of giving political power to those who are utterly incompetent to use it. Universal suffrage is well enough in New England, in the country towns, where there is general intelligence, and the people have been trained to voting in their town elections; but to give it to the ignorant creatures that are "dumped," like cattle, on our wharves, is the very insanity of democracy. We have found what a terrible curse it is in New York city, where we are overrun by these hordes that have not the remotest idea of American institutions. We import ignorance by the cargo, and set it up to rule over us. Mr. Hugh McCulloch, in his recent admirable volume, argues that the giving of the suffrage to all the immigrants that land upon our shores, is the great danger of the Republic.

But, as if it were not enough to commit one such folly, we must add another, and a greater, in giving the same unrestricted suffrage to the negroes of the South. Not that it is any worse to give the vote to ignorant blacks than to ignorant whites, [it is not the color I object to, but the ignorance wherever it exists, in white or black— the mistake is as great in the one case as in the other,] it is *worse* only in that it is far greater in amount; that whereas the immigrants in our Northern cities are counted by tens of thousands, the blacks in the South are counted by millions. One folly does not excuse another; it should rather be a warning against it; and the horrible blunder that was made in giving the vote to the "raw Irish," should have warned us against plunging into a still deeper abyss by giving it to the blacks without reserve.

But with a nation, as with individuals, there is sometimes a state of the public mind approaching to frenzy, which leads it to rush to fatal extremes. Such an access of rage and madness is apt to follow a civil war. It followed ours, and there was but one man who could control it—the man who had carried the country through the war, and thereby acquired a boundless popularity. Such a strong hand was needed in the critical period of reconstruction. How he would have acted in this very matter, it is not difficult to see: for all his ideas and habits of mind were conservative, and with his sense of humor he would have received a proposal to give the suffrage to the blacks just off the plantation, as a huge joke! This was something which he never dreamed of. When he wrote his Emancipation Proclamation, he promised the slaves their liberty, to be maintained by all the military forces of the United States; but it never entered his head that he was to divide with the newly emancipated the business of the government! On this point we are not left to conjecture, for he had expressed himself in no doubtful language. Long before the war, in his famous joint debate with Douglas, in answering the question whether he was "really in favor of a perfect equality between the negroes and white people," he replied in words which could not be more explicit: "I am not, nor ever have been, in favor of bringing about in any way the social and political equality of the white and black races. I am not, nor ever have been, in favor of making voters or jurors of negroes, nor of qualifying them to hold office, nor to intermarry with white people; and I will say, in addition to this, that there is a physical difference between the white and black races which I believe will forever forbid the two races living together on terms of social and political equality."

No doubt Mr. Lincoln's ideas may have been changed by the war, which brought an overturning of all things; but it could not change the "physical difference," which, in his view, would *"forever forbid* the two races living together on terms of social and political equality." Remembering this, it is safe to suppose that had he been living at the time this legislation was before Congress, his rugged common-sense would have perceived the fearful danger of committing political power to such untried hands. Here, as in the settlement of the many other difficult questions of reconstruction, the country was made to feel mournfully the want of that large, kind, gentle wisdom. The greatest calamity that ever happened to the South, was the assassination of Abraham Lincoln! When he was in his grave, another of quite a different stamp reigned in his stead, Andrew Johnson, who, with his perverse obstinacy and utter want of tact, soon succeeded in embroiling himself with Congress, where he was confronted in the House of Representatives by another man equally determined, Thaddeus Stevens, whose imperious will made him the ruling spirit in that stormy time, and able to lead his party to any extreme of rash legislation. Between the two, there was little place for prudence and moderation.

The plea for negro suffrage was one of necessity. It was the same argument that was used during the war to justify any violation of private rights or State rights, viz: that it was a "war measure," and was necessary to save the country! The ballot was declared to be a political necessity, "unless we would sacrifice the results of the war"! If all power in the Southern States were left in the hands of the whites, they would legislate the blacks back into slavery; or, if they did not, would impose such restrictions upon their liberty as would reduce them to a state of quasi-servitude. For this fear there was good reason. Hardly had the war closed, and the machinery of legislation been put in motion, before there were movements here and there to pass such laws as to neutralize the benefits of freedom. The black man was no longer a slave, but an "apprentice," who could be "bound out" to hard labor under conditions

almost as stringent as those of criminals in the chain-gang.*
Against this there was no insurmountable barrier but to
give the vote to the whole negro population. Ardent partisans reasoned that a people could not be juggled out of
their rights to whom the ballot was given without qualification, restriction, or limitation! How greatly they were
mistaken in this, the experience of a few years fully proved.

To make the matter worse, not only were the blacks
let into the citadel of power, but many of the whites were
shut out. To be sure, they could resume their former
position on easy terms. Says Mr. Blaine in his History:
"The great mass of those who had resisted the national
authority, were restored to all their rights of citizenship
by the simple taking of an oath of future loyalty; and
those excepted from immediate reinstatement, were promised full forgiveness on the slightest exhibition of repentance and good works." But even this requirement grated
harshly on the proud spirits that had been leaders in the
war, who held back from taking the iron-clad oath; and
when the blacks were admitted to the polls *en masse*, the
whites found themselves swamped as by an inundation.
This was a complete revolution. Power was taken away
from the upper classes, and given to the lower—the course
directly opposed to reason and common-sense. Nature
seems to ordain that in political societies, as in all human
affairs, intelligence shall rule over ignorance, and civilization over barbarism. But here this natural order was
reversed. Ignorance was set to rule over intelligence, and
thus the whole framework of society was turned upside
down. That which had been at the top was savagely

---

* For a full account of this Southern legislation, see Mr.
Blaine's "Twenty Years in Congress" (Volume II., Chapter V.),
wherein he gives such details as justify him in describing it as
"a virtual reënactment of the slave code."

thrown down and put at the bottom, and the bottom was dug out and put at the top. This, whatever the political necessity that compelled it, I cannot but look upon as anything less than the triumph of barbarism, and a crime against civilization!

The effect was what might have been expected. The poor people who received the ballot hardly knew what it meant. They could not read the names that were written on it, and were ready to vote as they were told, for anybody living or dead—for Andrew Jackson, or George Washington, or Moses, or Melchisedek! Of course they were the easy prey of demagogues, who could flatter them by appeals to negro vanity, or (what they understood still better) pay them for a vote, as they would for a day's work; and they made a pretty mess of legislation. I was in Richmond soon after the war, and went up to the old Capitol, and saw both houses filled almost wholly with negroes. It was not a cheerful sight, and as I turned away, I could but ask myself, Is this the highest result of free institutions in the New World?

Then the beauties of negro government were illustrated to the full. In South Carolina and the Gulf States it had a clean sweep; and if we are to believe the records of the time, it was a period of corruption such as had never been known in the history of the country. The blacks, having nothing to lose, were ready to vote to impose any tax, or to issue any bonds of town, county, or State, provided they had a share in the booty; and thus negro government, manipulated by carpet-baggers, ran riot over the South. It was chaos come again. The former masters were governed by their servants, while the latter were governed by a set of adventurers and plunderers. The history of those days is one which we cannot recall without indignation and shame. After a time the moral sense of the North was so shocked by these performances that a Republican Administration had to withdraw its proconsuls, when things at once resumed their former condition, and the management of affairs came back into the old hands.

Time is sure to bring its revenges; and there seemed a kind of Nemesis in the issue, by which the machinery so elaborately prepared to perpetuate a certain rule, had exactly the opposite effect. This amazing stroke of policy was intended to reduce the power of the white vote by raising up a colored vote to offset it. But owing to the greater skill of the whites in the manipulating of votes, or their power of coaxing or overawing their former servants, the course of the latter was speedily reversed, and thrown almost solidly on the side of their old masters. And inasmuch as the negroes were now counted in their full numbers—instead of at three-fifths, as before, in fixing the basis of representation—the addition of their votes swelled enormously the political power of the South in Congress and in the Electoral College, and thereby in the choice of President of the United States!

Here was a shifting of the scenes which completely upset the calculations of the politicians. The history of politics is full of surprises; but never was there a greater one than in the operation of negro suffrage at the South.

Since that time things have settled down into a regular "system," which is simply that of systematic disregard of the laws and the Constitution of the United States. But this slight discrepancy troubles no man's conscience, as every man, when questioned, declares himself, like the toper in Maine, "in favor of the law, but 'agin' its execution"! The matter is perfectly understood, and there need be no ambiguity about it. The negro vote, like the cotton crop, is always in the market, to be sold to the highest bidder. This seemed to be the first tangible idea which the

THE NEGRO SELLING HIS VOTE.

blacks had of the ballot—that it was something they could sell, and something which they have sold from that day to this, their chief ambition being to get a good price. The negro is for sale to-day as much as ever. He is put up at auction on the block, or rather he puts himself up. A New England pastor in Florida told me of a scene he witnessed at the polls. A negro got up on a box, and said: "I hasn't voted. Does any gemman want to speak to me?" Of course he found a "gemman" who was ready to whisper something in his ear. But he was not so simple as to take the first bid, and asked if "any oder gemman wanted to speak to him"; and after receiving several confidential communications, yielded to the arguments of the "gemman" who spoke the loudest, or in the way that he could best understand. All are not so unblushing as this. One colored brother, I was told, had a conscience about the matter, and made it a principle not to take more than two dollars and a half for his vote, saying that "that was all it was worth"!

In such hands the suffrage is a farce—not a farce in the sense that it is only a subject for laughter, but a horrible farce, in which the stake played for in this tossing of the dice is the government of a people that profess to be civilized, with the effect of a general demoralization of both races, whites and blacks, one of which thinks it is no harm to buy what the other is so ready to sell. So general has this buying and selling become, that many have told me that it was absolutely impossible to have an honest vote, and they had given it up in despair.

From buying votes, it is but a step to fraud in counting them, which is cheaper, and quite as effective ; or ballot-boxes may be emptied of the "wrong" votes, and stuffed with the "right" kind. There is but one step further—to intimidation, when men come to the polls with shotguns, not of course to do any mischief, but as a gentle hint to the other side that it might be safer to retire into the woods or to their cabins, and leave the business of electing public officers to those who understand it better. If this mere show of force does not prove sufficient, the guns are used in a more effective way. We hear of violence not unfrequently ending in murder; of midnight assassinations committed by masked marauders—Ku Klux Klans, or whatever they may be called. These outrages have produced at the North such a feeling of indignation, that there is a general outcry that stern measures be taken for their suppression. Of course such cowardly crimes should be punished with all the power of the law. The only question is, By what power shall they be punished? Murder is a crime against the State, to be punished by the State. If a murder is committed in the streets of New York, we do not send to Washington to ask for aid in bringing the murderer to justice. There may be a case of crime so extreme, and comprehending so many persons, that the State authorities are powerless, and the General Government may be asked to interfere. Thus if there were a riot in this city, such as we saw in 1863, which should threaten, if unchecked, to overthrow all law, and perhaps lay the city in ashes, the President might order the troops from Governor's Island to give support to the police in enforcing order; but surely we do not look to that source of authority to manage the internal affairs of our State. No more can it be called to perform police duty in the South. There, as at the North, crimes must be punished by the States in which they are committed. If the General Government can give indirect aid, of course it will; but with the best intention, it can hardly be expected to reach out its long arm from Washington to lay hold of fugitives in the swamps and cane-brakes of the South.

DEMAND FOR A FREE BALLOT.

But the demand is for the President, supported by Congress, to interfere to secure a free and honest ballot at the South! This might well set us at the North to thinking whether we are not responsible for this complication of affairs. We have forced universal suffrage upon the South, and now are asked to step in to save it from the natural consequence of our own blunders and mistakes.

Have we well considered what it means to "regulate elections" at the South? Do we mean to send an army there, and have soldiers stand guard at the polls? The experiment of military government has been tried with a result that is not encouraging. After the war, the power at command was almost absolute. When General Grant was President of the United States, and Commander of the Army and Navy, he had lieutenants in the South (all brave in fighting battles, but who had a limited experience in civil life) that were ready to declare martial law in every city from Richmond to New Orleans; to surround every State-house with soldiers; and to dictate the choice of rulers at the point of the bayonet. Such extreme measures were not resorted to (except perhaps in one instance, by Sheridan at New Orleans); yet during the whole of General Grant's eight years of power, there was in the South what amounted to a military occupation, with all the pressure that it brings to bear on legislation. But so utter was the failure of this policy of coercion, that scarcely had Mr. Hayes been inaugurated when, under the advice of his distinguished Secretary of State, Mr. Evarts, it was abandoned as absolutely beyond the power of the National Government.

"Ah, then," say some, "there is no hope for the emancipated slaves—emancipated only in name! If the South *will* not do them justice, and the North *cannot* enforce it, they are left to be ground between the upper and nether millstones!" Not quite so bad as that! Injustice always brings its own punishment. The South is suffering to-day from the lawlessness within her borders. Every "outrage" that is sent on the wings of lightning to the North, stirs up anew the feeling of indignation, and is a warning to Northern people and Northern capital to keep away from a land thus smitten by the pestilence. Of course, in this sweeping condemnation the good people of the South suffer with the bad: because it is assumed that these foul deeds are upheld, or at least condoned, by public opinion. In this there is a degree of injustice. Quiet and peaceable men express their horror and disgust at them, but say that they are the work of lawless ruffians, such as infest every community, and who are not more numerous at the South than the class of professional criminals at the North. But however few they may be, they seem to be strong enough to defy the law: for I have yet to hear of a single man punished for his part in these midnight assassinations! And so long as murderers walk abroad in the light of day without fear, the whole community must bear the odium. If the Southern States have not the power or the will to arrest the perpetrators of such crimes and bring them to justice, let them take the responsibility. They are the agents for the punishment of evil-doers, and ought not to bear the sword in vain. If they fail in their duty, it is their fault, and not ours. If they will not punish violence and blood, on them will rest the shame and the disgrace, and theirs will be the inevitable punishment: for such things cannot be done in a civilized community without provoking a terrible retribution in the demoralization which always follows unpunished crime.

CHAPTER XI.

CAPACITY OF THE NEGRO—HIS POSITION IN THE NORTH. THE COLOR LINE IN NEW ENGLAND.

I should have more hope of the progress of the African in the future, if he had made more progress in the past. But his history is not encouraging. What he has done on his native continent is all a blank ; but what has he done since he was transplanted to America?—for he has been here as long as the white man. The first slaves were brought to Jamestown, Va., in 1619, the year before the Pilgrims landed on Plymouth Rock. Thus the two races began their career together on the Western Continent, and yet who can for an instant compare the achievements of the one with those of the other! During the long lapse of two hundred and seventy years, the negro race has not produced a single great leader. It will not do to say that this has been because they were kept down. A great race, numbering millions, cannot be kept down. Besides, in half the country there was no effort to keep them down : for slavery in the North was abolished a century ago, and yet the same inferiority exists. I do not mention this with any feeling of pride in the superiority of the white race ; on the contrary it is with extreme regret that I recognize the backwardness of my colored brethren. But I cannot draw pictures of fancy that are not borne out by facts. I must see things as they are : or at least as they appear to my eyes ; and so seeing, it seems to me that the few colored people that are scattered here and there in the villages of New England, do not compare well with some splendid old types of the race whom I knew in my childhood. If the reader will indulge me in the episode, I should like to give him a picture or two of pure African genius half a century ago.

Although we of the North know much less of the colored people than those who live at the South (as they are so much fewer in numbers here than there), yet we know something of them, and I for one have personal reasons to remember them with a very strong feeling, as to one of that race I owe a debt which I can never repay, since she took me almost from the moment that I was born. When I opened my eyes on this world, almost the first human face into which I looked wore a dark skin. As my mother was very ill, and it was feared nigh unto death, I was taken away from her to the little cabin of a poor negro woman, who watched over me with a mother's tenderness ; and when a few weeks later I was carried to the old meeting-house to be baptized, it was in her black arms that I was held, while my sainted father sprinkled the water on my little head, and gave me the name of an English missionary, whose fame was then in all the Christian world.

As this black woman, who was known by the name of Mumbet (a contraction, I suppose, for Mammy Betty), was no ordinary person, I may briefly tell her history. She was born a slave, not far from the Hudson River —in what year she never knew—but was bought by Col. Ashley of Sheffield, Mass., when she was still such a

THE COURAGE OF MUMBET.

child that she was carried on the straw in the bottom of a sleigh over the mountains to her home in the valley of the Housatonic. As she grew up she was noted for her activity and courage, and her high spirit, as if the blood of old African kings was flowing in her veins. She was ready to do any amount of hard work, but would not submit to cruelty, and on one occasion, when her mistress in a fury of passion struck at her sister with a hot shovel, she threw herself between them, and received the blow on her arm, that left a scar which she carried with her to her grave. From that moment she left the house; neither commands nor entreaties could induce her to return, till her master resorted to the law to gain possession of his slave. Judge Sedgwick of Stockbridge defended her, on the ground that the Constitution of Massachusetts, then recently adopted, had declared that "all men were born free and equal." The court sustained him, and declared that she was free. Thus slavery was abolished in Massachusetts, not by a direct act of legislation, but by the decision of the courts. In gratitude to her defender and liberator, she attached herself to his family, in which she remained for many years. Devoting herself to the care of his children and his property, she became his defender as he had been hers. On one occasion, in Shays' Rebellion (which caused so much trouble after the close of the Revolutionary War), a party of insurgents came to the house to search for the Judge, and went into every room, running their bayonets under the beds to find him. But this old black servant, who had the heart of a lioness, confronted them at every step, following them up-stairs and down-stairs, into garret and cellar, armed with a huge shovel with which she could have dealt a tremendous blow. Hearing them speak of a favorite horse which they would take with them, she flew to the stable, and led it to the road, and then with a blow sent it flying till it was out of sight. Thus she outwitted them, and sent them away with scorn, remaining "solitary and alone," proud mistress of the scene.

But the greatest proof of gratitude to her benefactor was her devotion to his children, who, owing to the prolonged illness of their mother, were left almost wholly to the care of this old family servant. Better care they could not have had. So attached to her did they become, that it is safe to say that, next to their mother, they loved this faithful creature.

It was long after the youngest of that family had been reared to manhood and womanhood, that I fell into the same loving hands, and what she did for them she did for me. Thus my acquaintance with the colored race began very early, indeed with my very existence. And though so long ago, it would be ungrateful even at this distance of years to disown the obligation.

In the village burial ground, where are gathered in one enclosure the members of that distinguished family, this old negro woman is laid by the side of Miss Catherine Sedgwick, the celebrated authoress—I presume at her request, from a natural feeling that even in death she would nestle in her old nurse's arms. On the plain stone that marks her grave is the following inscription:

ELIZABETH FREEMAN
known by the name of
MUMBET
died Dec. 28, 1829.
Her supposed age was 85 years.

She was born a slave and remained a slave nearly thirty years. She could neither read nor write, yet in her own sphere she had no superior nor equal. She neither wasted time nor property. She never violated a trust, nor failed to perform a duty. In every situation of domestic trial she was the most efficient helper and the tenderest friend. Good mother, farewell!

ANOTHER NOTED CHARACTER.

Was ever a more beautiful tribute paid to womanly fidelity and devotion? As I stand by that grave I think what I too owe to that fidelity which "never violated a trust, nor failed to perform a duty." As after her death, one of the Sedgwicks, paying a tribute to her memory, said, "But for her care I should not now probably be living to give this testimony," so it may have been in my case. When I think of this: that I may have owed my life to the care that watched over my helpless infancy, I cannot recall the name of that faithful woman without a feeling of love and of gratitude, that predisposes me to a kindly interest in all her unhappy race.

But the genius of those old Africans did not run wholly to the woman side. There was a man in the town who was an equally noted character. This was "Agrippa Hull," whose life began towards the middle of the last century, and who had been in the Revolutionary Army from near the beginning to the very end of the war, though not for the most part as a soldier, but a servant, in which capacity he was for four years attached to Kosciusko, whom he accompanied in his Southern campaigns. He used to tell of bloody scenes that he witnessed, especially at the hard-fought battle of Eutaw Springs, where his part was to hold the wounded as they were laid upon the operating board to have their limbs amputated—"the hardest day's work," he said, "that he ever did in his life."

These trying scenes were sometimes varied by those of a different character. He used to tell a story that reflected on himself, but showed in a pleasant light the good nature of Kosciusko. On one occasion the General had been invited by a neighboring planter to go with him on a hunting excursion, and rode off, expecting not to return till the next day. Having the field all to himself, Agrippa set out to make the most of it; and arrayed himself in his master's uniform, with the military cap on his woolly head and sword in hand, wherewith he figured as a foreign officer, even to imitating the broken English of the distinguished Pole—a performance that was greatly to the amusement of the soldiers and camp-followers; until suddenly the General, having been overtaken and driven back by a thunderstorm, rode up! Poor Agrippa was ready to sink into the earth, expecting severe punishment. But to his surprise, the General entered into the humor of the thing, and burst into a hearty laugh, adding "This is too good to keep," and immediately had his black imitator mounted on a horse, and sent through the camp, to the unbounded merriment of the soldiers. This was worse than being flogged or put in irons, and Agrippa used to say that he would rather have been drummed out of camp to the tune of the Rogue's March, than be made such a laughing-stock. However, the joke answered one good purpose, as this mirthful scene was a relief to grim-visaged war, and made a welcome diversion to the monotonous life of soldiers far from home, in the gloom of the Southern forests.

Of course Agrippa had many stories to tell of the great men whom he met at the headquarters of Kosciusko. He was very proud when now and then he had the honor of holding the bridle for Washington, as he mounted to ride to the field. It was one of the delights of my boyish days to go to the little house of this old African, and hear him tell of those times of war, with all their scenes so strange and stirring.

He had a great deal of mother wit, which shone out most at weddings and other festive occasions, when he passed round the cake and wine—for sixty years ago there could be no wedding without wine: the parties would hardly have thought themselves legally married. As he made the circuit of the company, he had some joke for every one; he even noticed poor little me, for I was then a very minute specimen of humanity, and I counted it a mark of distinction, when he patted me on the head, and bestowed his approbation in the highly musical lines—

> "Henry Martyn
> Is a gentleman for sartin,"

which I cherish to this day, as the first and only instance in which my name has been embalmed in poetry!

Though he knew his place perfectly, yet he could hold his own with the best of white folks; and if anybody snubbed him for his color, he would not be offended, but answer pleasantly that "many a good book was bound in black, and that the cover did not matter so much as the contents," ending the brief passage of words by asking, "Which is the worse: the white black man or the black white man—to be black outside or to be black inside?"

Agrippa and Mumbet! what a couple they make! When I think of these dear old souls, how can I help loving them? Both ripened with age, as religion came to give the crowning grace to their characters. Agrippa was not, when young, at all religiously inclined. The army was not a good school of religion or of morals, and many of those who came back from the wars were more given to drinking and cursing than to prayer. But a more quiet and peaceful life, with the influences of his New England surroundings, made him a new man; and in the prayer-meetings no one was more fervent than Agrippa. The memory of his past life seemed to be a constant source of humiliation, and his penitence showed itself in his confessions and prayers for forgiveness. Sometimes his language was a little too strong, as when he thanked God that "white folks were so kind to a poor old black nigger"; and again he used homely phrases, as when he besought the Lord "that every tub might stand on its own bottom"; which, however, was not so grotesque as the prayer of a noted Baptist preacher of the county—a white man at that—Elder Leland, who (if we may believe the rustic chroniclers of the time, and who would doubt them?) once prayed "that we might all hitch our horses together in God's everlasting stable"! But words are little where the heart is found, and quaint as might be the words of poor Agrippa, none who heard him could doubt that his prayers went up like sweet incense to the throne; and as for Mumbet, though her skin was black, her heart was white, and she too, like so many of her race, is now without fault before the throne of God.

Of course there were not many such characters anywhere. But here and there the like of this old nurse might be found in the early days of New England. Generally they were the retainers of rich families, in which they had lived for years, till they became an important, and almost necessary, part of the establishment. As I have taken one instance from my own very limited experience, I will venture to add another from fiction, inasmuch as the character is drawn from real life. Many of my readers are familiar with "The Minister's Wooing," by Mrs. Stowe, the scene of which is laid in Newport: that, before the Revolution and some years after, was the chief Northern port for the importation of slaves from Africa; and here were found in the godly families of Puritan New England, servants that had been born on the other side of the ocean, on the dark slave coast; some of whom, in disproof of the common idea that native Africans are all of a low type of humanity, possessed great natural intelligence; and though, like Mumbet, they "could neither read nor write," showed such strength of character that they became the stay and staff of their households, and were "in every situation of domestic trial the most efficient helpers and the tenderest friends." Such an one was "Candace,"* who proved herself in her new sphere a true "Queen of Ethiopia." The first picture we have of her, presents her as "a powerfully built, majestic black woman, corpulent, heavy, with a swinging majesty of motion, like that of a ship in a ground swell. Her shining black skin and glistening white teeth were indications of perfect physical vigor which had never known a day's sickness : and her turban, of broad red and yellow bandanna stripes, had a warm tropical glow."

This robust exterior was the fit embodiment of a mind of great native independence, which did not hesitate even to wrestle with the hard theological problems of the day. As she was under the ministry of old Dr. Samuel Hopkins, the great theologian, she was put duly through the Catechism, or "Catechize," as she called it, in which there were some things hard to be understood, and some which she flatly rejected, as, for instance, being held responsible for Adam's sin, to which she said :

"I didn't do dat ar', for one, I knows. I's got good mem'ry—allers knows what I does—nebber did eat dat ar' apple—nebber eat a bit ob him. Don't tell me!"

It was of no use to tell her of all the explanations of this redoubtable passage—of potential presence, and representative presence, and representative identity, and federal headship. She met all with the dogged

"Nebber did it, I knows; should 'ave 'membered, if I had. Don't tell me!"

And even in the catechizing class of the Doctor himself, if this answer came to her, she sat black and frowning in stony silence even in his reverend presence.

* The original of this remarkable character, I am told, was an old servant in the family of Dr. Lyman Beecher, when he lived in Litchfield, Conn.

140 A REMARKABLE CONVERSION.

From this error she was reclaimed by a personal influence which has been known to change other than dark-skinned unbelievers. It was a mysterious conversion, which came in this way :

Candace was often reminded that the Doctor believed the Catechism, and that she was differing from a great and good man; but the argument made no manner of impression on her, till one day, a far-off cousin of hers, whose condition under a hard master had often moved her compassion, came in overjoyed to recount to her how, owing to Dr. Hopkins's exertions, he had gained his freedom. The Doctor himself had in person gone from house to house, raising the sum for his redemption; and when more yet was wanting, supplied it by paying half his last quarter's limited salary.

"He do dat ar'?" said Candace, dropping the fork wherewith she was spearing doughnuts. "Den I'm gwine to b'liebe ebery word *he* does!"

And accordingly, at the next catechizing, the Doctor's astonishment was great when Candace pressed up to him, exclaiming,

"De Lord bress you, Doctor, for opening the prison for dem dat is bound! I b'liebes in you now, Doctor. I's gwine to b'liebe ebery word you say. I'll say de Catechize now—fix it any way you like. I *did* eat dat ar' apple—I eat de whole tree, an' swallowed ebery bit ob it, if you say so."

If those who read this with a smile infer from it that the faith of such a woman was a mere assent to whatever she was told, they would be greatly mistaken. Religion was the very core of her being, but it was a religion which had an African type. It did not come through the intellect, by any form of reasoning, but through the heart, and was hence far more powerful than any conversion worked out through a process of the understanding, as it enabled this poor black woman to be a minister of consolation, when the great divine, to whom she looked up with awe, would have driven a poor, unhappy soul to despair.

THE SHIPWRECKED SON.

The crisis came in the family of Squire Marvin, in which Candace lived, when the report came that a son who had run away and gone to sea, had been lost. Far away on the other side of the world, the ship had gone down with all on board. The terrible tidings threw the poor mother into an agony of despair, which was not relieved at all, but rather intensified, by her religious belief, for it compelled her to think that her son had not only lost his life, but his soul! The cold, hard creed of the day made light of human suffering. Human beings were but "worms of the dust," mere animalculæ, cast into the great crushing machine of the Almighty decrees, to be ground to powder and blown to the winds. What mattered it? Though this "machine" crushed man to atoms; though it broke every bone in his body; though his flesh was torn and bleeding, and his very soul doomed and damned; yet the mild-eyed preacher looked on with serene complacency, believing that it was all for the glory of God, in comparison with which the happiness of the whole human race was not of the slightest consequence.

This might be orthodox divinity, but it was terrible for a mother in agony for her son. What comfort could she find in a great machine, rolling on piteously, crushing human hearts and hopes? Under this strain the poor woman was driven almost to insanity. Her husband, well meaning (but awkward and clumsy, as men are apt to be in such circumstances), came into the room, and tried to take her in his arms; but she pushed him away, with the piercing shriek, "Leave me alone! I am a lost spirit!" What followed can only be told by the writer, whose powerful pen alone is adequate to describe the scene:

At this moment, Candace, who had been anxiously listening at the door for an hour past, suddenly burst into the room.

"Lor' bress ye, Squire Marvyn, we won't hab her goin' on dis yer way," she said. " Do talk *gospel* to her, can't ye?—ef you can't, I will.

" Come, ye poor little lamb," she said, walking straight up to Mrs. Marvyn, " come to old Candace!"—and with that she gathered the pale form to her bosom, and sat down and began rocking her, as if she had been a babe. " Honey, darlin', ye a'n't right—dar's a drefful mistake somewhar," she said. " Why, de Lord a'n't like what ye tink—He *loves* ye, honey! Why, jes' feel how *I* loves ye—poor ole black Candace—an' I a'n't better'n Him as made me! Who was it wore de crown o' thorns, lamb?—who was it sweat great drops o' blood?—who was it said 'Father, forgive dem'? Say, honey!—wasn't it de Lord dat made ye?—Dar, dar, now ye'r' cryin'!—cry away and ease yer poor little heart! He died for Mass'r Jim—loved him and *died* for him—jes' give up His sweet, precious body and soul for him on de Cross! Laws, jes' *leave* him in Jesus' hands! Why, honey, dar's de very print o' de nails in His hands now!"

The flood-gates were rent; and healing sobs and tears shook the frail form, as a faded lily shakes under the soft rains of Summer. All in the room wept together.

" Now, honey," said Candace, after a pause of some minutes, " I knows our Doctor's a mighty good man, an' larned—an' in fair weather I ha'n't no 'bjection to yer hearin' all about dese yer great an' mighty tings he's got to say. But, honey, dey won't do for you now; sick folks mus'n't hab strong meat; an' times like dese, dar jes' a'n't but one ting to come to, an' dat ar's *Jesus*. Jes' come right down to whar poor ole black Candace has to stay allers—it's a good place, darlin'! *Look right at Jesus.* Tell ye, honey, ye can't live no other way now. Don't ye 'member how He looked on His mother, when she stood faintin' an' tremblin' under de Cross, jes' like you? He knows all about mothers' hearts; He won't break yours. It was jes' 'cause He know'd we'd come into straits like dis yer, dat He went through all dese tings—Him, de Lord o' Glory! Is dis Him you was a-talkin' about?—Him you can't love? Look at Him, an' see ef you can't. Look an' see what He is!—don't ask no questions, an' don't go to no reasonin's—jes' look at *Him*, hangin' dar, so sweet an' patient, on de Cross! All dey could do couldn't stop His lovin' 'em; He prayed for 'em wid all de breath He had. Dar's a God you can love, a'n't dar? Candace loves Him—poor, ole, foolish,

COMFORTING THE BROKEN-HEARTED MOTHER. 143

black, wicked Candace—an' she knows He loves her"—and here Candace broke down into torrents of weeping.

They laid the mother, faint and weary, on her bed, and beneath the shadow of that suffering Cross came down a healing sleep on those weary eyelids.

"Honey," said Candace, mysteriously, after she had drawn Mary out of the room, "don't ye go for to troublin' yer mind wid dis yer. I'm clar Mass'r James is one o' de 'lect; and I'm clar dar's consid'able more o' de 'lect dan people tink. Why, Jesus didn't die for nothin'—all dat love a'n't gwine to be wasted. De 'lect is more'n you or I knows, honey! Dar's de *Spirit*—He'll give it to 'em; an' ef Mass'r James *is* called an' took, depend upon it de Lord has got him ready—course He has—so don't ye go to layin' on your poor heart what no mortal cretur can live under, 'cause, as we's got to live in dis yer world, it's quite clar de Lord must ha' fixed it so we *can*, and ef tings was as some folks suppose, why, we *couldn't* live, and dar wouldn't be no sense in anyting dat goes on."

This was the very oil of consolation poured on the wounds and bruises of that great agony. The poor black woman had done what the learned theologian could not do. To the mother in her anguish, this simple Gospel was better than the whole Hopkinsian theology. What does one care for any "system" when the heart is breaking? It needs only to be brought into the immediate presence of Christ the Consoler. It is one great gift of the African nature, that it takes hold of the Living Person, rather than of the abstract idea. It does not come to its perfect trust by any logical process, but by the instinct of love and gratitude, clinging to the Master as a shipwrecked sailor clings to the life-boat in a stormy sea. There are times when the tropical fervor of the African "fuses" the Gospel so as to take in its vital glow and heat when the larger brain of the Anglo-Saxon would remain cold and insensible.

These are pleasant pictures to dwell upon of the colored

race in the early days of New England, recalling as they do the sweet Arcadian simplicity of that olden time which has passed away. Who of my readers has not known such dear old saints in black, who have long since 'gone to glory," and who that remembers them can help feeling the warmest regard for this simple and affectionate race?

From the past we turn to the present, and ask for the children of these fathers and mothers. With such grand characters as examples, they would seem to need only to have their limbs unbound by the abolition of slavery, to start forward in a career of progress that should furnish the decisive proof of the capacity of the African race. And yet here we are doomed to a great disappointment. The black man has had every right that belongs to his white neighbor : not only the natural rights which, according to the Declaration of Independence, belong to every human being—the right to life, liberty, and the pursuit of happiness—but the right to vote, and to have a part in making the laws. He could own his little home, and there sit under his own vine and fig-tree, with none to molest or make him afraid. His children could go to the same common schools, and sit on the same benches, and learn the same lessons, as white children.

With such advantages, a race that had natural genius ought to have made great progress in a hundred years. But where are the men that it should have produced to be the leaders of their people? We find not one who has taken rank as a man of action or a man of thought : as a thinker or a writer ; as artist or poet ; discoverer or inventor. The whole race has remained on one dead level of mediocrity.

If any man ever proved himself a friend of the African race it was Theodore Parker, who endured all sorts of persecution and social ostracism, who faced mobs, and was hissed and hooted in public meetings, for his bold championship of the rights of the negro race. But rights are one thing, and capacity is another. And while he was ready to fight for them, he was very despondent as to their capacity for rising in the scale of civilization. Indeed he said in so many words: "In respect to the power of civilization, the African is at the bottom, the American Indian next." In 1857 he wrote to a friend: "There are inferior races which have always borne the same ignoble relation to the rest of men, and always will. In two generations what a change there will be in the condition and character of the Irish in New England! But in twenty generations the negroes will stand just where they are now; that is, if they have not disappeared. In Massachusetts there are no laws now to keep the black man from any pursuit, any office that he will; but there has never been a rich negro in New England; not a man with ten thousand dollars, perhaps none with five thousand dollars; none eminent in anything, except the calling of a waiter."

That was more than thirty years ago. But to-day I look about me here in Massachusetts, and I see a few colored men; but what are they doing? They work in the fields; they hoe corn; they dig potatoes; the women take in washing. I find colored barbers and white-washers, shoe-blacks and chimney-sweeps; but I do not know a single man who has grown to be a merchant or a banker; a judge, or a lawyer; a member of the legislature, or a justice of the peace, or even a selectman of the town. In all these respects they remain where they were in the days of our fathers. The best friends of the colored race—of whom I am one—must confess that it is disappointing and discouraging to find that, with all these opportunities, they are little removed from where they were a hundred years ago.

In the above I have spoken only from my own observation, and am therefore equally surprised and gratified to find that others, with wider opportunities, find more that is hopeful and encouraging. Thus Mr. A. H. Grimké, a colored man, who is a lawyer in Hyde Park, near Boston, reports as follows :

"There are about a dozen colored lawyers in Massachusetts, a majority of whom are justices of the peace. There has been a colored man in the Legislature every year since 1882. Prior to that period, there was a colored member of the Legislature every second or third year since the close of the war. Twice during these periods, two colored men were members at the same time. Every year there are three or four colored members of the Republican State Convention, and this year there was a colored member of the Democratic State Convention as well. Mr. J. C. Chappelle is at present a member of the Republican State Central Committee. In my own town of Hyde Park, a colored man is Sealer of Weights and Measures. If you will allow a personal reference, I am one of the trustees of a public institution (the Westborough Insane Hospital), recognized as one of the most important in the State, and I am, in addition, Secretary of the Board. The expenditures of this hospital are about $100,000 a year. Judge Ruffin was appointed Judge of the Charlestown Municipal Court in 1883, and filled the position with credit to himself and the community until his death about three years afterwards. Dr. Grant is one of the best dentists in Boston, and has a large practice among both races. He is a man of inventive skill in his profession. His invention in relation to cleft plates is well known here and elsewhere. Besides, he has been for years an instructor in the Dental College connected with Harvard University—mechanical dentistry being his department. John H. Lewis has a merchant tailoring establishment in Washington street, Boston, and does the second largest business in New England. His transactions annually exceed $100,000; he has just started a branch store in Providence, R. I. Mr. Joseph Lee is owner and proprietor of one of the first-class hotels of the East. The richest people of the State are guests at the Woodland Park Hotel, at Auburndale. His business is rapidly increasing, he has already enlarged the original building, and is about

NOT TWO RACES, BUT THREE. 147

to enlarge a second time to meet the increasing demands of the public. The property is valued at about $120,000. Beside Mr. Lewis above mentioned, there are three colored merchant tailors doing a handsome business in Boston.

"In New Bedford, one of the largest and finest drug stores is owned and conducted by a young colored man. In that city the colored people are butchers, fruiterers, grocers, master shipbuilders, etc. Colored young women have taught in the public schools of Boston within the past few years, and one, Miss Baldwin, has been for some years one of the most popular teachers in the public schools of Cambridge."

This is very gratifying : and it is from no wish to belittle its significance, that I suggest, that if it be made a test of the capacity of a race, it would be necessary to press the inquiry a little farther. Dr. Blyden, who has himself no tinge of whiteness, and is very proud of his pure African blood, says : "You talk of *two* races, but there are *three !*" Such is the division in Jamaica, where they are distinguished as the whites and the blacks and *the browns;* and it is said that the browns are much more particular than the whites in standing aloof from the blacks. It is to the credit of the mulattoes of this country, that they cast in their lot with the weaker race, but in distinguishing what is due to native genius, we must recognize that it is not commonly the pure African who comes to the front. Of this Mr. Grimké is himself a proof : for the colored men in the North who bear that honored name, have the best white blood of South Carolina in their veins. But putting every one of these to the account, how far could a dozen or two of isolated individuals, go to prove the capacity of a whole race, the mass of whom are still far, far behind?

With this experience of slow progress here in our own New England, it might be in better taste to be a little more guarded and careful in judging our brethren of the South, where the failure of the blacks to improve their condition is ascribed to "unjust laws," to "race-prejudice," to the "color-line," and to every other cause except natural incapacity or want of application. But can we truly say that they impose hardships upon the negro from which he is free at the North; that he has here rights and opportunities that are denied to him there? Do a few degrees of latitude make so great a difference in his position?

The first charge in the indictment against the South, is "unjust laws"! But what laws? Are not the laws affecting human rights the same in all parts of the country?

I am now writing in New England, where the very air that blows over the hills is an inspiration of liberty. This grand old State of Massachusetts, in which I was born, is my model of a free commonwealth, a genuine democracy of the highest kind, in which there is an absolute equality of civil rights, and the nearest approach to an equality of conditions. This is a reflection very gratifying to our State pride, all the more as it is in such contrast with what we are accustomed to think of the South, but just emerged from the barbarism of slavery.

But as I am indulging in this comparison, so flattering to ourselves and so disparaging to others, I begin to reflect that perhaps I have forgotten the changes wrought by the war: the great Act of Emancipation, and the amendments to the Constitution, which guarantee to all the same civil rights, "without distinction of race, color, or previous condition of servitude." This is broad enough to cover "all sorts and conditions of men." It is the law, not for one State alone, but for all; and hence it follows that the status of the negro at the South is precisely the same—so far as the law is concerned—as at the North; he has exactly the same rights in South Carolina, that he has here in good old Massachusetts!

The statement put in this frank, blunt way, is somewhat

startling : it is what Dick Swiveller would call "an unmitigated staggerer," and we do not quite like to admit it, and would not, if the words were not so plain that there can be but one interpretation.

But here a friend, seeing my perplexity, comes to my relief by saying "Oh, well! it is not *the law* of which we complain—that is all right enough ; but it is the color line that runs through everything at the South—the bitter prejudice against the black race—which is so unjust and so cruel."

This gives a new turn to my thoughts, and as I sit brooding over it, I am happy to see another friend appear, who can enlighten me on the subject. It is General Armstrong, the head of the famous Hampton School in Virginia. He is a typical American ; born in the Sandwich Islands, the son of a missionary ; educated at Williams College in Massachusetts, which he left to enter the army, and fought bravely at Gettysburg ; and at the end of the war was placed in charge of the "contrabands" who were gathered in great numbers at Fortress Monroe, out of which grew in time an institution for teaching them both to read and to work. To this he has given more than twenty years of the hardest labor, till under his care it has grown to great proportions ; sending out from year to year hundreds of young men, with an education sufficient to be able to teach others ; and who, at the same time, while supporting themselves by manual labor, have learned some useful industry, by which they can afterwards take care of themselves. In carrying out this grand design, General Armstrong has been a public benefactor. No man in this country has done more for the education and elevation of the colored race. No man understands better all the conditions of the Race Problem, as it is now being worked out in the Southern States. To him therefore I turn eagerly, enlarging with virtuous indignation on the "color line" that is kept up at the South and the race-hatred, when I am taken aback at hearing him say that "There is a great deal more antagonism between the two races here at the North than at the South!" "What?" I ask with surprise, almost doubting if I heard him correctly, when he repeats the remark as positively as before: "I find much more mutual repulsion between the whites and blacks here in Massachusetts than down in Old Virginia." This was another "staggerer," which set me thinking, and has kept me thinking ever since.

Is this statement true? Can it be that there is a color line in Massachusetts? Alas! I am afraid there is even here, in dear old Stockbridge, which is so near heaven that I have heard some of my neighbors say they were not impatient to make the change. It does not show itself much, because we have but few colored people; if there were more, the feeling would be more pronounced. True, they have the same rights of person and property as white folks. I never heard of their being subject to any injustice because of their color. On the contrary, if anybody were to attempt to do them wrong, it would be the impulse of many, as it would be mine, to befriend them just because they are fewer and weaker. Here then is absolute equality before the law; but that does not imply social equality, of which (in the sense of social intercourse) there is none.

In making these comparisons, we are able to strike a balance between the North and the South as a field for the negro; and now I ask my colored brother if, looking about him at the whole situation, he does not agree that, with all its drawbacks and disadvantages, he has just as good a chance to make a man of himself in Georgia and South Carolina, as in Massachusetts or Connecticut?

EXCLUSION FROM HOTELS.

True, there are some things which grate harshly, such as the exclusion of negroes, even though they may be men of education, from places of entertainment—from hotels and theatres, and seats in drawing-room cars—a grievance so great that it has been thought deserving of a special enactment for its punishment. The Civil Rights bill, of which Charles Sumner was the father, and which he left on his death-bed as a sacred charge to his party to carry through Congress, made it a law that the blacks should have the same rights in hotels and on railroads as whites, disregard of which was to be punished by fine and imprisonment! As the law was soon declared unconstitutional by the Supreme Court of the United States, it fell to the ground; but if it had not, it would have been difficult or impossible to enforce it. Nor can we of the North blame the South for this: for whether the exclusion of colored people from hotels be right or wrong, just or unjust, we cannnot reproach others for doing what we do ourselves. So long as negroes are not received at the principal hotels in the North, it would be a piece of pharisaical hypocrisy to require that they should be at the South. We must not try to enforce in the St. Charles Hotel in New Orleans, what cannot be enforced in the Fifth-avenue Hotel in New York!

Why, even here in New England, we find the same race-prejudice. Take our own happy valley. If a colored man were to come from the city to spend a few weeks in the country, and should apply for rooms at the Stockbridge House, would he be received? There might be no objection to him personally, but the landlord, though he is one of the most obliging of men, would say that the admission of a colored man to the same rooms and the same table, would give offence to his white guests; and that, however he might wish to do it, he could not.

As to equality on railways, there is more ground for complaint, as cases are frequently reported in which colored men, who are as decent and well-behaved as the common run of white passengers, and even ministers of the Gospel, are turned out of cars, for which they have paid full fare, with a degree of roughness and violence which has excited indignation, not only at the North, but among the best men at the South. There is a plain rule of justice, which ought to be recognized and enforced, viz: that every man is entitled to what he pays for. If there be on the part of the whites an unwillingness to occupy the same cars and to sit in the same seats with the blacks, let them be separate; only let equally good cars be provided for both, if both pay for them. In Georgia I am told that this is now required by law; but the law, it would seem, does not always suffice to protect the blacks from the violence of ruffians who invade the cars, and drive them out from seats for which they have paid, and to which they are legally entitled. Here is a case for those who have framed a righteous law, to see that it is enforced. A black man's money is just as good as a white man's, and if he pays the same fare, he is entitled to the same accommodation.

Whatever inequality there may be of rights and privileges at the South, I certainly do not mean to apologize for any wrong or injustice to the colored man. I wish simply to show that the color line, of which we hear so much, is not peculiar to one section of the country; that it exists at the North as well as at the South; and that, if we would be just, we must recognize the fact, and not ascribe what we call race-prejudice to the peculiar perversity of our Southern brethren. I ask that we judge them by the same rule that we adopt for ourselves, and that we do not condemn them for the very things of which we are guilty.

WE CANNOT FIGHT AGAINST INSTINCT.

As a basis of comparison, I have taken the highest standard. New England is my mother, and my model of all that is good. I am proud not only of the freedom, but of the equality, that exists among these hills, where it matters not if a man be rich or poor, white or black. I am willing to give to the black man every right which I ask for myself; but I cannot compel my neighbor to invite him to his house; nor indeed do I feel at liberty myself to invite him to a company, in which there are those who would be offended by his presence. This would be rude to them, and would make all uncomfortable. A gentleman must be governed by a scrupulous delicacy, and that would dictate that he should not give pain on one side or on the other. Social intercourse cannot be regulated by law; it must be left to those natural attractions and affinities which the Almighty has planted in our breasts. That the whites should desire to keep to themselves, is not to be ascribed to arrogance; it does not even imply an assumption of superiority. It is not that one race is above the other, but that the two races are different, and that, while they may live together in the most friendly relations, each will consult its own happiness best by working along its own lines. This is a matter of instinct, which is often wiser than reason. We cannot fight against instinct, nor legislate against it; if we do, we shall find it stronger than our resolutions and our laws.

CHAPTER XII.

THE EXPATRIATION OF A WHOLE RACE.

The shadow of the African still darkens the South, casting over it a gloom, by which some are so burdened and oppressed with the foreboding of what may come hereafter, that they mildly propose, as the only remedy for the danger, to remove the race altogether. If the negro is left to multiply in the land, he may become too powerful, and so let us get rid of him while we may by his wholesale expatriation. Thus Senator Hampton of South Carolina, speaking of a movement of the negroes from some of the cotton States, says: "An extensive exodus would be an inconvenience to the South, but not an injury. We would gladly see the colored people move elsewhere, and we should be willing to suffer any reduction of representation that might result from their departure. It would deprive us of much of our labor, and make it a little harder for the present generation; but it would be the salvation of the future. I do not wish any harm to the negroes, but I would sacrifice whatever votes we get in the Electoral College or in Congress by reason of them, if they would go off by themselves. I would gladly vote to appropriate $50,000,000 for the purchase of Cuba, or some other place for them to settle in."

WHERE SHALL THE NEGRO GO? 155

This is certainly very generous—to offer a whole race, which it is proposed to exile, all the world in which to choose a home, except the country in which they were born, and the only country that they know under the sun! But by what right do we make this startling proposal? Has the Creator given it to us thus to dispose of different portions of the earth? God has formed the world for the habitation of men—not of one race only, but of all the tribes and kindreds of mankind. Has He given to the Anglo-Saxon an exclusive right to lord it over this continent, and to expel all races but his own? First, to drive out the Indian from his forests and his hunting-grounds; and then, after having imported the African to be a slave, and kept him in bondage for eight generations, to turn him adrift, to seek a home in the West Indies, or in the pestilential swamps of South America? The descendants of the Africans who were landed at Jamestown, Virginia, in 1619, are as pure "native Americans" as the proud descendants of the Huguenots, who settled in South Carolina. On what ground can the latter invite the former to depart, and leave the continent to them alone?

But as this suggestion of "getting rid" of the black race is made in other quarters, and in all seriousness, it is worth considering what it implies.

You who would expatriate the negro, tell us, Where shall he go? Two generations since, it was the belief of many good people that the Africans had been brought to America to be Christianized, and were now to be returned to their native land, to be the heralds of the Gospel over the Dark Continent. The idea had been conceived in the last century by Dr. Samuel Hopkins, that brave old champion of the faith and of human liberty. In his parish at Newport (which might have been called Slave-port, from the number of cargoes of slaves that were landed there from Africa), his soul was kindled with indignation; and he longed to see the day when these unhappy children of an oppressed race should be sent back to the land from which they had been torn. But he did not live to see his hope fulfilled. After his death, the project was revived by some of the best men in the country, such as Bishop Meade and Charles F. Mercer of Virginia, and Rev. Dr. Finley of New Jersey; and in 1816 a Society was organized, with the great name of Washington (Bushrod Washington) as its President. A deputation was sent to Africa to select a site for a colony, and chose the best on the western coast, with five or six hundred miles on the Atlantic, and extending three hundred miles into the interior. Instead of being all swamps and jungle, it was a high, rolling country, with hills covered with forests, and a number of navigable streams. In 1820 eighty-six colonists were sent out, and in the course of a few years it had transported ten thousand free colored people. In 1847 it was organized as an independent Republic, to which was fitly given the name of Liberia. Then, as for many years before and after, it bore the illustrious name of Henry Clay as its President. It seemed a most benign and happy project; and when, now and then, a ship sailed away, bearing a reinforcement to the colony, devout men and women gathered on her deck, and sang hymns, and offered prayers and thanksgivings, in blissful hope that the day of Africa's redemption was drawing nigh. But since the foundation of the colony, seventy years have passed, and the day does not seem to be much nearer than before.

Since the war the Colonization Society has faded from the public notice so entirely that many will be surprised to learn that it is still in existence. But the visitor at Washington, as he rides down Pennsylvania avenue, will see its sign still on the corner, where it has hung so long;

and once or twice a year (perhaps oftener) it sends a small contingent to the shores of Africa. Nor is the work that it has done to be despised: for it is no small thing to plant a colony which, in spite of all obstacles, still lives, and has grown strong; which has a good government, with schools and churches, with eighteen or twenty thousand people born in America, or their descendants, forming the nucleus of a civilized and Christian State; and that has a million of natives under its beneficent rule. This is a great deal to be accomplished within three-score years and ten—the life-time of a man—and is worth all that it cost.

As such, Liberia will remain a beacon-light on the African coast, to attract all who may wish to go. But their going should be a matter of perfect liberty. Whoso is "called," either by Providence or his own inward yearning for the land of his fathers, let him go. But let no man be compelled to choose what seems to him exile from the land of his birth. If of his own unfettered will he elects to go, let him depart with the blessing of all Christian people upon him, assured that on the other side of the ocean he will find a home and a welcome, and may become a missionary of civilization and Christianity to a continent. To those who thus go as volunteers, the change may be a good one, and their coming may be a valuable accession to the colony; but as reducing the colored population in this country, the effect would be infinitesimal.

To anticipate anything beyond this limited and voluntary emigration, seems to me quite visionary. I know that a high authority, a man of great intelligence and learning, Dr. Edward W. Blyden (a full-blooded African, though born in the West Indies), who has spent the greater part of his life in Liberia, argues that colonization on the widest scale is the true, and indeed the only, exit for the negro race. He says in so many words that the only hope of the African is *in Africa;* that so long as he remains in America, he must be an inferior; but that once transferred across the sea, "the whole boundless continent" is his, in which to build cities and found empires. He does not tell us how it has happened that the African race has held the continent, to the exclusion of all other races, for hundreds and thousand of years, having had at one time the benefit of the highest civilization, when Northern Africa was a part of the Roman Empire; but that, instead of building cities and founding empires, it has sunk to the lowest degree of barbarism.

The project of a general emigration to Africa as a final settlement of the Race Question, may therefore be dismissed as a beautiful dream—beautiful indeed, but none the less a dream. The undertaking is beyond the power of all the Southern States combined, even supported by the resources of the National Government. The thing is physically impossible. There are not ships enough in all the navies and all the commerce of the world, to transport seven millions of human beings—men, women, and children—across the Atlantic. What heavy-laden fleets would need to accompany this Grand Armada, to feed the poor creatures on their miserable voyage! And then, when landed, what would you do with them? You could not leave them to perish. You must prepare the way for them by subduing the forests, and clearing the jungle along the coast for hundreds of miles; you must plant millions of acres, and build towns and cities for human habitation; while the African fever—a destroyer more terrible than all the lions on the continent—would lay the miserable exiles by tens of thousands in their graves. I do believe that one half of all the emigrants would die the first year, and the other half the next. This would be a settlement of the negro question by universal destruction.

But the idea of colonization is not one conceived only in the brains of the old masters, eager to expel the poor people whom they can no longer control—a decree of banishment to be passed by the State Legislatures or the National Government, and carried out by the arm of the law, no matter what degree of suffering it may inflict; it is a favorite idea with many of the colored people themselves, who, feeling that they have no home here, that they must always be an inferior race, cast their eyes round the horizon, to see if they can find some place of refuge. Some colonies have already been sent to Kansas, where they are reported as doing fairly well; others seek homes farther south, in the less occupied parts of Texas, or it may be even across the border in Mexico.

To such movements it seems to me the whites should interpose no obstacle, but rather aid those to whom they have stood in such close relations, and bid them farewell in the sincere hope that they may find happiness in the new homes to which they are bound. But here, as in the emigration to Africa, the few that go make no perceptible reduction of the mass that remain. The emigrants go in small companies, by dozens or by scores, that are not missed by those that are left behind. What impression can these little detachments make upon a population that is increasing at the rate of over a hundred thousand a year?

But Senator Hampton suggests a nearer home for the exiled race. Let us buy Cuba, which is but a few hours' sail from our coast, and transport them there, where they could have the island all to themselves, and govern their own country in their own way. This looks more feasible, but the result, I believe, would show that the black race cannot stand alone—separate from the help and guidance of the more intelligent white race. In the West Indies there has been already an experiment of a government by blacks, the history of which is written in blood. Do we desire to turn the fair island of Cuba into another St. Domingo?

But some think these dangers might be guarded against, and the experiment made a success, if the emigrant population were to retain a political connection with us, not as a colony under the protection of the United States, but as an integral part of the Union. One of the most distinguished men of Georgia, who has given a great deal of attention to this subject, recently explained to me in some detail the plan which he would like to see brought forward in Congress, and adopted by the Government. It was briefly this: that we should purchase from Mexico one or two of its outlying provinces, covering a territory as large as Texas, to which should be removed the negro population of the Southern States, where they should be a people by themselves, their own masters in every respect, forming a pure African State, with no intermixture of alien blood. This would relieve the feeling of humiliation from which their young men of high spirit now suffer: for they would have open to them all the honors and dignities of the State; they could be governors and judges and legislators. The State would be as "sovereign and independent" as Georgia and Virginia. As such, it would send its representatives to Congress, where they would be no longer looked upon with a race-jealousy. On the contrary, a black senator would be a picturesque object, as much as if he were a Moor from Africa, and would be looked upon with the same admiring curiosity that we now bestow upon a Chinese or Japanese ambassador.

So reasoned this delightful Southerner. The picture which he drew was so dazzling that I did not wonder that it blinded him to all the difficulties in the way, which melted before his ardent imagination like mists before the rising sun. If Mexico would not sell us a portion of her territory, there was land enough to be had for the asking, or for purchase, and the price was nothing to a country rich as ours. In what is known as Central America there are two States, Honduras and Nicaragua, either of which is larger than the island of Cuba, the former having 50,000 square miles, and the latter 58,000—both magnificently situated between the two oceans, with vast coast-lines opening on the Atlantic and the Pacific ; while Guatemala has 44,000 square miles, and yet (although its population is reckoned at nearly two millions), it has but 20,000 whites. The country, in fact, is said virtually to belong to a few Spanish families, that perhaps might be induced to part with their possessions for a reasonable consideration. Even little Costa Rica, with but 21,500 square miles, is a good deal larger than Massachusetts, Connecticut, and Rhode Island put together. Here then are four States, all in that tropical climate which is suited to the negro. May not one of them be finally the Promised Land for the Lost Tribes of our African Israel?

This is indeed a brilliant scheme, but which, I think, would encounter both a material and moral objection that would be fatal. If it is to be carried out by the General Government, it must have the support of the North, whose people form a very large majority of the whole population of the country. Now the Northerners are a careful and a prudent race, and before entering into such an enterprise, would scrutinize it very carefully, and would soon conclude that it would not only cost more than a dozen Panama Canals, but that it would be very doubtful in its results. But, behind and above all, is the moral sentiment of the North, that would never consent that the colored population should be removed in any other way than by their own free choice. Here, as in the case of whoever wishes to seek a home in Liberia, the country would say: If you desire to go out from among us, go, and the blessing of Him who is the God of all the races of men, go with you! But you shall go as a freeman, as an emigrant, and not as an exile!

Suppose then, before this general deportation is begun, it should be left to the negroes themselves to vote upon it, what do our Southern friends think their choice would be? They are not a venturesome and enterprising race, ready, like the sea-rovers of the North, to start off on great expeditions, and sail away to plant colonies on distant shores; and however they might listen with wonder to the fascinating story of the palm-groves and the free-and-easy life to which they were to be transported, when it came to the point of breaking away, they would draw back and linger about the old plantations, rather than seek new homes in some unknown "land of the sun."

If the sanguine projectors of these grand schemes of expatriating a whole race, are surprised and disappointed that the negroes do not eagerly accept the offer, they may yet find their disappointment a blessing: for this removal of the blacks would be the greatest possible calamity to the South, as it would take away at a blow what is the first necessity in every civilized country: a vast laboring population—a race especially fitted to the climate and accustomed to the labor. Take the African from the rice and the cotton fields, and the sugar plantations, and in spite of the golden visions of Mr. Wade Hampton, a large part of Georgia and Mississippi and Louisiana would relapse into a howling wilderness. Thus expatriation would be, not a blessing, but an unspeakable curse—a curse to both races, as the banishment of one would be the ruin of the other. Nor is there any need to resort to a measure so extreme and so cruel. The two races are necessary to each other, and any policy which would divide them and separate them, would entail untold misery on succeeding generations; and therefore I protest against all schemes of banishing the negroes from the soil on which they were born. A race that has been here for two hundred and seventy years, and that has multiplied till it has become like the stars of heaven for multitude, is not to be driven off the continent into the sea, or beyond it, at the bidding of any power. When I hear the politician casting words of contempt and of ignominy upon the negro, and predicting that he will "die out," and perish from off the New World in which he has lived so long, I see a dusky figure rising up in the gloom of the Southern forests, and hear the voice of one who believes in his race, and in Almighty God as its Protector, making answer, "I shall not die, but live, and declare the works of the Lord!"

Is it not time to drop these visionary projects, and to recognize the hard fact, however unpleasant it may be, that *the negro is here, and here to stay?* He has as good a right to be here as we have. He was born on this side of the Atlantic. He knows no more of Africa than we do, nor half as much. The only country he knows under the broad canopy of heaven, is America. Has he not a right to say, "Here my fathers have lived for many generations; here was I born; here were my children born; and here, by God's help, will we live, and here will we die"?

Recognizing this fact as one that cannot be changed by any amount of agitation or of legislation, the only question is, Whether the two races, white and black, can live side by side without constant collision? Some will tell us that it is simply impossible; that the juxtaposition of two races, alien to each other in nature as in blood, yet living on the same soil and having the same political rights, means perpetual war—a war like that between the Spaniard and the Moor, which lasted for eight hundred years, to end, like that, only in the extermination of the one or the other. Is this the inevitable doom of the black race? Or is it possible that the two races should live through all the coming generations, not only the closest of neighbors, but the best of friends? This is the Race Problem which confronts us to-day—the most difficult and perplexing problem that ever stood across the ascending path of a great nation. We are making a tremendous experiment, and one, some tell us, foredoomed to failure. If so, then civilization is a failure; and, what is worse, Christianity is a failure. But we shall not fail. Our faith is in God and in the American people. He who guided our fathers in all the crises of their history, will not forget us in this supreme moment of anxiety and of fear. He will still lead us on through this last great danger, to the end that our government may be "settled upon the best and surest foundations; that peace and happiness, truth and justice, religion and piety, may be established among us for all generations."

CHAPTER XIII.

LOOKING FORWARD.

From the dark background of a gloomy past, it is a relief to turn our eyes towards a brighter future. It is a quarter of a century since the negro received his freedom. Since then he has been, as it were, on trial, to prove whether he was worthy of the liberty that was given him, or whether it were better that he had been kept in slavery. And with all his imperfections, I think he has stood the test pretty well. He has proved himself, not only a good hand at his old business of the shovel and the hoe, but has shown a good deal of "grit" and "staying power." He has not died out, as some of his kind friends were sure that he would do as soon as he was left to himself; but, on the contrary, his descendants have multiplied like the children of Israel in the land of Egypt. Nor has he shown himself the indolent creature that we were told he would be as soon as the pressure of servitude was taken off. True, there are numbers of idle, shiftless, worthless negroes, lying about the streets of every city and large town in the South, just as there are numbers of idle, shiftless, and worthless white men in our Northern cities, that could be spared without a loss to civilization. Those who prophesied his helpless and hopeless indolence as soon as he was set free, forgot that he would come under another pressure the moment that he had to take care of himself. In the old days, when "Master" provided everything, he could lie about, and feign sickness, and shirk his day's task; but when it came to this, that "if he did not work, neither should he eat," he began to stir himself, and has worked to some purpose, in proof of which it is necessary to give but one single fact : that in Georgia the negroes are taxed on property to the amount of ten millions of dollars! As the property subject to taxation is generally estimated at little more than half its real value, this would indicate that the negroes of one Southern State are to-day worth twenty millions of dollars! This does not look like idleness and waste in the years that they have been free.

It is not to be supposed that all these well-to-do blacks are mere laborers on the old plantations. Many of them are mechanics, wherein they have an advantage over their brethren at the North. In New York city there are few colored mechanics, and these work in a very small way. General Armstrong recently said to me: "Northern competition is harder on the negro than Southern prejudice." Colored men here complain bitterly of the way in which they are driven out of all the better class of trades. They say that not one of them can find employment in any store or shop; nor be an apprentice to learn a trade; indeed that they cannot do anything except the most menial labor. The cases recently given us by Mr. Grimké would show that it is somewhat better in New England; yet even The Congregationalist of Boston says:

"The difficulties in the way of just treatment of the negro are not confined to the South. In some respects he is not so well off in the Northern States. It is affirmed that even in Boston hardly a single colored boy can be found learning a trade, because, except hotel-waiting, boot-blacking, and barbering, the trades are all closed against him. No negroes, with a single exception, were observed in the ranks of the processions representing the different trades on Labor Day. In the South they are shut out of hotels, and compelled to ride in inferior railway-cars; but they can learn trades without hindrance. Such a state of things is not a credit to Northern civilization."

In Georgia the negroes find no such barriers in their way. They can enter any trade, and, if they become skilled mechanics, can find plenty to do. Their old masters, instead of a feeling of resentment at their being free, seem to like to have them about, and encourage them in every way. This is greatly to their honor. When we think how many of these old masters were themselves impoverished, and some of them literally beggared, by the war, it shows a generous disposition that they take so kindly to the new situation; and it may be in part ascribed to their friendly counsel, as well as to the industry of the blacks, that so many of the latter have got along so well, and been able to make themselves comfortable and independent.

But the brightest light on the Southern horizon, is the education of the colored race. Before the war this was unknown. A few house-servants might be taught to read and write, to make them more useful in the business of their masters; but anything like a general education of the blacks, would have been viewed with alarm. Indeed a school for teaching them, however small, even if it were on a plantation, and conducted by members of the planter's own family, was an object of suspicion. A servile race must not be allowed to become intelligent. Ideas are explosive. For this reason schools for the blacks were forbidden by law. But when the war was over, this was one of the first things that engaged the attention of philanthropic people at the North; and teachers were sent

South, who, at the cost of social ostracism in the communities into which they went, began the work of negro education.

But these schools, few and scattered as they were, could make but little impression on the mass of the colored population. All together, they could reach but a fraction of the children. It was reserved for the South itself to do the work on a much grander scale. Governor Gordon of Georgia, in a recent address, says: "When her people secured possession of the State government, they found about six thousand colored pupils in the public schools, and her school exchequer bankrupt. To-day, instead of six thousand, we have over one hundred and sixty thousand colored pupils in the public schools, with the exchequer expanding and the schools multiplying year by year!" If it be said that the negroes themselves are taxed for these schools, I answer: "Yes, they pay one-thirtieth of the expense; the other twenty-nine-thirtieths are paid by the whites!"

Nor is Georgia alone in this work. The same spirit is reported in South Carolina and Tennessee, and other of the more thickly-settled States; so that in all the South there are no less than sixteen thousand colored schools! Of course the burden of supporting all these is enormous, especially upon States that are not rich. It is to the honor of the North that she has claimed a share in this truly national work. There is the Peabody Fund, and the Slater Fund, and the Hand Fund, besides hundreds of thousands of dollars that are given every year. But after all is said and done, the greater part of the burden has to be borne by the South, and to her belongs the honor, which no Northerner should be so base as to try to take from her. Let her have the full glory of this magnificent work, done in such a magnificent way.

After such an exhibition of kindness and generosity, it would seem as if the South was ready to do everything for the negro—to give him every right, every opportunity, and every privilege possessed by the whites. Yes! yes! every right but one—that of the ballot! Even to this they have no objection when he is in a hopeless minority, so that his vote "can do no harm." But the moment he is in the majority, he becomes dangerous. Now there are four Southern States—South Carolina, Alabama, Mississippi, and Louisiana—in which he outnumbers the whites, so that a combination of the black voters would give them the election of the Governor and Legislature, and thus the control of the State. Here in these States any attempt on their part to exercise the right of suffrage on a large scale, and thus to gain political power, is to be resisted to the last extremity.

My readers do not need to be told that I have never been in favor of universal suffrage among whites or blacks—among the ignorant creatures who arrive here by every ship from Europe, or the equally ignorant negroes of the South; and I still adhere to that opinion, even though the country has, in both cases, decided otherwise. A man who is defeated always thinks he is right: he may at least be allowed that small privilege, when those who differ from him have won their case. It is too late to argue the matter now. Good or bad, wise or unwise, the thing is done, and cannot be undone. If a ship is overtaken by a storm in the middle of the ocean, and in danger of going to the bottom, none but cowards would sit down in the cabin, and lament the folly of setting out on the voyage. The duty is to save the ship!

So in the present case. Everybody now sees that the giving of the vote to raw immigrants, who could not even speak our language, was a stupendous folly; but what are we going to do about it? Mr. McCulloch thinks Congress should pass a law requiring them to reside here a number of years before being naturalized and allowed to vote. That would be indeed a wise precaution, but it is easier said than done. It will not be easy to pass such a law, for the opposition will come from the places where such restriction is most needed, viz: in the great cities, where demagogues find this ignorant mass of foreign voters the very material which they wish to use.

Nor is there any more hope that the vote will be taken from the blacks at the South, than from the newly imported Irish at the North. I know that some cling to such an idea, and measures have been proposed to this end. There is indeed one way in which it could be done, that would be fair and just to all parties, by which our Southern friends could be immediately disembarrassed of the negro vote, viz: by passing a law to restrict the ballot to those who can read and write, and who have some small amount of property. This would not be universal suffrage, but it would be impartial suffrage, which would be far better. But this change is opposed by the politicians, on the ground that it would exclude thousands of the whites who are as ignorant as the blacks! So there is no hope of relief from that source. Universal suffrage is the law, and such it will remain, and we have got to take it, for better, for worse. We are in for it, and must make the best of it.

This is the situation which the South has to contemplate. Her leading men are old soldiers, trained to military discipline, and they know that the only way to meet danger, is to look it squarely in the face. They cannot run away from it if they would, nor is that the temper of men whose courage has been proved on many a battle-field. In the same cool and determined spirit the South should understand the dimensions of the power that it has to deal with, before it enters on a struggle in which it may have to measure strength, not only with a subject race, but with a whole nation behind it. It would therefore simplify the situation, if it would recognize the fact, which it can no longer ignore, that the policy of the country in regard to the civil rights of the negro is settled, and will not be changed.

The only question that remains is, What is the South going to do about it? Will it accept the situation, and make the best of it? Or will it try to nullify the law by fraud, by miscounting of the vote, or by violence and intimidation? I do not like to ask this question, as it is a sore point at the South, whose people sometimes think it a great impertinence in us at the North to trouble ourselves so much about Southern elections. We beg to assure them that we have no disposition to meddle in what is none of our business. We believe in home rule for Georgia as well as for New York, and that in the management of her political affairs the South must work out her own salvation. At the same time we cannot forget that the North and the South are parts of one country; members of the same body; and that if one member suffer, all the members suffer with it; and that political demoralization cannot prevail in half a dozen States without poisoning the whole national life.

I admit that the South has reason to distrust the colored vote. It has had one experience of negro rule, and once was enough. A friend recently told me of an incident within his own personal knowledge. It was some years since, in a town in Mississippi, where the blacks being largely in the majority, swept the board, electing none but negroes, save one who was a carpet-bagger—a combination that went to work at once to loot the town, beginning operations by imposing a tax of twenty-five per cent. "for municipal purposes"! As the whites had been so impoverished by the war that they could not pay, the next step was to put up their lands and houses to be sold for taxes, which the carpet-bagger, being the only man who had any money, stood ready to buy! Here was as nice a scheme of plunder as ever was planned, which the old masters met in the only way possible: seeing that they had fallen into the hands of a gang of thieves, they went to the chief brigand, and putting together all they could rake and scrape, bought him off by paying him blackmail, giving up a part of the little they had to save the rest!

Such performances shock all our ideas, not only of decent government, but of civilized society; and we do not wonder that men of spirit and independence will not submit to what is no better than highway robbery. But this was an extreme case, from which it will not do to draw a general rule—one that will justify the same "buying off" whenever it is needed to carry an election. One of the evil consequences of universal negro suffrage, is that it has begotten such a general demoralization in political matters, that buying votes is not only winked at, but done openly, without the least scruple; with no conscience about it, as if it involved anything wrong. I cannot get over the impression made at hearing one of the most intelligent and honorable gentleman I met in the South, say, "The negro vote is easily controlled *by the use of money.*" It was a surprise, and a painful one: for while money breaks no bones, it works fearful mischief upon one's manliness. Indeed few things are more demoralizing than bribery. It is not, like mercy, "twice blessed," but twice cursed, in "him that gives and him that takes."

But this is not the worst of the case. There are de-

NO APOLOGY FOR CRIME.

grees in evil; and bad as it may be to bribe a man, it is still worse to kill him. Yet to this extent has the race-hatred sometimes gone, by which the worst men in the South have placed themselves, and the States of which they are taken (very unjustly it may be) to be fair representatives, beyond the pale of Northern sympathy or support. Do our Southern friends realize how hard such violence makes it for *their* friends at the North to defend them? The intelligent people in New York and in New England fully appreciate the difficulties of the South, and are ready to make all reasonable excuses and palliations. But no sooner do we get the temper of the Northern mind a little subdued, than there comes a story of a negro shot in cold blood, or a white man assassinated for no other reason than that he voted the Republican ticket, and all our arguments are knocked into flinders. We cannot apologize for such dastardly crimes; nor can we keep our own blood from boiling when we hear of them. Those who connive at them, play into the hands of the most fiery element at the North. If Southern politicians wish to keep the North solid against them, they have but to let their Ku Klux Klans and "Regulators" continue to furnish fuel to kindle the fires of popular indignation.

I have had many talks with Southern men in regard to these matters, in which they have spoken with the utmost frankness. They all deprecate violence, and regret any violations of law. They admit that it is a hard necessity which compels them to extreme measures for their own protection. But they say, "Self-preservation is the first law of nature. We must fight fire with fire. If we cannot keep our self-government in one way, we must in another. It is all that is left us, and we should be less than men if we did not fight for it." Sometimes a planter describes his own situation, surrounded by blacks, whose votes would quite overwhelm him and all the whites he could muster; and then he turns to me abruptly, and says, "*Put yourself in my place! what would you do?* Would you let everything go to ruin, or do all in your power to prevent it?" This is an embarrassing question, and if, through delicacy, I remain silent, he will perhaps think that it admits of but one answer, and justifies any measure of repression or suppression of what would prove so great a calamity. Wherefore candor compels a reply.

As my Southern friends are so frank with me, they will not be offended if I am equally frank with them. They know me, not only as a personal friend, but as a friend of their people. Perhaps I may presume so far on my friendship as to say a few words in the utmost kindness to those whose prosperity is very near to my heart.

Is there not a better way to deal with the negro vote than to suppress it, viz: to admit it, and see if you cannot control it by some legitimate means? You say, "This is a white man's government, and we will never submit to be ruled by an inferior race." Very well! Certainly one who himself belongs to the white race, will not object to its retaining its supremacy if it be by fair means, by superior intelligence or character; but he does object to a supremacy that can only be kept by fraud and by force.

Suppose you should try an experiment. At the risk of your smiling at my simplicity, I will venture to ask, Is there not a way of giving the negroes some sort of political education? If I were an old planter, surrounded by my former slaves, it *seems* to me (perhaps if I had tried it, I should be a sadder and a wiser man) that I would not only put no obstacle in the way of their voting, but encourage them to vote—only I would try to persuade them to vote what I thought the right ticket. Some may think it useless to waste argument on those who are so

EDUCATION THE ONLY REMEDY.

dull, or so dogged in their prejudices and hatreds; but after all the negro is not a fool, and I will not believe, until convinced to the contrary, that he cannot be led to see what is for his own interest.

If the blacks are suspicious of special instruction, as if you wanted to gain some advantage over them, at least they cannot resist the uplifting force of general education, which will act upon them as it does upon the latest and freshest and rawest of our foreign importations. Here in New York we have shiploads of ignorance emptied almost daily upon our shores. What do we do with them? There is but one thing that we can do—*convert that ignorance into intelligence.* This will take a whole generation, but it is the only possible means of safety.

What is wise at the North is wise at the South. The negro stands on the same ground as the foreign emigrant, both utterly unfitted to be entrusted with the ballot. But since they *are* entrusted with it, it must be ours to see that they know how to use it. We must deal with the negro vote as we do with the foreign vote. The only remedy for ignorance is knowledge; and as we have a vast system of education for the children of the poorest who come to us from foreign shores, so the same system of common schools, not only furnished, but *enforced,* for a whole generation, will elevate the African race. The South is at this moment using the most effectual measures to remove the unfitness of the negro for the suffrage, by its widespread system of colored schools. Let the good work go on When the schoolmaster is abroad in the land, there will be raised up in time a laboring population, no matter how poor or how humble, not below the rank and file of the foreign contingent of our New York democracy, and quite intelligent enough to exercise the right of voting without danger to the State.

FEAR OF NEGRO DOMINATION.

In discussing this question, we are embarrassed by the apprehension which seems to pervade the South, of negro domination—a fear that surprises us in a people of such unbounded courage. Setting one race over against the other, such a transfer of dominion seems not within the range of possibility. No matter how the blacks may increase, they can never be a match for the superior intelligence and power of organization of the whites. Yet even Mr. Grady, (whose death, while these pages are going through the press, has awakened universal sorrow,) a man who had seen too much of public affairs to be easily frightened, thought it necessary to sound the alarm. Mr. George W. Cable, who, though a Southern man, now lives at the North, and takes what some of us would consider an extreme Northern view of the case, in a recent address said:

"My opinions have been uninfluenced by the talk about the 'New South.' The only 'New South' is the industrial South, and the change there is only partial and along the line of the mineral belt. Henry W. Grady's speech at the New England dinner at New York, meant little. At the Texas Agricultural Fair a few months ago, he called on an audience he was addressing to defend to the last drop of their blood the principle of the white man's domination of the negro!"

This was certainly a stirring appeal; but was there any occasion for our eloquent friend to anticipate a change so overwhelming? Is there really the slightest danger of negro domination at the South? If it ever comes to a contest of arms, there would not be a battle, but a massacre. I must say that Mr. Cable expressed himself with more justice as well as moderation, when he said:

"My own notion is that the true Southern problem is not whether the white man shall dominate the negro, or the negro the white man. If it were, I suppose I should have to declare in favor of the whites. But the problem is whether American citizens shall not enjoy equal rights in the choice of their rulers.

It is not a question of the negroes' right to rule. It is simply a question of their right to choose rulers; and as in reconstruction days they selected more white men for office than men of their own race, they would probably do so now."

But as Mr. Cable is just now out of favor at the South, I will quote another and a very high authority on Southern questions, Dr. J. L. M. Curry of Richmond, late Minister to Spain, and now Administrator of the Peabody Fund for Education at the South, who, if he has not so much of the ardor of youth, has the wisdom of age, and who, in an address before the Legislature of Georgia, used these plain words:

"I want to say to you in perfect frankness, that the man who thinks the negro problem has been settled, is either a fanatic or a fool. I stand aghast at the problem. I don't believe civilization ever encountered one of greater magnitude. It casts a dark shadow over your churches, your government, and your future. It is a great problem, which will tax your energies. Georgia was once Shermanized. Georgia, with the South Africanized, as it may be, would be a thousand times worse than Shermanized.

"But you may make the outlook as black as possible, and yet ignorance and poverty are not remedies for the situation. Better have the negroes educated; better that they should have intelligent preachers, intelligent industry, improved homes. Which is better—to brutalize and pauperize, or humanize, civilize, and Christianize? I leave it to you to settle the problem.

"There are people who say this ought to be a white man's government. I am not prepared to contest that proposition; but I beg you to remember that the negroes—and I am glad of it—have friends at the North who are befriending them. But they are not coming to your relief. You must help yourselves, if you are helped at all.

"I know that the indications are prophetic of a race conflict. God save us from it! I know that dark shadows of the future are flung across our pathway. It is idle to shut our eyes. It is better to meet such dangers half way, even though they come no further. There is nothing *per se* in a white skin unless behind that skin lie the hereditary experiences of centuries of good government. I know that the negro of Africa has no invention, no discovery, no law, no literature, no government, no civilization. Why? If you put the Caucasian under the same environment, and keep him there ten or twenty centuries, there will be no invention, no science, no discovery, no history, no civilization, among Caucasians. Your ancestors and mine were once pagans and cannibals. We have become what we are, not by virtue of a white skin, but by improving government and good laws. Let the negro children get an education where yours do not—let the negro be superior to you in culture and property—and you will have a black man's government. Improvement, cultivation, education, is the secret, the condition and guarantee, of race supremacy. I shall astonish you, perhaps, by saying that if the negro developes and becomes in culture, property, and civilization superior to the white man, the negro ought to rule. You are to see to it that he does not become so. The responsibility is with you."

This puts things in rather a different light. It lays the responsibility of the superiority of the negro race (if that should ever come) upon the whites themselves; while it fixes the period so far away that it would need an inspired prophet to tell the date of its coming. As the time at which a race is attaining maturity is put at "ten or twenty centuries," I think our Southern friends may safely postpone the catastrophe of negro domination to the next generation!

CHAPTER XIV.

OLD MASTERS CARING FOR THEIR OLD SLAVES.

"You people of the North do not know the negro. You draw a fancy sketch, as Mrs. Stowe did in her Uncle Tom's Cabin, and fall in love with the picture of your imagination. But that is not the real African. The negro, pure and simple—that is, apart from all romantic associations—is not an attractive creature. He is gross in body and dull in mind. He may do well enough as a laborer in the lowest kinds of work, when guided by the superior intelligence of the white man; but if you seek for anything higher than that, you will not find it. There is no fire in his eye, and no thought in his brain. If you wish to make a man of him, you must put a soul inside of his body. And his moral state is as low as his intellectual. In short, he is very far down in the scale of humanity: poor and ignorant; low of origin, and bad by nature; debased by every vice, and capable of every crime!"

Such are the colors, blacker than the skin he wears, in which some would paint the negro of the South. As these harsh words grate upon the ear of the stranger, he is tempted to reply in terms equally emphatic. But it is better to keep silence, at least until the speaker is done. Let the blast blow itself out : it is not till the storm is past that there is any chance to hear the still, small voice of reason and of truth. Even then I should begin my protest very modestly by confessing that this wholesale depreciation has some faint shadow of truth, just enough to give it plausibility. You say that the negro is "poor" —it is true ; that he is "ignorant"—it is true ; that he is "low of origin"—that also is true (although it is nothing new in human development—we can even trace back our own "great race" to a period at which it began its process of evolution at the lowest point); and if he were "bad by nature," that would be only the natural result of conditions so unfavorable. That he should be "debased by every vice, and capable of every crime," is what could be said with equal truth of thousands in all our great cities, who are born and bred under conditions equally unfavorable to virtue. I only wonder that the negro is what he is, when I think whence he came, and through what ages of suffering he has passed.

If you set out to paint him as black as you can, the materials are at hand. You may treat him as a naturalist would treat a singular variety of the human species, and set him down in your scientific catalogue as a freak of nature. You may confirm your theory by tracing his history: beginning far back in the wilds of Africa, and seeing him come out of the slime and ooze of the jungle, with his very blood poisoned by malarious swamps, and his imagination haunted by murky superstitions which reflect the gloom of the forest. Traces of such an origin you may find in him still, in which he bears a resemblance to his fathers, who offered human sacrifices. I admit it all: that he is the dark child of a Dark Continent, with the stamp of oppression, if not of degradation, on his brow. But is that any justification of wrong? However low and degraded he may be,

"A man's a man for a' that";

and the fact that he is poor and ignorant, is no reason why we should take advantage of him, to cheat him, or rob him, or oppress him. On the contrary, his very helplessness appeals to the generosity of the stronger race to reach out its powerful arm to lift him up.

And here, if I were replying to one who had pronounced this sweeping judgment on the whole African race, I would add one parting word: "If this be the result of your experience with your negroes, did it never occur to you as just possible that you were partly responsible for their intellectual and moral degradation? Good masters make good servants: why is it that yours have turned out so badly? In condemning them, you condemn yourself; and the best, indeed the only, atonement you can make for your neglect in the past, is to befriend and help them in the future."

But I will not trust myself to enter into an argument with men who in the days of their power were violent and cruel, and whose attitude towards their former dependents is still that of hatred and contempt. Nor will I be so unjust as to reckon all old masters with them. In the days of slavery slaveholders were like other men; having among them a mixture of good and bad. There were all sorts of masters as there were all sorts of men. There were hard masters, and there were kind masters: and it would not be fair that one class should suffer for the sins of the other.

Nor have their characters changed with their condition. The old master who was hard and selfish, will be hard and selfish still. But from such a poor example, I turn to one of another stamp. Those whose memories reach back to a former generation, will recall many a master who was borne to his last resting place by his faithful servants, who, as they laid him down, shed bitter tears over the grave of one who had been their greatest benefactor. This feeling may have been changed in some who survived the war. There were those who were so soured by the loss of their slaves, that they could hardly bear to hear them spoken of, and muttered with a savage brutality, "Let them take care of themselves; let them go to the dogs!" But others there were who had been kind and gentle before, and were kind and gentle still. Had you by chance met one of them, you might have heard him say, "These poor people served me faithfully while they were bondmen: I will be their friend and helper now that they are free." In losing the ownership of his slaves, he did not lose his interest in them; but still cared for them, and tried to smooth their path, even though they had passed from under his control. The rupture that had come between them, was like the tearing asunder of the parts of the human body, leaving the feet to walk and the hands to seize the implements of labor, with no eyes to see, and no brain to guide them. It is hardly possible to conceive of a more helpless human being than the newly-emancipated slave—houseless, homeless; without food, with not even a hoe-cake in the cabin; having nothing, doing nothing, and earning nothing. Then it was that he needed more than ever a friend, and a friend he found in his old master, who was the first to give him something to do. He had not a sixpence to buy a peck of corn; his old master gave him wages. Above all, he needed direction, and to whom should he turn so soon as to the one who had been his guide for so many years, and who now took him by the hand like a child, and led him on till he could get strength to walk alone? I do not say this was the case with all old masters—perhaps not with the majority; but it was with enough to redeem the race from the reproach of selfish indifference to the suffering of their fellow-creatures. These are the representatives whom I have in mind as "caring for their old slaves." And if any of my Southern friends think it presuming in a Northerner to make suggestions to them as to how they should treat their former dependents, I answer that I only give you back what you gave to me; that I have taken my models and examples from among yourselves, and taken them only to give them the honor which they deserve, and to hold them up to universal imitation.

What has been done before can be done again, and on a much larger scale, and with much greater effect. The help which the old master can give his old slaves is not help in money. That perhaps he has not to give; and if he had, it would only do mischief to scatter it about among them, for it would only make them more careless and improvident. He can serve them better, not merely by making fair bargains with them and paying them promptly, but by taking a kindly interest in their welfare, and helping them in their little economies. What they want is intelligent guidance—a little of the white man's brains to show them how to pick up something for themselves, and how to keep it till they get enough to buy a little cabin and a few acres of ground, to make a home, for that is the starting-point of all that is good in them. Perhaps they do not need to be urged to send their children to school, for they are said to be very eager that they should learn; but a little encouragement never comes amiss as a means of help, both intellectual and *moral*. I place an emphasis on the last word, as it marks the point of greatest weakness in the ex-slave, where he needs most the benefit of his master's example. It is not in "book-education," but in the training of character. The complaint that I hear constantly may be thus expressed: "The negro has no moral stamina. There is no way in which you can get hold of him, legally or morally. You engage him to work for you a week, and he will work two or three days, and then leave you with no reason except that he takes it into his foolish head that he'd rather go a-fishing! He has no conscience about it, no moral sense, and no force of will, or persistence in anything that he undertakes. Such a creature is hardly a responsible being, and you must create the elements of a moral nature—reason, conscience, and will—before you can deal with him as an intelligent subject of law and a member of civilized society."

You say they are wanting in moral stamina; but where should they get moral stamina but from you, their former masters, who are still in their eyes the highest types of manhood, their heroes and examples? The negro is at once a very observing and a very imitative creature. He can see the difference in white folks—between the "poor trash" and the man to whom all look up; and so he can see the difference between what used to be called on the plantation a "low-down nigger," and a black man whom the whites as well as the blacks regard with respect. At the same time his very habit of mimicry, which is a peculiar gift of the race, leads him to imitate what others admire. He apes the air and the style of his old master. If *he* was coarse and vulgar, his chief show of manhood being his swearing and swaggering manner, he cannot expect the old slave to improve upon his model. On the other hand, if he possessed that highest virtue, self-control, which never burst out into a furious passion, but was always quiet and restrained, it had, and still has, a powerful effect upon his old slave. In order to command others one must first command himself, and his example will be more powerful than any authority.

Of course in dealing with a people that are so careless and heedless, there will be many things very discouraging. Some of my Southern friends are getting weary of this constant pushing up-hill the heavy stone, that, the instant it is let go, comes rolling to the bottom. But I venture to say to them, Be a little patient! Lay aside your contemptuous manner towards the colored brethren, even if you have to put up with some manifestations of joy in their new-found liberty that may provoke a smile. It is the natural consequence of that "holy estate" of liberty whereinto they have come, that they should be at first somewhat dazed and bewildered. They are "like them that dream," and in the intoxication of their first sense of freedom and independence, it would be strange indeed if some of their performances were not rather grotesque. All this is in the course of nature, and is no more to be resented or criticized than the caperings of a young colt that "feels his oats," and being let loose, starts off on a run. By-and-by he will sober down, and be subdued to the quiet and dignified jog of a useful worker in the world.

Recognizing all this, the colored people of the South are to be treated with the greatest possible kindness. The negro is not an abnormal specimen of humanity: he is simply a child, and to be treated as a child. If you have a child that is rather dull and slow of improvement, you do not beat him, but teach him, and have long patience with him, till finally you make a man of him. So these Americans " of African descent " are but children in understanding, and are to be treated like children, not with severity on the one hand, nor fond indulgence on the other. Treat the negro as a brute and a savage, and you make him one. Hunt him as a wild beast in the swamps

186   THE HARDEST TRIAL OF PATIENCE.

with bloodhounds, and you may yet feel his vengeance in the deadly shot fired on a lonely road, or in the flames of your burning dwellings. But treat him kindly, and trust to the better nature that is in him to respond to kindness. If he does *not* respond, so much the worse for him; but you at least have done your duty. But do not then, in the excess of your good nature, turn round and flatter him, so as to fill him with conceit, for that is the worst possible thing for him. It is worse than cruelty—indeed it *is* the greatest cruelty. The negro—ignorant, simple creature that he is—is easily flattered, and while under this influence, he loses the little sense that he has; he does not know whether he stands on his head or his feet, and is easily made the tool of a demagogue, who wishes to use him for his own selfish purposes. Ignorant people are apt to be suspicious, and are often shy of their best friends, whilst giving their confidence and their votes to impostors and deceivers; and it would not be strange if the negroes were at first to shake their heads, and think that the old master had some selfish purpose to gain by his unexpected kindness. All this is a state of things which requires the most delicate handling. Such distrust can only be removed by degrees. But in time unfailing kindness will do its work, by bringing the old masters and their former slaves into a mutual understanding and good feeling, that will be for the prosperity and the happiness of both.

Perhaps the most severe trial of patience is to labor for those who are not grateful for it. Ingratitude is an infirmity that belongs to our poor human nature, and we must not expect the colored people to be free from it. Coupled with this there is often a self-sufficiency that is very discouraging. Northern teachers who have gone South to teach the colored people, thereby exposing themselves to social ostracism, have acknowledged to me that their greatest trial was, not the hostility of the whites, nor even the ignorance and stupidity of the blacks, but their self-sufficiency Not long ago I visited a University, which had some hundreds of colored students, and as I watched the long procession of young men filing out from their halls, a Professor said to me, "There is not one of them who does not think that he is competent to run the whole concern!" Naturally, their teachers are pained at this want of appreciation and of gratitude for the services which they render at very great cost to themselves. But what of that? If we wait for gratitude as the reward for doing good, we shall accomplish but little in this world. Even Christ pleased not Himself, and it is enough that the disciple be as his Master, and the servant as his Lord.

"But this is very slow business!" Of course it is slow, as all the great processes of nature are slow. "It may take years!" Yes: and it may take generations. But is not the end worth all the toil and the delay? To educate one mind, to form one character, to bring one sinner home to God, is often the work of a lifetime, and that life is not spent in vain. What then is it to lift a whole people out of the depressed state in which they have been for ages?

The first condition of doing anything is to appreciate the greatness of the work. We are too ready to rush to the conclusion that everything was done for the negro by the war, whereas the work was only then begun. It indeed emancipated the slaves; it gave them the same rights that belong to other citizens of the Republic; but it did not change their nature any more than it changed their color; it did not make one hair white or black. Those who were ignorant and degraded before, are ignorant and degraded still. In order to change that condition, we have to educate, not by units, but by millions—an undertaking that may well appal us by its magnitude.

Here is the great opportunity of the Republic, and of Christian civilization—to raise up an inferior race to the level of our own. This is at once the greatest and the most difficult work that was ever attempted by man. But it is the work that God has given us to do, and blessed is he who has a part in it. And to have a part, it is not necessary to be in a public station—a governor or a legislator: for it will be accomplished in private spheres, by the personal influence of good men of one race coming in contact with the masses of the other. You may make all the laws in the world, and enforce them by all your power, civil and military: they do not touch the seat of the disease. The poison is in the blood; in the profound mutual distrust which divides the two races. How is this to be overcome? How are they to be brought together? In the advance towards a better understanding, the stronger race must lead the way. The white man, in his intercourse with the blacks, never forgets his own superiority. Then he must accept its obligations. *Noblesse oblige,* and the first of all its obligations is courtesy to inferiors. Kindness disarms distrust, and begets confidence—a warm atmosphere in which prejudices and animosities dissolve and die. There is no heart so hard that it can resist a love which "never faileth." The true solvent of the Race Problem, as of all social questions, is gentleness, not the gentleness of weakness, but the gentleness of power. "Thy gentleness hath made me great," is the Divine method; and so in human relations, a gentleness that is at once subdued and strong is the very breath of God. It is the South wind, causing the spices to flow out. And what healing influences will come from the schoolhouses! Already "the woods are full of them," humming like so many hives of bees; in which the noble army of teachers, faithful men, and faithful women, too—God bless them! — are working in the spirit of their Master for the uplifting of a lowly race. Work on, brave hearts! We send you our word of cheer and of hope. There is a better day coming, though we shall not live to see it. But whatever any of us can do, little though it be, will not be lost. Long after we are dead and gone, the seeds of kindness, sown by voice or pen, will spring up and blossom from the dust. And at last, in some far-off future year, will the desired end come, when no man shall vex his neighbor, since universal love brings universal peace. Then—in the middle of the next century, it may be— a generation not yet born may see those happier times which our eyes are not permitted to behold.

CHAPTER XV.

A CAMP-MEETING IN THE WOODS, WITH A FEW WORDS TO MY COLORED BRETHREN.

The desire to do full justice to one side of a question, often leads to injustice to the other—a danger I have felt from the beginning of this discussion. While trying to present the case of the whites of the South in the most favorable light, I have feared that I might seem unsympathetic with those who had suffered from the more powerful race. If it were a mere question of sympathy, I should always be on the side of the weak against the strong. But it is not a matter of feeling, but of truth and of justice, in which one needs to be on his guard against being led away by his sympathies, so as to impair the value of his judgment.

Have I really leaned to the stronger side? Then I will try to restore the balance by leaning to the other; and my last words shall be to my colored friends. In these I hope they will not think that I assume a condescending or patronizing tone. I do not wish to pat them on the back, or delude them with high-sounding promises to the ear, that will be broken to the hope. I love them too much to deceive them. As the only true kindness is in perfect frankness, I wish that my parting words should at least bear this proof of what I feel so deeply.

But it is very awkward to talk in a familiar way with those at a distance: it seems as if I were shooting into the air, and over the heads of everybody within hundreds of miles, with a vague idea that *somehow* and *somewhere* I should hit *somebody*. Now if I am to talk, I like to have my hearers near enough to see the whites of their eyes; and so, if you do not object, I will, for the purpose of this familiar talk, suppose ourselves to be assembled in a big camp-meeting, in a grove of live oaks— those magnificent trees which are the glory of the Southern forests, and which, when bearded with moss, seem like the veterans of another generation, looking down upon their puny descendants at their feet. Here there is ample space for you all to rest at your ease, leaning against the trees, or sitting on the ground, if perchance the talk should be a little dull, or you can prick up your ears if there be anything worth listening to. I can promise only that it shall be the advice of a sincere friend. With this I begin:

Men and brethren! The Lord has brought you out of the house of bondage! He has set before you an open door, leading to a straight path of safety and of peace; but He does not compel you to walk in it: it is left to you to take your own course. Hence my first word to you— *and the last also*—is this: Your fate is in your own hands; the great work for your race must be done by yourselves. If any of you have got an idea, because of the way in which you were cared for by your old masters, that you are to be "carried" as long as you live, the sooner you get rid of it the better. Even if they were ever so kind and ever so willing, they could not do everything for you, and they ought not if they could, for it would only keep you in a state of perpetual childhood. The sooner you come to a "realizing sense" that you have got to take care of yourselves, the better it will be for you. Nor must you look to the Government to provide for your wants. It is not the business of the Government to feed black men any more than to feed white men. There is but one law for white and black: He who will not *work* neither shall he eat. This little word of four letters is the key to Paradise.

As I am saying this, I see a man of large stature and great bodily strength standing on the outskirts of the wood, in doubt whether to accept this hard doctrine. Let him not be in a hurry about it; but go off a little way, and sit down under a solitary oak, where nobody will disturb him, and he can do " a heap o' thinking." Indeed, if we can "let up" on the talking for a few minutes, and vary the exercises with a spell of singing (which stirs the blood, when rolled out by such magnificent voices), I will go and sit down by him for a little private conversation.

"Well, Abraham"—I use this name as one that is familiar to me and has pleasant associations—"how do you like being a free man?" He answers slowly, "Things ain't quite so easy as they used to be on the old plantation." "Yes: I know it, but think what you have gained by the exchange. True, you've got only a mere patch of ground with a log-cabin upon it. It's 'mighty little.' Yes, but it's *yours*. And Dinah, who keeps it for you, is yours, and no man can take her from you; and the little merry faces that I see around, grinning with their white teeth, and laughing out of their eyes—all are yours! They may not be as well dressed as white folks' children, but Dinah will patch up their tattered garments; and as long as you can scratch ground in that garden patch fast enough to keep them in hoe-cake and corn-dodgers, and they are plump as so many rabbits, you need not be troubled. Isn't it something to work for 'your own self'? You are no man's slave, and can sit before your humble door when the day is done, and sing:

> 'We own de hoe, we own de plough,
> We own de hands dat hold;
> We sell de pig, we sell de cow,
> But nebber chile be sold.'

What a motive you have in that wife and children to work, since you can enjoy all the fruits of your labor which God giveth you under the sun! Then work, and work hard! That's the price of anything that is to be gained in this world. Quiet industry will make you comfortable and respectable. That is the way you are to make your own position, without 'calling on Cæsar for help,' unless it be the Cæsar and Pompey in the next cabin.

"And now, Abraham, remember this one word: You must work out your own salvation! No man can do it for you: you must do it for yourself. You must fight your own battles, not with sword and gun, but 'wid de shovel and de hoe.' That old hoe is the best weapon that was ever put into the hands of a man, white or black. The Lord put it into the hands of Adam when he got into a bad way in the Garden of Eden, and it has been a mighty instrument to keep his descendants from going to the bad ever since. As long as you keep hold of the hoe-handle, you keep your hands out of mischief, and that is no small thing in this wicked world."

As this kind of talk seems to make an impression, when I go back to "the stand," I look about and spy another huge, lumbering fellow, and fixing upon him my "glittering eye," I talk to him in the same direct fashion: "Is it not a shame that you, an able-bodied man, should 'lie around' and waste your time, when once you could work like a hero? You, who could be a slave for your master—can you not be a slave for yourself, and for your wife and children? Think about it, and keep on thinking till you get the idea so deep into your head that it will stay there. If, as some sneeringly say, your slowness in receiving ideas is because nature has provided you with a better protection for the brain than for us thin-skinned and thin-skulled white folks, the same physiological fact ought to make it easier for you, when once you have got hold of an idea, to keep it locked up in this secure repository of the most precious things which you have to carry.

There is another idea which I would like to drop into that iron-bound chest, viz : that you not only work now and then, by fits and starts, but *regularly*, as white men do—every day in the week, and so many hours a day. If you only work three days, and are idle the rest, you will always be a vagabond, a loafer, and a beggar. What you need is to form a habit of industry that will become to you a second nature.

A third idea, which is literally worth its weight in gold, though I shall charge you nothing for it, is, Save what you earn! Your wages may be small ; but no matter how small they be, you can save a little of them. Do you not spend some of your hard-earned money for drink? That is a great deal worse than throwing it away. Keep away from those vile dens in the woods, that are worse than rattlesnakes' holes! If you can save the sixpences that go into that bottomless pit, in a few weeks they will count up some shillings, or even dollars, enough to put into a savings bank. That marks the point where a black man's fortune begins to turn. His name will no longer be prefixed with a word spelled with two *gs ;* and when it gets around among his people that he has money in the bank (!), they will speak of him as Mr. Jones!

But I do not urge you to save your money in order to make a miser out of you; but that you should get a *home*, which is, or ought to be, the aim and end of every hard-working man, white or black. It will be the happiest moment of your life when you can go into a little cabin, and look round on the rough walls, and say, "This is mine! It isn't Master's. *I'm Master!*" Ah, my friend, I know not what transport you may feel when you pass over the waters of death, and your feet touch the heavenly shores; but *this side of Jordan* there is no keener pleasure than when you enter your humble dwelling. It is yours. Nobody has given it to you : nobody except the Creator, who gave you strong arms and a strong will to take care of yourself.

But perhaps some of you are not content with the log-cabin, however neat and trim it may be, or with the shovel and the hoe. It is too much like being on the old plantation. Well, for my part, I consider the cultivation of the earth to have been, from the time of the Garden of Eden, the most honorable occupation of man. But if your young fellows look for "something higher," there is no law to keep them in the cabin, or on the five-acre lot : they can go into the towns and cities, where they will find mechanical employments open to them. The danger is that, having no trade to work at, they will not find anything to do, and so will wander about the streets, and become just as useless as would the same number of white vagabonds. But if they are in earnest to work, and ready to take whatever comes to hand, they can soon make a place for themselves. They can become, not only hostlers and teamsters and draymen, but skilled mechanics. In Atlanta colored men are blacksmiths, masons, carpenters, and house-builders, and work side by side with white mechanics, with no friction between them.

In this way the negro can soon take care of himself. If he is a good mechanic, he will find plenty to do. Of course, if he is a poor workman, he must not expect to be employed simply because of his color. But let him show superior skill, and he will not stand idle. If there be in Atlanta a bright-eyed and strong-limbed son of Africa, who has got the reputation of being the best blacksmith in the city, the Southerner who has his stable full of blooded horses will ride by the open forges of all the white blacksmiths, to find the man who can shoe his horse in the best way. No man ever hated the negro to such a degree that he did not prefer a good black mechanic to a poor white one!

My next word may surprise you: Be kind to one another! I should not presume to say this, as if you were in any special need of it, if it were not for what I hear about you. But some who have had to do with colored people all their lives, tell me that, however subservient they may be to white folks, they are by no means gentle among themselves; that fathers whip their children without mercy; and that negroes placed over others do not prove the most indulgent "bosses"; that a little authority turns their heads; that they like to show their power, and that this makes them hard, often to the point of cruelty. They tell me that on the old plantation a slaveholder could do nothing that would so soon create a panic on the place, as to give his people a black overseer, as he was pretty sure to be more rough in the field than a white man. A friend from Virginia recently told me that if a negro was arrested on a charge of crime, his first request was that there should be no one of his own color on the jury; that his instinct told him that white men would be more lenient to his infirmities, big or little, than those of his own race.

PLAYING WITH FIRE.

These are not pleasant things to hear. I do not know that they are *true*. You know better than I. But if they *are* true, you can hardly expect your white friends, however kind-hearted they may be, to be very considerate of your feelings or your interests, when you are indifferent to the feelings or interests of your colored brothers and sisters, who may be in a condition of the greatest poverty and helplessness. "Bear one another's burdens," and you will find your white neighbors very willing to bear your burdens with you.

And that leads to another point that is all-important to your comfort and happiness: Do not let anybody persuade you that white folks are unfriendly to you. Some of your own race go about saying such things, and stirring up hatred. But whoever whispers this to you, be he white or black, is a very bad adviser. If you listen to him, you will always be in hot water; in a sour, ugly mood, making threats, and watching for a chance of retaliation.

Be careful! You are playing with fire in the midst of the most inflammable materials. It is very easy to stir up passion; it is not so easy to control it. If ever there should come the awful calamity of a race-war, it will come by the preaching of this fiery gospel of hatred and revenge. Of course there is enough to stir up the excitable African nature. Here is a powerful negro, who is not a bad fellow at heart, but is maddened by the memory of cruelties in the old days of slavery, when perhaps he was subjected to the lash to "break his spirit." Such a man may easily be converted into a desperado, lurking in swamps, only to emerge now and then to do some deed that thrills the land with horror. It is easy to see where his career will end; but were it not better to tame this African lion before he becomes so desperate and so terrible? And if he cannot be tamed by the whites, the very sight of whom rouses all the hatred within him, let him be held in check by his own kindred. If I had the ear of your leaders—for you have leaders as much as we—I would implore them, in the name of God and of their race, to restrain the fury of the more violent among you, lest it become a contagion of madness, spreading rapidly and wildly, and involve your whole people in one common ruin.

But for you who have no wrongs to embitter you, these suspicions are as foolish as they are wicked. Throw all this stuff to the dogs! When the tempter comes, say, Get thee behind me, Satan! The white men are *not* your enemies, but your best friends. They help you by giving you work to do ; they pay you wages ; they tax themselves for schools for your children ; they encourage you to help yourselves ; and if you would only listen to the advice they give, and follow it, it would be a great deal better for you and for your children.

But I have said nothing yet about your political duties : these I have left to the last, because I think them the least of all God's mercies, and the most unimportant to your *present* well-being. "But," you ask, "do you mean that we shall *give up* the rights that have been given to us by the laws of the country?" By no means. But there is a difference between having a right and exercising it. The latter is a matter of time and judgment. I may not surrender a single one of my legal rights, and yet there may be reasons sufficient to myself why I should defer asserting them to a more convenient season. And so, my good friends, the less you talk and think about "politics," the better it will be for you. If you can go to the polls and vote quietly, without getting into trouble with your white neighbors, do so ; but do not go armed, for the good reason that in a pitched battle you will be sure to be beaten—

[no matter what your numbers may be, they will be no match for the superior intelligence and organization of your adversaries]—and further, you will gain more by waiting than by fighting. For the present your strength is to sit still. Time will do for you more than you can do for yourselves.

We sometimes get wisdom from an unexpected source ; and not long ago I found this nugget of gold from Mr. C. P. Huntington, one of the half dozen men who built the first railroad to the Pacific. Some months since he was down in Mississippi, and happened to be present at a gathering of colored people, whom he addressed in a few plain, homely words, that seemed to cover the whole case. He said :

"Boys, you must be industrious! Save your money, and put it into land. If you do this, you will soon own the soil, and command the respect of your enemies and the confidence of your friends. You will have to learn to deny yourselves the gewgaws which it seems so easy for you to spend your money for. If justice is slow, do not get impatient, for it will come in the course of time. *Go to the polls, but do not take your guns!* If you are not permitted to vote, *go again*, and *keep on going* patiently as a silent protest against this political injustice; and in time you will have your rights, with the capacity to use them wisely."

As to this whole political business, one word of caution : Don't expect too much from the General Government! I know it is the most natural thing in the world, when you get into straits, to call on the power at Washington to help you out, and party papers echo the cry. Just now we hear a loud call upon Congress to secure to the negroes at the South " a free ballot and an honest count "—an admirable thing to do, if there were not several big stumbling-blocks, veritable boulders, in the way, which no one has pointed out more clearly than President Harrison, who in a speech in the Senate, March 3, 1886, showed the difficulty, even the impossibility, of doing this very thing. He said :

"I have looked hopefully in the old times to the forcible intervention of the General Government. I have thought that it might be possible under that stringent legislation which Congress adopted, by the forcible intervention of the Federal authority, to protect them [the negroes] in those rights of which they were so cruelly deprived. But I have ceased to have faith in the possibility of that intervention in their behalf, constituted as this Government is, with its complex organization of Federal and State governments, independent within certain limitations. In the States and in the tribunals which they establish, and in the venue where the offences are committed, crimes against the colored people must be tried. Of necessity the successful vindication of the rights of these people fails unless there is a sentiment in the locality where the offences are to be examined into and punished that reprobates and condemns them."

If such be the language of our Chief Magistrate, who was elected partly because of his pronounced political opinions in regard to the rights of the colored people, to the defence of which he is pledged, not only by party ties, but by his personal sympathies and all his public career, we may well hesitate in urging the Government to a policy which the head of the Government has already declared to be impossible. Better wait a little longer, even though it be at the cost of some hardship, than precipitate a conflict, which can only end in disaster and defeat.

Meanwhile is there not something else to think about than going to election? Does it really make any difference in your corn crop? "De yam will grow, de cotton blow," no matter who is Governor; and if you should stay at home on election day, and spend it in your garden, while others go tearing by on horseback, you will have no reason to be ashamed if, when they come riding home at night a little the worse for wear, they see the pretty picture of a neat little cabin, with roses in the window, and vines running over the door!

But brighter than the roses are the snapping eyes of your children, as they shine when they come home from the little school-house in the woods. They are big with the sense of knowing something which "Daddy" did not know; and as they climb upon his knees, and prattle of the lessons in spelling and in reading they have learned, the old creature's heart swells, half with sadness and half with pride, that they have opportunities that were denied to him. The most touching picture in the New South is that of a former slave, with grizzled head bent fondly over his child, listening eagerly as he hears the first words read out of the Bible from those tender lips!

With such elements of happiness, my poor friend, your lot in life is not very hard, even though you should not have the honor of voting or being voted for. Take what you have, and be thankful to God for it, though there may be other things which you desire, but do not possess.

To make your happiness complete, I would that you could be lifted up, not with pride, but with genuine, manly self-respect. To this end I beg you, do not try to be what God never made you to be, and what you cannot be, however much you try. The great trouble with the colored people of the South, is that they want to be white folks. But can the Ethiopian change his skin? In this foolish desire to be what they can *not* be, they lose the opportunity to be what they *can* be: to take a position of their own, in which they can keep their independence and their self-respect.

Can anything be more childish than to complain that we are not treated with proper consideration? I sometimes hear a good honest colored man say "white folks don't treat him 'spectful," by which he means that they wont have anything to do with him socially. Well, then, my good fellow, if I were in your place, I wouldn't have anything to do with them. They like to be by themselves, and so do you, for you feel a great deal more free, and enjoy yourself better; and if I were in your place, when I wanted to have a good time, I wouldn't have any white folks around!

In this matter of social position, those of the colored people who are most worthy of respect, have a becoming pride, which leads them to hold themselves in a position of reserve. One of them writes to me: "As to social equality it is a mistake to suppose that the colored people, either North or South, have any desire to intrude themselves upon the whites. They have intelligence enough to know that social equality is a matter which must be regulated entirely by individual preference." If all had this feeling of dignity, there would be no trouble: for, as our friend truly indicates, these are matters regulated by an instinctive feeling on the one side and on the other; and the less attempt there is to use force or compulsion of any kind, the better. There are things which the law cannot do: it cannot change a man's skin; it cannot make him white or black; nor can it eradicate his natural instincts; so that we need to be careful, in our zeal for humanity in general, not to attempt the impossible, nor to force a union which nature does not permit.

Nor should your equanimity be disturbed if white folks should have the bad manners to speak of you with an affectation of contempt. What if they do? Hard words don't kill anybody. Perhaps they laugh at your efforts to take care of yourself. Never mind! Only just work a little harder, and by-and-by the laugh may be on the other side. A man who *is* a man—whose heart is clean, and whose hands are used to toil—can hold his own against the world!

THE CREATOR'S STAMP ON YOUR BROW.

Now it is very easy to give advice, and to say what *we* would do if we were somebody else; but I sometimes like to think what I would do if I were a black man. I would not try to make myself white, nor would I regard my color as a degradation. What's in a name? One of the most famous regiments in the English army, is known as the Black Watch, as one of its greatest heroes was called the Black Prince. Was not the name as honorable as if he had been called the White Plume, or any other fancy title that might be given to him as a leader of chivalry and romance? The Bible speaks of one who was "black but comely." So there are many of a darker skin than ours, but of splendid physique, as fine types of manly strength and beauty as any that we can show. If I were black, I would not ask my Creator to change my skin by a single shade. I would say, This is the badge of my descent; this is the stamp which the fiery sun of Africa has burned upon my brow. I accept it as the token by which the Creator would distinguish mine among the races of men, and I will make it honored in the sight of the world!

And so it *is* being raised up to a place of honor and respect. With all that is dark in the sky above, there is light breaking all round the horizon. If your race has long seemed to present a dead level of inferiority, there are heads cropping up here and there that will not be kept down. Young men are taking advantage of the opportunities for a higher education than that in the common schools. At the South there are numerous institutions for colored students, such as Lincoln, Howard, and Biddle, which are thronged by those eager to obtain the benefits of knowledge; while from Hampton, General Armstrong sends out hundreds of lusty fellows, strong of limb, and not at all deficient in intelligence, who are both ready to work and apt to teach, to be teachers in the schools which are being established everywhere in the South for the children of their race. At the North, here and there one has entered a college, in which all the teachers, and almost every one of the pupils, are whites. At the last Commencement at Williams I saw a black student come on the platform with the class, and receive his diploma from the hands of the President. Another has graduated at Harvard with such honor that he has received a Government appointment in Washington. Another has been chosen by the present Senior class as its orator at the next Commencement—a very high honor, which, we are assured, he owes to no favor or party feeling, but to his own indomitable spirit: for it is said that he began by working in a barber's shop, to earn money to get an education. This is the stuff that men are made of, and a race that produces many such cannot be kept down.

All this is progress in the right direction. To be sure, it may be asked, What are these among the millions to be raised up out of the depths of ignorance? Little indeed; but it is something that there are signs of life stirring in the sluggish mass of that vast population. In this new exodus from bondage, the emancipated slaves have a long road to travel before they reach the Promised Land. But it is something to see the head of the column coming up out of the wilderness, with their faces turned to the rising sun.

In that column you can be in the front rank, if you are worthy of it. My ambition for you is that you should rise to a true manhood; that you should become, not *white* men, but MEN, who will respect yourselves, and so compel the respect of others. This is not to be gained by selling your votes at the polls, or being flattered and cheated by demagogues, but by the humbler method of tilling the soil, in which will grow, not only corn, but every manly virtue.

The continual struggle with nature, which developes the physical strength, also developes character. He who casts his seed in the ground, and hath long patience for it, waiting for the early and the latter rain, thereby learns a lesson of trust in God; and so that which is a school of industry, becomes also a school of faith and hope. In such lowly places springs up the consummate flower of piety. A beloved minister, now dead and gone, used to tell me of a parishioner of his, a colored man who was very old, but who was never so happy as when working in his little garden, singing to himself in a low voice,

> "Dis one ting I find:
> Dat He can't go to glory
> And leave me behind."

That faith is a light springing up in a dark place. It makes the humblest home full of peace and bright with hope. If any among you be so poor as not to have a roof to cover you; if you have to sleep on the cold ground, and rest your head, like Jacob, on a stone, yet even then you may, like him, dream a dream in which you shall see a ladder reaching from earth to heaven, and the angels of God ascending and descending upon it.

Dream on, weary sleeper! There is more wisdom in your dreams than in the pride of your waking hours. Anchor your hopes fast to the throne of God, the beginning and end of all that is good, and of all our hopes for your race and for mankind. When I think of all the difficulties and perplexities that beset this Race Problem, the prospect is very dark; the sky is black with clouds; and I am almost in despair, and should be utterly so but for my temperament and my faith. But I am an incorrigible optimist, with a temper that rebounds like a spring from the heaviest weight the instant the pressure is withdrawn. But this buoyant spirit, however agreeable, would not be very wise, if it had not something to rest upon. That something it has, for it rests on the eternal foundations. I believe in the future, because I believe in God. When all is dark, I turn my eyes upward and see a Power above, as I see the sun in heaven; and seeing that, I believe that all the wrongs of ages shall be made right in the better ages to come.

We have all been reading lately of the wonderful march of Stanley across the Dark Continent. Pushing his way from sea to sea, he found himself entangled in a forest of apparently illimitable extent, which proved by actual measurement to cover four hundred miles of latitude and as many of longitude, so that it was as large as the whole of France! Into this wilderness he plunged without a guide, forcing his way through deadly swamps, through thickets so dense that every foot of advance had to be cut with an axe, and where it was dark even at midday, as trees a hundred, and even two hundred, feet high almost shut out the light of heaven. Yet sometimes he had a vision in the night that reanimated his courage. Lying on the ground, he looked up through the branches of the trees, and saw the stars keeping their eternal march. As some great orb rose and hung in the deep sky, it seemed as if it were the eye of God looking down upon him; and the faith taught in his childhood came back, and he believed that God would carry him through. So after more than five months, he came out at last on the highlands that overlook the clear waters of the Albert Nyanza, one of the great lakes of Africa.

It is not often that human courage has to face such difficulty and danger. But there is a wilderness right here in our own country more dense and dark and impenetrable, than the Forest of the Congo. It is in the Black Belt, with its population of millions. Here is darkness that may be felt. It is a part of that greater mystery of the African race—a mystery which casts its dark shadow, like the sun in eclipse, over one-quarter of the globe, and one large portion of the human race. How is it that a whole Continent should be foredoomed to eternal night, and a whole race to misery without measure and without end? Here we are lost in a wilderness so deep and dark that we cannot find our way out, but *God can lead us out, and He will.*

To my colored friends I say, Be of good courage! I do not mean to belittle your hardships; to make light of them as if they did not exist: they *do* exist. But whatever they may be, bear and forbear even to the end. If you have to suffer a thousand humiliations, remember that it was by far greater humiliations that the Saviour of mankind wrought out the salvation of the world. So the salvation of your race is not to be lightly won: it must be gained by silent endurance; by toiling and suffering; by industry, by patience, and by peace.

And so ends our camp-meeting. If it has seemed to you a little long, you can shake off your weariness by rising to your feet, and making the woodland arches ring with a parting hymn. To you has been given, whatever else be denied, the gift of song, by which you touch the heart of the world. Those melodies tell the story of your race, as in their plaintive tones are heard the wail of the captive and the sighing of the bondman. They strike a chord of pain, till through them there breaks a strain of hope, that swells at last into a song of jubilee. Who that has ever been present at a camp-meeting of our colored brethren, can forget the multitudinous voices that mingle in the mighty Hallelujahs, that make the air to tremble, to which we listen enchained till they die away in the depths of the forest? That dying strain is our mutual farewell.

Here I leave this mighty Race Problem, over which I have been brooding for months, but which I make no pretence to have solved. No man on earth is wise enough to solve it. But when we are in darkness, we must grope towards the light, and even then the light comes only by degrees. One thing I hold to be fixed: that the Problem, however difficult, is to be wrought out and to be settled *here*. We are not to get rid of it by shipping off a whole people to die miserably on some distant shore. This is their home as much as it is ours; and it is written in the book of fate, that the two races are to remain on the same soil, inhabitants of the same country, and sharers of the same destiny. So it ought to be. The two races are not natural enemies: on the contrary, they are indispensable to each other; and as they are the nearest neighbors, they ought to be the best friends.

We have seen that the African race, which we have been wont to regard as doomed to inferiority, is capable of elevation, and that under the stimulus of education, it is steadily rising, so that, even if it should not become the equal of our boasted white race, it may yet attain to an honorable place among the races of the world. As to the social and political antagonisms, which are complicated by race antipathies, by jealousies and hatreds, if we cannot extinguish them, we can relieve the strain of the situation by a strict regard to justice and humanity; by kindness and gentleness. Thus we can soften bitterness, and slowly removing obstacles out of the way, may "turn the hearts" of the two races towards each other. But when we have done all, we have still to confess that there hangs over the future a veil through which no human eye can see. The final solution must be left to God and to time.

CHAPTER XVI.

THE BATTLE OF FRANKLIN.

When I left Atlanta, and turned northward, it was delightful to feel that, at last, after two months absence, I was homeward bound. My friend, Mr. Cunningham, who had met me on my way South at Chattanooga, now met me again, and accompanied me to Nashville. Our last day together had been on Lookout Mountain, and now we were to pass over other historic scenes. Middle Tennessee is full of war memories. Here is the field of Murfreesboro, which tells its story silently in thirty thousand graves. As we approach Nashville, the crumbling remains of old earthworks that once girdled the city, remind us how two great armies were once camped on these hills. But just now my eyes were turned in another quarter, to the town of Franklin, a few miles south of Nashville, that had been the scene of a battle near the close of the war, which, though less in the number of those engaged than some others, was contested with the most desperate courage on both sides, and was one of the most important in its results to the Union cause. In this battle Mr. Cunningham had borne a part as a Confederate soldier, and he had told me so much about it, with such details as

VISIT TO FRANKLIN.

brought it all vividly before me, that I had it in mind, if I came this way again, to pay a visit to the historic ground, that from a study of its geography, and of the position of the contending armies, I might be able to appreciate the tremendous conflict, and do full justice to the brave men on both sides who perished in it.

Accordingly we fixed a day for the visit, when he brought a friend, Major Vaulx (pronounced *Voss*), who was Inspector-General to Cheatham's Division, which bore a leading part in the battle. Franklin is but eighteen miles from Nashville, and a half hour's ride brought us to the station. As we entered the town, we had the good fortune to meet Col. McEwen, an old resident, who was here when the battle was fought, and from his front door witnessed it all, and who now kindly consented to accompany us over the field, and give us the benefit of his personal observations. Later we had also Mr. Carter, whose house was such a centre of fire from both sides, that he and his family fled to the cellar for safety. Of these four persons, three were eyewitnesses of the battle; and the fourth, if he did not *see* so much, it was only because the roar of conflict was going on over his head; but as soon as the battle was ended, he had the fullest opportunity to visit the field while it was yet covered with the dead and wounded, and his observations will come in in the proper place.

As the points to be visited were at some distance from each other, my first step was to engage a carriage with two horses, with a negro following on an extra horse in case any of our party preferred to make his observations from the saddle. Thus provided with the best of guides, we set out on our morning's ride, driving directly to the line of entrenchment, along which General Schofield, who commanded the Union army, drew up his line of battle.

THE CRISIS OF THE WAR.

To make the description intelligible, we must recall the general position of the armies in the South in the Fall of 1864. That was the crisis of the war. While Lee held Richmond, he could do nothing to sustain the fortunes of the Confederacy in any other part of the field, lest he should leave the Capital to his vigilant and powerful enemy. Hence the active campaign was transferred to the farther South, where Sherman in a series of battles had pushed Johnston back to Atlanta—a movement which created such alarm that he was removed, and the command given to Gen. Hood, who had shown his courage on many fields, having lost an arm at Gettysburg and a leg at Chickamauga, but who in his mutilated body still carried the heart of a lion. He inaugurated his campaign by a new system of tactics. Instead of manœuvering and retreating, he believed that battles were to be gained by hard fighting, and at once took the offensive, and fought three bloody battles, but could not save Atlanta from surrender. Failing to shake the hold of his adversary by direct attack, he undertook a movement in the rear. Leaving Sherman in Atlanta, he crossed the Chattahoochee with an army of more than forty thousand men, and struck into Tennessee, intending to cut his adversary's communications, and thus compel him to retreat in self-defence. It was a brilliant plan of campaign, and might have been successful if the Confederate leader had not been dealing with a wary old soldier. But Sherman was then planning his march to the sea, and did not mean to be diverted from it. That was a bold stroke, but not without its danger, for the farther he got away, the more he left the enemy free to sweep the country; and so it might have been that while Sherman was marching through Georgia to the sea, Hood should be marching through Tennessee and Kentucky to the Ohio! The letters of Grant written at the time, show that he was full of anxiety as to the result.

To guard against the danger from that quarter, it was necessary that Sherman should leave in his rear a sufficient force to deal with such a movement. Accordingly, Thomas was left in command at Nashville, and Schofield *

* If proof were needed of the great value of institutions for the training of officers who are to be at the head of armies, it would be afforded by the late Civil War, in which the same Military Academy furnished the leaders on both sides. In the battle that is here described, the opposing commanders were not only both graduates of West Point, but *members of the same class, entering on the same day*, and had spent four years together, little dreaming that they should ever be arrayed against each other in the field.

General John McAllister Schofield is a son of the State of New York, having been born in Chautauqua county, Sept. 29, 1829. He graduated at West Point in 1853—when General Robert E. Lee (then only a Captain of Engineers, though a Colonel by brevet for his services in the Mexican War) was Superintendent, and General George H. Thomas Instructor of Artillery and Cavalry—in the same class with General Hood, and also with General McPherson and General Sheridan; while in the next class were O. O. Howard and Thomas H. Ruger, afterwards Generals in the Union Army, and on the Confederate side Generals G. W. Custis Lee, John Pegram, J. E. B. Stuart, the famous cavalry officer, and Stephen D. Lee, who commanded a corps at Franklin. On his graduation, Schofield was assigned to the Second Artillery, and yet such was his standing as a student that for five years he was retained at West Point as Instructor in Natural Philosophy; and then obtained leave of absence from the army, that he might go to St. Louis, and there fill the same chair in Washington University. But at the breaking out of the war, he returned to the army with the rank of Captain, and was almost immediately promoted to be Major of the First Missouri infantry. He subsequently became chief-of-staff to Gen. Lyon. In November, 1861, he had been promoted to be brigadier-general, and was assigned to the command of the Missouri militia, and in April, 1862, became commander of the district of Missouri. In was sent with two corps to his support. But even with this reinforcement, Thomas did not feel strong enough to deal the crushing blow which he afterwards gave in the battle of Nashville, and so sent Schofield as far south as Pulaski, a distance of eighty miles, to keep watch of Hood, falling back as he advanced, and thus check his march northward. At Columbia the two armies were separated only by a river, which furnished an excellent line of defence against the pursuer, if he should try to force a crossing at that point. But instead of this, Hood moved east to a ford five or six miles above, from which Schofield at first supposed that he would turn along the north bank of the river, and attack him in his position; but he soon learned that, instead of this, his antagonist had struck northwest towards Spring Hill, the point where the road by which he was marching, would strike the main road from Columbia to Franklin. The object of this movement was plain: it was to place Hood between Schofield and Thomas, who was at Nashville, and thus cut the Union army in two. This would give him an opportunity to fight

the Fall of 1862 he was given command of the frontier, including the Kansas as well as Missouri troops. He was made a major-general of volunteers Nov. 29, 1862, and after distinguished services in different fields (especially in the campaign of General Sherman against General Joseph E. Johnston in the Summer and Autumn of 1864, which ended in the capture of Atlanta, and in the Battle of Franklin), he was breveted a major-general in the regular army. In July, 1867, he was appointed to the command of the first military district. In 1868 he was Secretary of War. The following year he was assigned to the command of the Department of the Missouri, and was made a full major-general. When General Hancock died he was assigned to the command of the Division of the Atlantic. Since the death of General Sheridan, he is the senior officer in the national service, ranking as General of the United States Army, and has his headquarters in Washington.

them separately, and to gain a victory over both. If he could only reach the road before troops could be sent to head him off; or while they were defiling along it; he would have his adversary at a terrible disadvantage, and attacking him in the flank, might strike a fatal blow, and therefore he gave orders that, as soon as the head of the army reached Spring Hill, it should begin an immediate attack—an order the execution of which was committed to General Cheatham, one of the bravest and most trusted leaders of the Southern army; and to the fact that this commander did not make the attack, and that the Federal Army was able to pass undisturbed, Hood ascribes the loss of his opportunity to win a great, and perhaps decisive, victory. In his volume entitled "ADVANCE AND RETREAT," which now lies before me, he gives a full history of the campaign, and dwells at great length on this failure, which seems to have been the sore point of his whole military career. He says that he led the army in person to within two miles of the Columbia turnpike, " where, sitting upon my horse, I had in sight the enemy's waggons and men passing at double-quick along the Franklin pike"; and said to Cheatham, "General, do you see the enemy there, marching rapidly to escape us?" and ordered him at once to push on and seize the road and hold it. What was his amazement and indignation, an hour later, when, as "twilight was upon them," Cheatham rode up, *not* having executed his command, and Hood "exclaimed with deep emotion," "General, why in the name of God have you not attacked the enemy, and taken possession of that pike?" to which Cheatham replied that "the line looked a little too long for him, and that Stewart should first form on his right." This was his unpardonable crime. The brave soldier had failed in the hour of need, and to his dying day he suffered from the imputation of culpable negligence!

THE OTHER SIDE OF THE STORY.

This is one side of the story, which is very good until you hear the other. But the friends of General Cheatham by no means admit its truth, but reply with much indignation that it was merely an attempt to throw on him the blame which should have been assumed by quite a different person; and they think it due to the good name of the brave old soldier, now that he is sleeping in his grave, that this unjust imputation should be removed. Major Vaulx writes to me from Nashville, as an eye-witness of that which he describes, that the responsibility for not attacking Spring Hill (if it *was* a fault, which he seems to doubt) should rest not on Cheatham, but on the Commander-in-Chief. He says:

"Cheatham's corps was in advance on the march. As it approached Spring Hill, he was ordered by Gen. Hood to form it in line of battle in front of the Federal army, which was already in position—an order which he promptly obeyed, forming it from left to right as each division came up: Bate on the left, Cleburne in the centre, and John C. Brown (who commanded Cheatham's old division) on the right. As Brown was the last to arrive, Cheatham pointed out his place to the right of Cleburne, and then gave him orders, as soon as his division was formed in two lines, to move his right brigade forward and attack the Federals, who were posted south and west of Spring Hill, with their line curved round on the east side of the town. Cheatham told Brown that he would order Cleburne to attack *on hearing his guns;* and that as soon as Cleburne became engaged, he would order Bate also to advance. With this Cheatham turned and rode back to give the order to Bate, expecting every moment to hear the signal from behind that the battle was begun, and kept asking impatiently, ' Why don't we hear Brown's guns?' The reason was soon explained.

"While Brown was forming his division, General Strahl, who commanded his right brigade, reported to him that he had discovered a line of Federal infantry on a wooded hill, in such a position that the moment he (Strahl) swung forward to the attack, he would be exposed to a fire both on the flank and in the rear. On hearing this, Brown went to Strahl, who pointed out to him the position of the Federal line, and seeing it, sent two staff officers to report the situation to Cheatham, who, not hearing the guns, had said to his staff, 'Let us go and see what is the matter!' On the way to Brown, he met the officer who was coming to report the situation on the right, and hearing it, said 'Go with me, and report to Gen. Hood just what you have said to me,' which being done, Gen. Hood replied to Cheatham, 'If that is the case, do not attack, but order your troops to hold the position they are in for the night.'" [This explanation will be clearly understood by reference to the map.]

Such, according to Major Vaulx, is the true explanation of the reason why General Cheatham did not attack Stanley at Spring Hill. It was from no lack of courage, but because of the darkness coming on, and the bold front of the enemy. Another account indicates that, with all the rage that Hood showed afterward at his lost opportunity, he had himself an access of irresolution. Gen. Bate reports that on that night he had occasion to go to the headquarters, which were about two miles back from the road, and there found Hood in consultation with General Forrest, at the conclusion of which he turned to Bate and said that no movement would be undertaken that night: for that Forrest had just reported to him that he could easily seize and hold the pike at a point above Spring Hill, which would prevent the passage of Schofield, so that in the morning "they would bag the whole Federal army"!

While thus vindicating the good name of his old friend, the Major takes occasion to stamp out another cruel story which has been permitted to float about in different quarters. As if the imputation of unmilitary conduct in disobedience of orders, were not enough, the charge is made still more odious by the explanation given of this culpable neglect, viz: that General Cheatham was grossly intoxicated! This I myself have heard stated, not as a mere rumor, an idle report, but as something which

MARCH TO SPRING HILL.

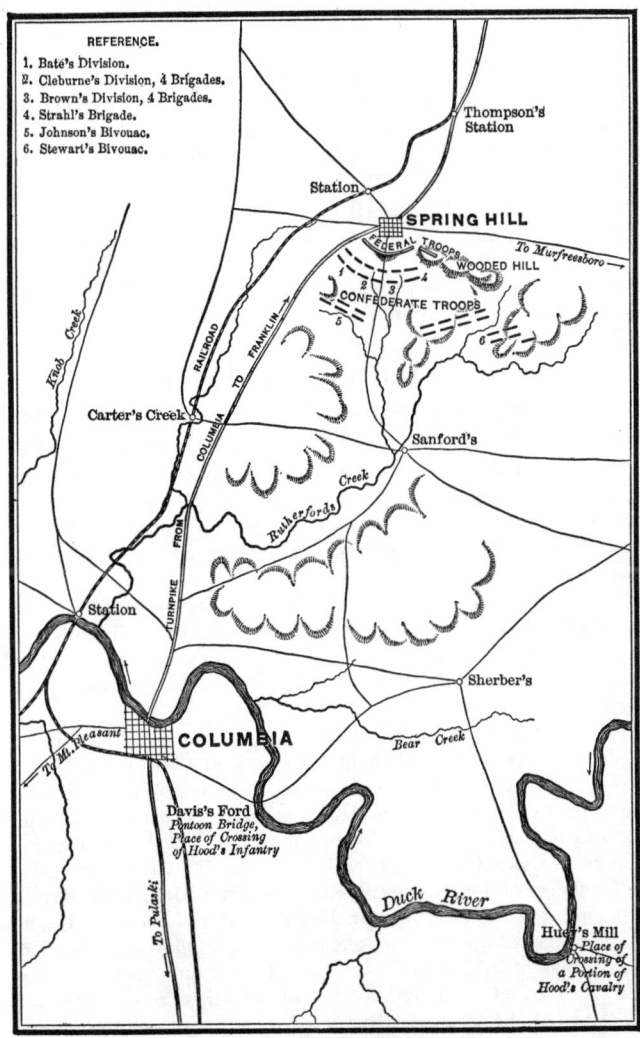

FROM COLUMBIA TO SPRING HILL.

"everybody knew" in the army. To this Major Vaulx gives a peremptory denial. He says:

"I was with Gen. Cheatham when he was giving his orders to Gen. Brown. The charge that he was intoxicated is false. I never saw him more self-possessed than on that afternoon. He gave his orders in a very plain and explicit manner. His words expressed just what he wanted, and in such a manner that no doubtful construction could be given them."

To the same effect, ex-Governor Porter of Tennessee writes:

"I was with Cheatham during the entire day from Columbia to Spring Hill, and he was not only *not* intoxicated, but I am positive that he did not taste nor see a drop of liquor of any kind."

The injustice of a Commander-in-Chief throwing upon a subordinate a responsibility which he should take upon himself, is answered by the Major with this telling remark:

"*General Hood was himself on the field*, but a few hundred yards from Cheatham's line, and if he felt that his orders were not being obeyed, he could have ridden to the front *in five minutes*, and in person ordered the charge which he blames Cheatham for not making."

[The whole subject is very fully treated in a paper read before the Southern Historical Society at Louisville by Major D. W. Saunders, who served upon the staffs of Generals Pegram and Walthall. Its vindication of Gen. Cheatham is complete.]

Major Vaulx adds these further particulars:

"Gen. Edward R. Johnson's Division was detached from Stephen D. Lee's Corps, then at Columbia, and arrived in front of Spring Hill after dark. Gen. Johnson was ordered by Hood to report to Cheatham, and Hood ordered Cheatham to have Johnson placed in position to command the turnpike road running from Columbia to Spring Hill. Gen. Cheatham sent his Staff Officer, Major Joseph Bostick, to order Gen. Johnson to take such a position (Johnson had gone into bivouac). Upon getting this order, Johnson vehemently objected to undertaking this movement in the dark; said he could not do it, as he had no idea of the country, or the position of the other troops; that he had reached the ground after dark, and knew nothing about directions; and if he went to moving about in the dark, he would be liable to run into some of our own troops, and they would fire into each other. Major Bostick suggested that he could show Gen. Johnson where the turnpike was, and point out where our lines were posted; but Johnson said he could not, and was not willing to undertake such a movement in the dark, ignorant as he was of the country and all surroundings. It was then suggested by Major Bostick that he had no decision in the matter, but that Gen. Johnson might give orders to his command to prepare to move, and then go himself to Gen. Cheatham, and lay the case before him, which he did, and impressed it upon Gen. Cheatham that he could not undertake the move intelligently or safely."

But the next morning, when Hood found that the great opportunity had been lost, he was unwilling to bear the reproach of its being due to any want of energy on his own part. Major Vaulx told me of a conversation which he had with General Brown as they were riding side by side, in which the latter said :

"General Hood is mad about the enemy getting away last night, and he is going to charge the blame of it on somebody. He is as wrathy as a rattlesnake this morning, striking at everything. As he passed along to the front a while ago, he rode up to me and said: 'Gen. Brown, in the movement to-day I wish you to bear in mind this military principle: That when a pursuing army comes up with a retreating enemy, he must be immediately attacked. If you have a brigade in front as advance guard, order its commander to attack the enemy as soon as he comes up with him; if you have a regiment in advance, and it comes up with the enemy, give the colonel orders to attack him; if there is but a company in advance, and it overtakes the entire Yankee army, order the captain to attack it forthwith; and if anything blocks the road in front of you to-day, don't stop a minute, but turn out into the fields or woods, and move on to the front'."

Aside from this Confederate testimony, it argues a certain simplicity in the commander of an army to assume that, while he is wide awake and urging on his soldiers, the opposing commander is not equally vigilant and equally determined. The whole argument of Hood seems to imply that the Union commander was quite unprepared, whereas General Schofield had had his eyes open all the time to the possibility of such a flank movement, and as soon as the cavalry reported that the enemy were crossing the river, he at once despatched General Stanley with a division comprising three brigades and all the reserve artillery of the Fourth Corps to Spring Hill, with orders to throw up intrenchments and hold the position.

As these bickerings between Gen. Hood and his corps and division commanders contributed so much to defeat the Confederate army, they suggest by contrast the opposite state of things in the Federal camp, where General Schofield was supported by Generals Stanley and Cox, on whom he relied with the absolute confidence that one brave man gives to another. The situation was critical. The Union army was threatened on two sides: by the flanking movement directed towards Spring Hill, and at the same time by the persistent attempt to force a passage of the river at Columbia, where the attack was kept up without intermission. Had Schofield withdrawn his whole force, the Confederates would have immediately crossed with all their heavy artillery, which could have been transported rapidly over the hard, macadamized turnpike. Against both these movements, aimed at points ten miles apart, he had to be equally prepared. As has been well said, "He must hold back his enemy at Columbia with one hand, and fend off the blow at Spring Hill with the other." So while Stanley marched with all speed to Spring Hill, Cox was ordered to hold on to the last moment at Columbia, to prevent the enemy crossing the river. It was to the admirable manner in which *both* these orders were carried out, that was due the success of this and the following day.

CALCULATING THE CHANCES.

To return to General Schofield: having anticipated the flank movement of the enemy, he calculated the chances. This he did, reasoning from his personal knowledge of the General pitted against him. He and Hood had been classmates at West Point, and he knew that, while a braver man never lived, his mind was not exact. At West Point he had no standing in mathematics; he did not calculate distances nor impediments; and *he had no idea of the value of time.* This he proved to-day: for while he and Stanley were aiming for the same point, and he had the start, Stanley got there before him. True, the latter had the advantage of a smooth, hard turnpike, while the former had to move by a country road, in which his artillery and baggage waggons would sink deep at every step. I say *would*, for in fact the baggage trains had been left behind at the river, and the artillery also, except a few light guns. Thus the army was stripped for a forced march. Can any one doubt that, if Stonewall Jackson had been in command, even though his men might have been barefoot, ragged, and sore, he would have carried them, dead or alive, to the point where the fate of the contest was to be decided? But Hood, as he tells the story himself, did not come in sight of the turnpike till three o'clock, when he was still two miles away, and then only to see "the enemy's waggons and men" streaming along the road of which he had been so eager to get possession! General J. D. Cox in his History * states that the division of Stanley

---

* This little volume, one of a series published by the Scribners, entitled "CAMPAIGNS OF THE CIVIL WAR," is the clearest account I have found anywhere of the battle of Franklin, and of the campaign of which it was a part. General Cox is one of the men who rank high both in military and in civil life. Since the war he has been Governor of Ohio and a Member of the Cabinet. His book is written not at all in the style of a partisan, but in

reached Spring Hill *at noon*, just in time to prevent its being seized by a party of cavalry. Thus he was fully three hours in advance of Hood. Those three hours saved the Union army. In that time the division had thrown up earthworks around the little town, and was preparing for an attack. If Hood was two miles away at three o'clock, soldiers can make the calculation how long it would take to move a large body of troops over that distance, and get it into line of battle. Still it is true that the head of the army approached the turnpike before sunset, within gunshot of the Federal troops, and opened fire, which was so vigorously returned that they found, to their surprise, that they were in the presence of an enemy that was well prepared for their reception.

The truth is that, although Hood tried afterwards to belittle the force in possession of Spring Hill, in order to throw the blame of his failure upon Cheatham, that vital point was held too firmly to be shaken. Stanley was a dangerous man to attack at any time, especially at the head of five thousand of those Western troops that had fought so splendidly in the Atlanta campaign. To add to his strength, all the reserve artillery of the Fourth Corps had been sent forward in advance, which enabled him to put thirty pieces in position: so that when Cleburne, the most dashing division commander in the Southern army, who led the advance, moving forward in obedience to Hood's orders, began the attack, he was received with such a tremendous shock that, brave as he was, he drew off and sent back for reinforcements; but before they could come up and be put in line of battle, night fell and pre-

the spirit of fairness and candor. As he took part in all the movements preceding the battle, and was in command on the line that bore the brunt of the battle, there can be no questioning facts that passed under his personal observation.

IN SIGHT OF THE CAMP-FIRES.

vented further operations. Thus it was that a large part of the Confederate army was camped within sight of the road along which the Union army was moving. Schofield found them there when he came up, and just after dark he walked to a slight ridge in front of his lines, and looked straight into their camp-fires. They could have thrown themselves upon his line of march, but it would have been a fight in the dark, with a result by no means so certain as they seemed to suppose.*

As night came on, the troops under Cox were ordered to withdraw from before Columbia in detachments, leaving

---

*If further light be needed on the disputed questions in regard to the incidents of the day before the battle of Franklin, it may be found in a very full and detailed narrative by Thomas Speed, Esq., of Louisville, Kentucky, who, as Adjutant of a Kentucky regiment in the Twenty-third Corps, took part in the battle, and who gives us, not only his personal observations, but the result of a careful study of the Confederate reports, all of which lead him to the conclusion that Hood found that to make that night attack, of which he afterwards talked as so easy to be made, would have been a pretty serious business. The paper was prepared to be read before the Ohio Commandery of the Loyal Legion, and is published in their Historical Transactions.

In a private letter Mr. Speed gives the testimony of an officer who was at Spring Hill, as to the preparations that had been made for an attack. He says: "A few years since General Cheatham came to Louisville to address his old companions-in-arms on this very campaign (an address that was listened to with equal interest by those who fought on both sides), in which he explained *why* he could not reach the turnpike that memorable night. On the platform sat General Walter Whittaker, a gallant Kentuckian, who commanded a brigade under General Stanley. As we left the hall, he came up to me and said in his characteristic way: 'Yes, the reason he didn't get *thar* was because he couldn't. I was *thar* myself—I was thar *with seven regiments*!'" The explanation appears to be quite sufficient.

till the very last a force sufficient to prevent the enemy crossing. The rear-guard did not leave till after midnight. There was no moon, but the stars were shining brightly; and the old soldiers, elated to be once more in motion, swung along the road rapidly. Three hours of this steady march brought them near Spring Hill, and as they caught sight of camp-fires in the distance, they began to cheer at the prospect of hot coffee and a night's rest. But the cheer had hardly been heard before it was silenced: as an officer at the head of the column put his finger to his lips, and whispered "Hist!"—a warning that passed quickly along the line, and hushed every voice: for those camp-fires were not surrounded by the boys in blue, but by those who, at the least alarm, would have seized the guns that were stacked at the edge of the woods, and fired into the crowded column that was moving along the highway: though, if the attack had been made, it would not have found the column unprepared: for even while on the march, it was kept ready for battle. "The divisions were all moving by the left flank, so that when they should halt and face, they would be in line of battle, and could use the road fences for barricades, if attacked. By this arrangement there was the least risk of confusion, and the greatest readiness for any contingency which might arise." But while the position had these advantages, the General could but feel that it was one of great exposure and of great danger. He never passed a night of greater anxiety. When it was all over, he telegraphed to Thomas: "I don't want to get into so tight a place again."

But just now he was *in* "the tight place," and it required the utmost promptness and skill to get out of it. The decision with which he acted showed that he had the resources of a soldier fitted for high command. He seemed to be present at every exposed point. Cox says,

"On hearing from Stanley that he was attacked by infantry, Schofield hastened to Ruger's division, which was nearest to Spring Hill, and led its two brigades in person by a rapid march to Stanley's support." Again, "Learning that some force of the enemy was at Thompson's Station [three miles beyond], he immediately marched with a division to that point, to open the way to Franklin." He returned to Spring Hill at midnight.

To add to his perplexities, he was without orders, and wholly ignorant of what the rest of the Federal army might be doing. It had been understood that as soon as General A. J. Smith, with his corps from Missouri, arrived in Nashville, he should push southward to Schofield's support. But whether this movement had been executed, the latter did not know, for he had received no recent communication from Gen. Thomas. Surrounded as they were by enemies, of course they could not telegraph to each other except by cipher—a cipher which they themselves did not understand: for Mr. Stanton (knowing how often important secrets leak out through the treachery of some one who may be a trusted agent, and in the very tent of a commanding officer) had, with an excess of caution, issued an order that the cipher should be known only to certain telegraph operators sent from the War Office in Washington; so that in one case Schofield received a message which no one in camp could interpret, and remained ignorant of its contents for forty-eight hours! So he heard nothing from Thomas, and knew nothing of the movements of Smith. But in the evening a train had come in, the conductor of which said that as he passed Franklin, he *thought* he saw troops there; but as it was after dark when he came through, he could not be positive. At once an officer was despatched with all speed to Franklin, to bring positive information; and if he found

General Smith, to order him (for he would have been under Schofield's command) to push on instantly to join him for the battle that must be fought at daybreak. But ruturning to the conductor, and questioning him more closely, the General felt that his information was too uncertain for him to rely upon, and at midnight he gave orders for the whole army to push on to Franklin.

In this forward movement the troops which had just come from Columbia led the way, the two wings of the army reversing their positions: Stanley, who had marched to Spring Hill in the morning, remaining where he stood; while the Twenty-third Corps, that had been keeping back the enemy at the river, as it now came up the road, filed behind the Fourth Corps, and passed to the front. Gen. Stanley, who had had the honor of leading the advance, now had the honor of guarding the rear—a position which might bring upon him the whole of Hood's army, but which he held till all of the Twenty-third Corps had passed, when silently regiment after regiment formed in column, and followed.

That night march will never be forgotten by those who were in it, or those who saw it; for it was in full view of the camp-fires of the enemy. If the army had marched in single column, with its baggage trains, it would have extended fourteen miles! This was shortened one-half by *doubling up,* for which there was room on the turnpike, so that the baggage train was kept in motion, with a column of troops marching at its side, ready for attack. The cavalry under Forrest were hovering along the line, trying to strike a blow. Cox says, "Forrest's troopers made an occasional dash at the long waggon train, but only in one or two instances did they succeed in reaching it"; and yet Hood says (as if he wished to emphasize the difference between this dashing cavalry officer and Cheatham),

ARRIVAL IN FRANKLIN.

"Forrest gallantly opposed the enemy to the full extent of his power." If so, it is a wonder that he did not accomplish more. Perhaps the explanation is that, as an old officer once told me, "cavalry do not like to attack infantry *in the dark*. The long roll of musketry empties the saddles and the horses rush about in confusion." And so it is not surprising that, in spite of such "dashes" here and there, the column continued its march. The night seemed very long, but the tramp never ceased till the troops halted in the outskirts of Franklin. The advance arrived before daybreak, and the officers who led the way rode up to the Carter House (the first that they came to), and woke up the old man, the father of the Colonel, who showed us over the battlefield (who had been in the Confederate army, and was then at home on parole), and politely informed him that they would take possession of his house as their headquarters, to which, knowing the usages of war, he did not object. One who was in that group says: "While sitting out in front of the house, waiting for the head of the column to arrive, everything was as still as the grave, and there was time to ponder on what the day would bring forth. Few anticipated the dreadful and bloody outcome, but rather looked for another flank movement, as at Columbia. Presently the tramp of horses in the distance, and the rattle of tin cups against bayonets, told us that the troops were coming." * As they came up,

---

*For this and many touches which give vividness to the picture, I am indebted to a most spirited account of the battle, and of the campaign of which it was a part, entitled "The Retreat from Pulaski to Nashville," a paper read before the Ohio Commandery of the Military Order of the Loyal Legion of the United States, December 1st, 1886, by Companion Levi T. Scofield, late Captain U. S. Volunteers. (Published by H. C. Sherick & Co., Cincinnati.) It is written in the style of a soldier, with all the fire of one who describes scenes in

they were turned to the right and left of the road, that the trains might pass through into the town. General Schofield at once pressed on to the river, where he had hoped to find the bridges standing, and pontoons, for which he had sent urgent messages to Thomas, ready to lay others, to pass over the artillery and baggage waggons. Instead of this, he found that the bridge connecting with the turnpike had been swept away, and that there was not a single pontoon with which to construct another. All that remained was the railroad bridge, which had to be planked to make it passable for waggons, and even then furnished but a slender resource for the passage of an army. Finding this condition, he returned to the front in a state of great anxiety. Thorough soldier as he was, he took the chances of war as they came, but for once he was taken aback at the unexpected position in which he was placed. "I never saw him," said General Cox, "so disturbed," as he now contemplated the probability, which a soldier dreads, of having to fight a battle with his back to a river, when a disaster is likely to prove fatal. [The orders of Hood were to "drive them into the river"!] But it was no time for idle regrets. Gen. Cox was placed in command of the two divisions of the Twenty-third Corps, his own and Gen. Ruger's, and ordered to entrench strongly on a line running to the right and left of the turnpike. This was a new task for the soldiers, weary as they were with their all night's march, covering a distance of twenty-three miles. They were almost dead with fatigue, but not a moment was to be lost. As soon as they had snatched a hasty breakfast, they were set to work with spades and shovels,

which he was an actor; and yet, we are informed on the best authority, that it is as accurate in its details as it is picturesque. It is these old soldiers who tell what they have seen, who furnish the most authentic materials of history.

and in two or three hours had dug a ditch a mile and a half in length, throwing up the earth on the inside to make a breastwork (to which some added a log on the crest, raised three inches to leave space for their rifles), along which at intervals there were openings for the batteries ; all which being done, they threw themselves upon the ground for a sleep which to many of them was to be their last.

General Schofield too was glad of a short interval of rest. For several days and nights he had had little sleep, except such as he got in the saddle. On the march he could clasp his hands round the pommel, and for a few minutes relapse into a state of forgetfulness, which, if not so refreshing as rest in a quiet bed or by the camp-fire, at least kept him from the point of utter exhaustion. So when the position had been made secure, he went to the house of a good Union woman (it was pointed out to us as we rode through the street), and threw himself on a bed and fell asleep, and rested for an hour and a half, till he was awakened for orders.

All the forenoon the troops came pouring in, the last to arrive being those that had remained at Spring Hill. The Confederate army was but a few miles behind, sometimes approaching nearer, when the Federal rear-guard turned at bay, and showed such a grim front, with its batteries ranged so as to sweep the road, that its pursuers kept at a respectful distance. It was not till a few hours later that they were to come to close quarters. As the different divisions reached Franklin, there was another reversal of positions ; for as those that arrived in the morning were now entrenched, they remained in their works; while the Fourth Corps under Gen. Stanley, which consisted of three divisions, was thus distributed : that of Kimball was placed at the extreme right of the line ; that of Wagner was cut in two (two brigades being stationed outside of the works where they met a hard fate ; while a third brigade, under Colonel Opdycke, was brought within the lines, and placed in the rear as a reserve ; and, as we shall see, made one of the most brilliant charges of the day); while Wood's division marched through the town, and took its place on the other side of the river, where Stanley joined Schofield, and remained with him till the afternoon, as both fully expected that the attack of Hood's army would be aimed in that quarter rather than in front. The disposition of the troops is indicated on the map of Franklin, that I have copied from General Cox's History. From this it will be seen that the position of the town is well fitted for defence, as it is surrounded on three sides by a river, and is open only on one. Across this open front, swelling out into a projecting curve, was drawn the line of entrenchments, to one end of which, near the railway, we had first driven to get a general view of the field.

From that point we had pushed on two and a half miles out of town over the Columbia turnpike, till we came to where the road passes over high ground between two hills. Here, leaving our horses in charge of our black rider, we ascended a hill on which were a few scattered trees, on the brow of which stood an old linden, tall and gaunt, with its naked arms lifted against the sky. "Here," said Mr. Cunningham, " on the day of the battle, I saw General Hood ride forward alone on his horse, and halting near this tree, take out his field-glass, and gaze long and earnestly across the plain at the position of the enemy. All who were in sight of him watched him with eager eyes, for on the decision of that moment depended the fate of thousands. Presently he turned back to General Stewart, to whom I heard him say, 'We will make the fight!' and who received his extended hand with a sadness, which seemed to say, 'We may not meet again!' The die was cast. The order was instantly given to the troops, who, as they came over the hill, deployed, stretching out to the right and left, and forming in line of battle. On the opposite hill a military band had taken its position, and played some stirring Southern airs as the brave men marched down into the valley, which was to be to thousands of them the valley of death. The whole scene was the most thrilling that I ever saw in war."

It was now the middle of the afternoon, and it took an hour for the army to defile into position. This hour, as may be supposed, was one of intense, though suppressed, excitement. We hear much of the noise of battle, but the stillness which precedes it is not less awful, as column after column, with measured step, takes its place in the ranks of death. It is the stillness which precedes the tempest, as thunder clouds gather darkly but silently. It is not till they touch each other that the storm bursts.

As the Confederate lines thus formed in front, General Hood rode forward to a hill, from which he could have a nearer view, so as to watch every movement, and be in position at once to receive reports and to give orders; while across the plain, on another hill overlooking the same scene, stood General Schofield, giving quick glances along his own lines, and away to the dark masses of men that were forming in mighty battalions for the death struggle.

It was now four o'clock, and as it was the last day of autumn, and therefore one of the shortest days of the year, the sun was sinking in the west; but as the light struck across the plain, it shone on one of the most dazzling sights in the world—a great army drawn up in

"Battle's magnificently stern array."

These preparations were not unobserved. As it was an open plain between the two armies, every movement of the enemy was distinctly seen. Going to a projecting angle of the works, General Cox mounted the parapet, and with his field-glass took a long look at the large bodies of troops that were being massed at the foot of the hills; then mounting his horse, he rode to every point of the line, to see that all was ready for the attack. He had not long to wait, for already the troops were in motion. The day was nearly done, but enough remained to gain an immortal victory, and at that moment the dropping of a flag by General Cheatham gave the signal for the whole line to advance.

The battle began on the extreme left with a premature attack, which failed from its very precipitation. Gen. Bate (afterwards Governor of Tennessee, and now Senator) was a dashing soldier, and, being eager for the combat, pushed forward his division only to discover, as it came within range of the enemy, that it was in advance of connecting lines. As his men looked to the right for a support, they saw that the other divisions were far behind; and as they had to take the whole fire, they retreated. Major Vaulx was an eye-witness of the attack and the repulse, and could not but regret, while he admired, the too impetuous valor of his brothers-in-arms.

But the fortune of war changed as the Confederates advanced in tremendous force, and it was now the turn of the Federals to experience a great disaster. In arranging the defences, two brigades had been placed outside of the town, across the turnpike, not as a position to be held, but simply to check and delay the attack. They were to fire a few rounds of artillery, and then to withdraw within the works and take their place in the line of defence, or to be held as a reserve. But as the approaching columns drew nearer, the officer in command, more brave than wise, (who seems to have thought it the proper thing for a soldier to fight the enemy anywhere, and with any odds,

WHO WAS IT THAT BLUNDERED? 233

even unsupported and alone,) ordered his infantry to open fire, as if the battle were to be fought on that ground.*

*That it was the commander of the division who blundered at this awful moment, is but too evident. The author of "The Retreat from Pulaski to Nashville," thus reports what he himself saw and heard: "The writer was standing on the parapet of the 100th Ohio Regiment, urging the men to strengthen their works, and talking with General Wagner. The General was reclining on his elbow, with a staff or crutch in his hand: he had fallen with his horse and was lame. We remarked that the musketry firing was becoming more rapid, also from the two guns in front. By-and-by a staff officer rode fast from one of the brigades, and reported excitedly, 'The enemy are forming in heavy columns. We can see them distinctly in the open timber and all along our front.' Wagner said firmly 'Stand there and fight them,' and then turning to me, said, 'And that stubbed, curly-headed Dutchman,' meaning one of his brigade commanders [General Conrad], 'will fight them too.' 'But, General,' the officer said, ' the orders are not to stand, except against cavalry and skirmishers; but to fall back behind the main line if a general engagement is threatened.' In a short time another officer rode in from the right in great haste, and told him the Rebels were advancing in heavy force. He received the same order. The officer added, 'But Hood's entire army is coming.' Then Wagner struck the ground with his stick, and said 'Never mind: fight them!' Soon we heard the Rebel yell and heavy firing."

It was a dreadful mistake, for which he had to suffer in the way that a soldier feels most: for in less than a week, General Thomas, after careful investigation, relieved him of his command, and that was the end of his military career. But soldiers are generous in their judgments, and quick to forgive the mistakes of one who has been brave, and so the writer of the above adds: "Wagner was a great fighter. It is said that bullets rattled out of his clothes for a month after the battle of Stone River. . . . . He is now dead; his soul is in heaven with the heroes; and let us draw over this one error the mantle of charity, and cherish the memory of his personal valor and dauntless courage on the hard-fought battlefields of the West."

The only explanation of his thus acting, not only without orders, but against orders, is that he "lost his head"— a very bad thing to lose in a battle.* It were better that

* This terrible disaster at the opening of the battle has often led to the inquiry, why these brigades were placed in such an exposed position ? And gentle home critics think that they detect here a fault of strategy. A word of explanation, with the help of the map, may relieve their minds, and show them that there was no mistake at all in the disposition of the Union army.

The reader must bear in mind the position of Gen. Schofield on that morning. He had not planned for a battle at Franklin, but had intended, in accordance with the orders of Thomas, to continue his march to Nashville, as he would have done if he had found bridges or pontoons to cross the Harpeth river. Disappointed in this, he had to change his plan, and prepare for the contingency of battle where he was. As yet he was wholly in the dark as to the intentions of the enemy. Judging from the movement of Hood at Columbia, in crossing the river and endeavoring to get in his rear, it seemed probable that he would repeat the same movement at Franklin; and instead of attacking in front, where the Twenty-third corps held a strong line of defence, would cross the river, and making a circuit, move round the town, so as to take the Federal army in the rear, and cut off its retreat to Nashville. In anticipation of such a movement, one division of the Fourth corps, to be followed by others, if necessary, had been got across the river to the bluff on the other side, where General Schofield, from the earthworks (designated on the map as Fort Granger, the only point of sufficient elevation to command a view of the whole field), was able to watch the advance of the enemy, and change his own movements to meet the attack from whichever quarter it might come.

It was with an eye in both directions, that the two brigades had been placed in front, to observe the movements of the enemy; and if he should turn towards the river, to swing round with him, keeping in his front, and fending off the attack till the interior lines could be reformed to meet the tremendous shock that must follow. The plan was perfect in every detail. As Gen. Cox, repelling the criticisms which had been made on his com-

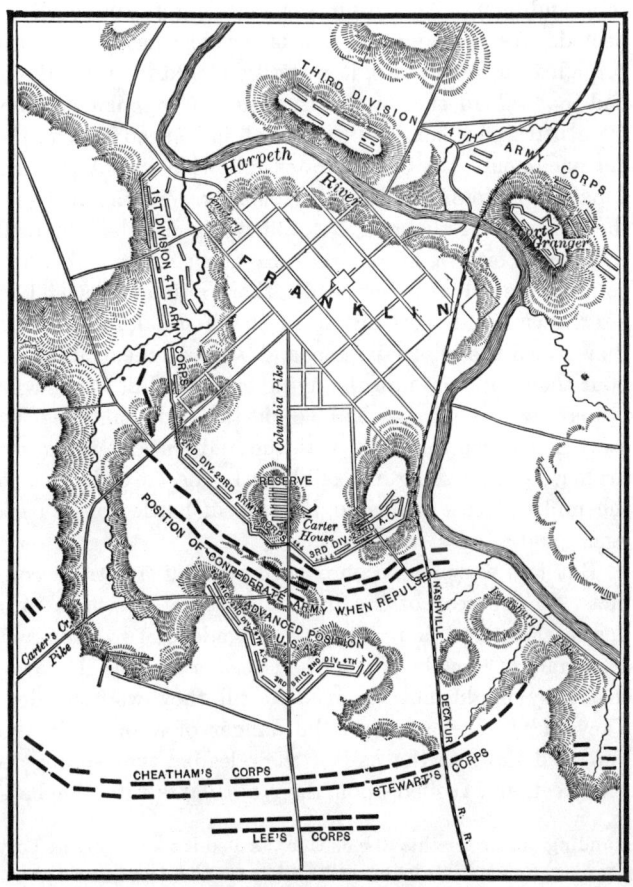

BATTLE-FIELD OF FRANKLIN.

he had lost his life, for by this act of madness he lost a thousand men! The result was what might have been expected. As the enemy's line of battle overlapped these brigades on both sides, it instantly closed in upon them, and poured in such a fire that in a few moments they were utterly broken, and rushed at full speed back to the entrenchments, the Confederates following in hot pursuit. This was a double disaster. Not only were the brigades themselves overwhelmed, but the whole line had to hold its fire for fear of killing its own men; and so when the column rushed into the works, their pursuers rushed in after them, and were inside of the Federal lines, where they seized the shotted guns, and whirled them about to pour their contents into the flying crowd. But in the wild uproar, even the horses had caught the panic, and tearing away fled down the road, with the limbers containing the primers, so that the guns could not be discharged; and in the midst of this confusion, the tide of battle rolled back again, and all was recovered.

But this was not accomplished without a terrific conflict. In the rear of the line the ground descends in a gentle slope, and here a reserve brigade of two thousand men, under Colonel Opdycke, had been ordered to lie down, that they might not be exposed till they were needed. They had been warned of the danger of a break in the line, and now, at the call of their leader, they sprang to their feet, and rushed upon their assailants with the bay-

manding officer for this disposition, as also for his being at Fort Granger instead of being with him at the front, said with emphasis, "General Schofield was exactly where he ought to have been, and the orders issued were exactly what they ought to have been." He might have added, that if those orders had been strictly obeyed, the result would have been not only the defeat but the entire destruction of Hood's army.

onet. So sudden was this apparition of armed men, starting up as if they had literally come out of the ground, and so tremendous their onset, that some accounts make their commander the hero of the battle. It would be more correct to say one of the heroes: for there is no need to exalt him at the expense of others, who shared in the same achievement. This brave officer now sleeps in a soldier's grave, and no praise can be too great for his courage at that decisive moment. But with his brigade were the portions of the two divisions under Reilly and Strickland that had been pushed back by the rush of Wagner's men, with the avalanche of Confederates behind; but who, as soon as the mingled mass swept by, so that they could distinguish friend from foe, reformed under those gallant soldiers. All those in high command did their duty on this great day. General Stanley had been so sure that the attack of the enemy, when it came, would be on the other side of the river, where he was, that he had remained there with General Schofield till the firing began. Then he mounted his horse, and spurred to the front just in time to meet Wagner's brigades (that belonged to his own Fourth Corps) in full retreat; and exerted himself with the utmost energy to rally them, when his horse was shot under him, and he was wounded, and compelled, very much against his will, to return to his quarters for surgical skill. This threw the whole burden of command upon General Cox at a moment when the fate of the army was at stake. The imminent peril inspired him to increased activity, so that he seemed to fly from point to point. The voice of command could not be heard in the uproar of battle; but soldiers along the line could see that figure waving his sword in air, and dashing wherever the combat was the deepest and the danger the greatest; and catching the inspiration, they reformed their broken ranks, and rushed upon the foe with a fury that was irresistible. The issue is briefly told : "There was a few minutes' fierce melée, but the guns were retaken, and all the men in gray inside the parapet were dead or prisoners."

General Schofield, who was watching the battle from the Fort, had felt his heart sink as he heard the yells with which the Confederates rushed over the works, and saw his own men swept away by the torrent. For the moment his heart stood still, for it seemed as if the battle was lost. But he soon breathed again, for though, at the distance he was, he could not see the forces engaged, since the roll of musketry was so incessant that friend and foe were wrapped in a dense cloud of smoke ; yet, as the space behind was clear, and he could see that *there were no more men running to the rear,* he knew that his troops had regained their position.

This tremendous attack, which had threatened to destroy the Federal army, had been made in the centre by General Cheatham. Those who saw it coming say that never was there seen in war a grander sight than that of this whole Corps, massed in one mighty avalanche, sweeping down with a force that, it seemed, must be irresistible. One who looked at it with a soldier's eye, in which admiration mingled with dread, draws this picture : "The day had been bright and warm ; the afternoon sun was setting on the distant hills ; and in the hazy, yellow light, and with their yellowish-brown uniforms, those in the front ranks seemed to be magnified in size : one could almost imagine them to be phantoms sweeping along in the air. On they came, and in the centre their lines seemed to be many deep and unbroken, their red, tattered flags, as numerous as though every company bore them, flaring in the sun's rays, with conspicuous groups of general and staff officers in their midst, and a battery or two in splendid line charg-

GREAT LOSS OF OFFICERS. 239

ing along between the divisions." This magnificence was terribly marred when the broken Federal line was restored, and the troops poured in their deadly fire. But still the charge was renewed with incredible fury. Again and again the Confederates rushed to the assault, even when it seemed hopeless, for the fire never slackened an instant. Instead of coming in fitful volleys, it was one continuous roar, sweeping away whole ranks of men; so that the survivors, as they staggered on, had to pass over the dying and the dead. Major Vaulx told us of the terrible slaughter in what passed under his own observation. He said: "Cheatham's old division (which still retained his name after he had been promoted to the command of a corps), was commanded by General John C. Brown. I was riding at his side when a ball struck him, and he fell forward on his horse's neck. I at once dismounted, and with others lifted him off and placed him in an ambulance, to be carried from the field, when I mounted and rode on, till of five general officers attached to our division, besides the commander, who had just been wounded, *three were killed,* and the fifth captured inside the Federal works; while of the staff officers attached to the division and to the four brigades, out of twelve, *all but one* were either killed or wounded! Such a loss of general and staff officers, I never saw before in any battle that I was in, and indeed do not think I ever read of in war."

While this murderous conflict was going on in the centre, another great Corps (that of Stewart), on the right of Cheatham, was converging towards the Federal lines. It came on with unbroken ranks till it got within range of the guns from the other side of the river, which swept that part of the field, and the heavy shot plunging into the solid columns, cut long lanes of death. But "officers on horseback and afoot were at every gap, trying to close them up," and the unfallen brave kept on till, as they came nearer and nearer the works, their numbers grew fewer. Never did men fight more desperately, and yet more hopelessly, as even Major Vaulx had to admit. To one who has shared in the fierce conflict of battle, it always seems as if there might have been done something more ; and in the morning, as we were overlooking the field, and he recalled every feature of the great struggle, he had felt again all the excitement of the hour. Standing up in the carriage, and looking intently at the ground in front, along which Stewart's men had swept up to the Federal lines, he took in the whole scene, and it seemed as if a little more *elan*, or a thousand or two more men, might have carried the day, and he exclaimed, "By the Eternal! Stewart ought to have broken through!" It was the natural feeling of a soldier, and yet in it he forgot that the Confederates, fearless as they were, were met with a courage equal to their own ; and later in the day, when we came to ride over the ground by which Stewart's Corps advanced, he saw at once the concentrated fire which it had to encounter, and was able to do more full justice to his brave companions-in-arms in recognizing that they had done all that human valor could do.

A gentleman recently living in New York, who was in command of a battery of steel guns, told me that as he moved forward, he passed over the hill on which General Hood had taken his position, in whose presence he suddenly found himself, and could not resist the impulse to pause a moment to see how a Commander looked in the midst of a battle. As he described the scene, "General Hood was sitting on a flat rock at the foot of a tree, his legs (one of which was of wood, to replace the original that had been lost in battle) extended in front, between which a fire had been lighted, and was still smouldering.

At the instant one of General Cheatham's staff rode up in great excitement to report that he had carried a part of the Federal line, but could not hold it unless immediately reinforced. 'How does Gen. Cheatham estimate his loss? asked Gen. Hood. 'At one-half of his whole command in killed and wounded,' was the reply. At this he raised his hands, clasping them together, and exclaimed ' O my God! this awful, awful day!' Then recovering himself, he turned to one of his staff and said 'Go to Gen. Stephen D. Lee, and tell him to move up to the support of Gen. Cheatham, putting in Johnson's division first, and Clayton's next.' As my battery was between the two, I knew that my time had come, and moved on with the rest."

And now the battle raged all along the lines. The first success of the Confederates proved their ruin, as it had been so easily gained that it led them to repeat the attack, pouring division after division upon the works, only to see them melt away under that terrible fire. After these terrific charges, came what was not less impressive — the lulls of the battle. First, there was a sound in the distance, as of a great multitude in motion, coupled with a fearful yell, which culminated in a rush and roar, as the living human wave struck upon the beach, and broke and rolled back again. Then for a few minutes there was a lull, as the enemy were gathering their forces to renew the onset—a comparative silence, broken only by the groans of the wounded and the dying. One who was in the battle writes me that the charge itself was not so dreadful as these moments of expectation. Then rose the same terrific yell, and on they came again with the same desperate courage, but not with the same confidence : for they came, not with erect, martial air, but with heads bent low, as when facing a tempest, and caps drawn over their eyes, as if to shut from their sight the fate that awaited them.

At some points of the line the fire was such as no troops could stand long. Mr. Fullton, of the Maxwell House in Nashville, told me that he belonged to a troop of cavalry, which, when earthworks were to be attacked, were dismounted, every fourth man being detailed to hold the horses, while the rest served as infantry. As they advanced to the attack, they had hardly come within range before twelve of his company fell, and it seemed as if the whole would be swept away if they had not been ordered to throw themselves on the ground ; and there, he said, "*we lay the greater part of the night*, not daring to raise our heads, nor to crawl forward even a few rods to give succor to the wounded and dying, whose groans we could hear distinctly right in front of us."

Driven back at one point, the charge was renewed at another with the same desperate courage, but always with the same result, until it was evident that further efforts were only a useless sacrifice of human life ; and still the rage of battle was such that the attacks were repeated at intervals far into the night.

All these incidents of the day were detailed to me with great minuteness, as we rode over that battle plain, by those who had been actors in the scenes they described.

As we came back along the Columbia turnpike to the edge of the town, Mr. Carter met us and conducted us to the old Gin-House, which figures in all the accounts of the battle ; and along the line of the entrenchments, pointing out where this or that Confederate division charged, and where the leaders fell. He had a theory of his own, according to which, if *his* plan had been followed, the result would have been otherwise. He was quite sure that if Gen. Bate, instead of rushing headlong into the fight, and getting severely crippled before the battle had really begun, had been a little less impetuous, and moved round *farther to the left*,

THE CARTER HOUSE. 243

he would have found the Federal line weaker, and might have made a charge that would have led to victory! Col. McEwen told how Forrest, the famous cavalry leader, went to Hood, and asked permission to cross the river with his mounted men, when, as he said, "he would flank the Federals out of their position in fifteen minutes!" But the Commander had made his own plan of battle; and being in an angry and imperious temper that day, was not in a mood to receive suggestions, or to listen to the proposal of any manœuvre other than that of direct battle, and answered haughtily to the bold trooper who would *flank* the enemy, "No, no! *Charge* them out!"

But leaving speculations as to what *might have been*, we proceed to observe what actually took place. Mr. Carter now led the way to his house, which was the very centre of the battle. As it stands fronting on the Columbia turnpike, which runs through the town, and was but a few rods in the rear of the Federal breastworks, it was in the angle of two lines of battle: for, when the brigades of Wagner came flying in utter rout, they swept past its very door, followed by the Confederates, and the two sides fought around the dwelling; and when the onset was stayed, that portion of the line which was nearest was still held by the Confederates, while the Federals formed another line a few rods in the rear, so that the house was left *between the two lines*, and received the fire of both.

At this time the house contained a large family. The mother had died ten years before, but the father was still living, and with him were a son (who was now our guide,) and four daughters, a daughter-in-law, and several children. Of course, had they foreseen how near the battle would come to them, they would have fled to the other end of the town, or across the river. But in the early part of the day, while this was the headquarters there was perfect discipline, nobody was disturbed, and they felt that they were safest under their own roof. And when at last the storm came, it burst upon them so suddenly that it was too late to escape. There was only one spot of safety, the cellar, and there they all took refuge. Here, self-imprisoned, they could not *see* what was going on about them, but they *heard* the roar above their heads, for the thunderings and lightnings were incessant. As the mass of soldiers surged round the dwelling, some who shrank from the awful fire crowded into the cellar way, when the family retreated behind a partition, but as there was no means of barring the door, the intruders pressed in there also, and into a third underground refuge, when, as Mr. Carter himself tells the tale, he "turned upon them and cursed them and drove them out!" But even in this dark hiding-place, he could look through the grated window, and ask the "Yankee soldiers" how the battle was going!

After a time the fury of the battle abated, for the first shock, which was the most tremendous of all, had spent itself in an hour. Then darkness came, so that the opposing lines were partly hidden from each other. But still they fought on, even when they could see to fire only by the flashing of each other's guns.

As we came up from the cellar, and went round the house, we saw that its southern side, which was exposed to the Confederate fire, was riddled with shot, as were all the outbuildings having the same exposure. How deadly it proved was shown by the fact that Mr. Carter counted fifty-seven dead, besides the wounded, in his door-yard the next morning.

Leading the way across the garden, my friend Cunningham stopped under a pear-tree, which recalled the memory of that fearful night. It was in the line of the earthworks thrown up by the Union soldiers, outside of which was a ditch. Of this part of the line the Confederates had got possession, and held it; but so terrible was the fire that again and again the parapet was swept of the heads that rose above it. The trench below was filled with the dying and the dead. Standing with one foot on the bodies of his fallen comrades, and the other on the bank, he rested his gun—a short Enfield rifle that he had been permitted to carry, as he was so young and small—on the top of the works. The line had been so thinned out that only a solitary fellow-soldier stood near him, and now *he* was shot, and fell heavily (he was a large man) against him, and tumbled over into the mass of dead below. Thus left alone, he asked General Strahl, who had stood for a long while in the trench, and passed up loaded guns to men posted on the embankment, "What had we better do?" The answer was "Keep firing!" But Strahl himself was soon shot, and while being carried to the rear, was struck again and instantly killed. He was succeeded by Colonel Stafford, who also was killed, and sank in such a position that he was braced up by the mass of bodies around him, so that when the morning came, he was standing there stark and cold, as if still ready to give command to the army of the dead!

These were ghastly memories to come back after the lapse of so many years. How changed the scene now! It was the month of March, and already the breath of Spring was in the air, and the little pear-tree, which had lived through all the storm and tempest of that fearful night, though scarred in many places, yet had healed its wounds, and was putting forth its leaves fresh and green, as if it had never heard the sound of battle. So, while men die, the life of nature keeps on, and even draws nourishment from their blood. Turning to my companion,

I said "Do you remember the lines of Byron on a friend of his youth who perished at Waterloo :

' And when I stood beneath the fresh green tree,
Which living waves where thou didst cease to live,
And saw around me the wide fields revive,
And earth come forth with promise of the Spring,
I turned from all she brought to those she could not bring' ? "

From the house, Mr. Carter and Colonel McEwen led the way past the farm buildings and across the back lot, that had been the scene of a fierce struggle, to a meadow, in which stood at the time of the battle a locust grove, where was planted a battery that inflicted a galling fire upon the Confederate lines. It was for the capture of this battery that Hood is said to have issued his order in the dramatic style of which Sam Jones makes such use in one of his sermons.*

* I quote from the little volume of Letters published three or four years ago under the title "BLOOD IS THICKER THAN WATER" (pp. 60, 61):

"It is said that the Confederate line as it advanced was enfiladed by a battery planted in a grove of the black locust trees so common in that region. Seeing his men cut to pieces, General Hood, who was watching the battle, sent one of his aids with the following order: ' Give my compliments to General Cleburne, and tell him that I ask at his hands the battery in the locust grove.' The aid disappeared, and quickly returned with the message, ' General Cleburne is dead, sir!' Again the Commander spoke, ' Give my compliments to General Adams, and tell him that I ask at his hands the battery in the locust grove.' Again the message is returned, ' General Adams is dead, sir!' Once more went the unflinching order to a third commander, with the same result. The moral is evident. The thrice-repeated command is meant to illustrate the duty of unquestioning obedience, and, as might be supposed, is used with startling effect on a Confederate audience, though the fiery preacher afterward introduced it in one of his great meetings in Chicago, when, after

But here is an incident which does not need to be told with an eye to dramatic effect, since nothing can add to its touching character. Mr. Carter, who was now walking at my side, had a brother, Theodoric, who when the war broke out was twenty-three years old, and though he had just entered the profession of law, was so carried away by the excitement of the hour that he threw down his books and enlisted in the ranks as a private (he afterwards became a quarter-master) in the Western Confederate Army. His service took him away from Tennessee, and I think his brother told me that he had not been home in two years. He was now in Hood's army, and perhaps, as he came over the crest of the hill, he caught sight of the old dwelling, where his family were troubled with anxious thoughts of the absent son and brother. In the night, word came that he had been wounded, and was somewhere on the field, perhaps dead or dying; and about two o'clock the father and son and one of the daughters went in search of him. Dividing into two parties, the son took one course, and the father and daughter another, and thus they went from point to point, turning the light of their lanterns into the faces of those scattered thickly over the ground. At length the father and daughter found him, mortally wounded, but still breathing, though unconscious. He had sacrificed his life to his chivalrous courage. His duties did not require him to be on the field, but he volunteered to serve as aid to General T. B. Smith, and was advancing to the charge when, about a hundred and sev-

winding up his hearers to the highest pitch, he gave the word of command somewhat after this fashion: 'As Adjutant of the Lord of Hosts, I ask at your hands the city of Chicago; that you compel it to surrender to the Lord Jesus Christ! —an undertaking more difficult than to storm any battery that ever hurled death in the face of a foe."

enty-five yards southwest of his dwelling, and eighty yards in front of the locust grove, he received two fatal wounds and fell from his horse. Thus it proved that, amid the horrors of that fearful night, when his family were cowering in terror at the roar of the battle around them, with an agony intensified by the thought of where *he* might be, he was in fact lying on the cold ground, bleeding his life away, near to the old home, almost within sound of their voices, yet beyond their reach and their aid. Tenderly they lifted him up and carried him to his father's house, where the next morning one who was an eye-witness tells me he saw the body of the long-absent son and brother, around which his sisters hung with the utmost tenderness, caressing the almost lifeless form, stroking the pale cheeks, and whispering gently amid their tears, "Brother's come home!" He had come home indeed, though it was only to die (he continued to breathe thirty-six hours); but it is something which is not always given to a soldier, to draw his last breath under his father's roof, and to be laid in his last sleep beside the dust of his kindred.*

* To these personal reminiscences of one of my companions, I may add this, told me by another, Col. McEwen:

"General Kimball occupied my house as his headquarters, at which occurred this strange incident. About four o'clock, after the General had left for the field, there lingered a Colonel from Indianapolis in my parlor; he was a lawyer, and a nice man; he asked my daughters to sing and play him a piece of music. They hesitated, but I answered for them, 'Yes.' My daughter asked what they should play? He replied that he had not been in a parlor since the battle of Oak Hill was fought, and that he did not know one piece of music from another, except field music. I then spoke and asked the young ladies to sing and play a piece which had recently come out, 'Just before the Battle, Mother,' telling the Colonel that it was a new piece. At my request, they sat down, and played and

About half past ten o'clock Gen. Schofield sent orders to Gen. Cox that at midnight the troops should be withdrawn—an order which the latter received with great pain, as he felt that there was now an opportunity to destroy Hood's army. The prisoners who had been taken, or who had come in and given themselves up, reported that they were all cut to pieces; that regiments and divisions were left almost without officers; and that the whole army was utterly demoralized. These reports were confirmed by the heaps of dead that lay all along the line. Seeing and hearing this, Cox felt that there was an opportunity such as seldom occurs in war, to end the campaign with a single blow, and he implored Gen. Schofield to remain, saying in the ardor of his confidence that he "would answer with his head" for the result of the next day. The answer of Schofield was all that could gratify the pride of a soldier. He said: "Tell Gen. Cox he has won a glorious victory, and I have no doubt we could do as he suggests in

sung the piece about half through, when I stepped to the door, and a shell exploded within fifty yards. I immediately returned and said, 'Colonel, if I am any judge, it is just about that time now!' He immediately sprang to his feet, and ran in the direction of his regiment, but before he reached it, or by that time, he was shot through the lungs, the bullet passing quite through him. He was taken back to the rear, and on to Nashville. Eighteen days after I received a message from him through an officer, stating the fact of his being shot, and that the piece of music the young ladies were executing was still ringing in his ears, and had been every moment that his eyes were open since he left my parlor the evening of the battle. In April, four months later, after the war was over, he had sufficiently recovered to travel, when he came to Franklin, as he stated, expressly to get the young ladies to finish the piece of music and relieve his ears. His wife and more than a dozen officers accompanied him. He found the ladies, and they sang and played the piece through for him in presence of all the officers; and they wept like children."

the morning. But my orders from Gen. Thomas are imperative, and we must move back to Nashville as soon as possible." So the order was reluctantly issued, and at midnight the troops were ready to move. But at this moment a fire broke out in the town—a building had perhaps been set on fire for the purpose—which cast a light over the place so as to expose every movement to the enemy. This caused a delay, but at length the fires sank down in their ashes, and the wearied soldiers once more strung their knapsacks on their backs. The trains had been already got across the river, and the broken columns resumed their march.

Ignorant of all this, Hood, who was brooding gloomily over the events of the day had called a council of war at midnight, at which the commanders of the three corps, Cheatham, Stewart, and Lee, reported their several commands as half destroyed. As he listened to tale after tale of disaster, his temper, soured before, became almost savage. Still he bore up with an unconquered mind; and, even while one-fourth of his army were stretched in their blood upon the ground, he declared that he would renew the contest the next morning. One thing he had to give him confidence. His heavy artillery, of which he had felt the want the day before, was now coming up, and he said he "would open the battle with a hundred guns!" Indeed he could not wait for the break of day, but at three o'clock startled the town with a tremendous roar. Said Col. McEwen, "I thought it would take my head off." But to his amazement there was no reply, for the Federal army was across the river, and on its way to Nashville, and only heard in the distance these last thunders of impotent rage and fury. The sound did not hasten their steps an instant, nor evoke a taunt or a cheer. Still they plodded on silent as the stars that were shining above them. In that long procession there was none of the pomp and circumstance of war, nothing of that which might be expected in an army a few hours after a great victory. But I believe it is Wellington that has said, "Next to a great defeat, the saddest thing in the world is a great victory." As there was no shout of triumph for the living, there was no mourning for the dead. "Not a drum was heard nor a funeral note." The soldiers were weary and worn : many of them had been wounded ; some had their heads bound up ; others carried their arms in slings ; some, leaning on their comrades, dragged themselves slowly along. Sadder than all, as they took their places in the ranks, they missed many from their side : comrades that but a few hours ago were "full of lusty life," were now lying in their new made graves, or unburied on the plain. An army thus stricken, was in no mood for exultation. What a contrast was this night march to that of the night before! Only twenty-four hours had passed, but in that time they had lived years! Thus blood-stained with the wounds of battle, *yet victorious*, in the gray of morning they found rest in the camps round the city of Nashville.

This withdrawal had been wholly voluntary, yet Hood had the weakness to telegraph to Richmond, "We attacked the enemy at Franklin, and drove him from his outer line of temporary works into his interior line, which he abandoned during the night, and rapidly retreated to Nashville!" as if he had gained a victory. But this pretence deceived no one, for it was impossible to hide from his own soldiers the awful carnage of that day. As soon as daylight made it visible, they had before their eyes the horrors of the battlefield, on which lay six thousand dead and wounded! Though used to war, they had never seen such a sight before. There were places where the dead lay one upon another, five deep ; while for some distance the ground was covered. A Confederate officer tells me that the next morning he mounted his horse to ride to the front, but as he drew near the horse started back, affrighted at the smell of blood, and at the human figures that stared at him from the ground, with every look of agony in their faces; and he dismounted and endeavored to pick his way on foot, but so thick were the slain that he said, "I do not think it extravagant to say that for two hundred yards from the line of the intrenchments, I could have walked on the dead, stepping from one body to another!"

As it was along this part of the line that the first rush of the Confederates came, here was the first shock of battle, and here many of the leaders fell. Cleburne, as might have been expected, was in the front. He was the bravest of the brave, and he had been stung to the quick by the angry reproof of Hood for his failure to attack at Spring Hill; and now, with his Irish blood hot within him, he mounted his iron-gray stallion, and putting himself at the head of his men rode straight at the foe, to fall in the sight of both armies, dying as a soldier might wish to die, "amid the battle's splendor." Knowing that his chivalrous daring had made him the idol of the Southern army, I could appreciate the feeling of my companions when Mr. Carter stopped us and said, "This is the very spot where Cleburne fell!" But a few rods distant Gen. John Adams was in the very act of springing his horse over the works, when both fell together, he being thrown over into the ranks on the other side, while his horse was left literally bestriding the works. "Old Charley" was the very type of a war-horse, and was almost as well known in the army as his master; and the figure of the powerful creature was very striking in death, as he lay at full length, his hind legs reaching to the bottom of the outer ditch, while the long neck was stretched on the slope, the head on the very top of the parapet, as if still breathing defiance at the foe :

> "There lay the steed with his nostril all wide,
> But through it there rolled not the breath of his pride;
> And the foam of his gasping lay white on the turf,
> And cold as the spray of the rock-beating surf."

That war-horse would make a figure for a sculptor, almost as striking as the lion of Thorwaldsen ; and the State of Tennessee ought to have it wrought in marble or cast in bronze, as a type of the courage of her sons on the field of battle.

Hardly less striking than this were the groups scattered far and wide over the field: for the dead lay in heaps, torn to pieces by shot and shell, till they had almost lost the semblance of humanity; with the brave creatures that had carried them into the battle stretched beside them:

> "Rider and horse, friend and foe, in one red burial blent."

In the presence of such awful misery, it seems an unworthy intrusion of human pride to dispute the honors of the day. It is not an hour to boast when thousands of our fellow-beings are lying on the ground in the agonies of death. The object for which the battle was fought—to destroy the Union army—had utterly failed, and so far it was a Union victory. But if only the glory be considered, there is glory enough for all : for never was there a more splendid display of courage and devotion, than in the Confederates who that day sacrificed their lives in vain.

The army that fought the battle of Franklin, was not yet quite at the end of its campaign. The last shot had not been fired. Only two weeks later—on the fifteenth of December—it was to have a part in one more battle and one more victory : when the army of Thomas, doubled in strength by that of Schofield, poured forth from Nashville, and swept all the encircling hills, by which the army of Hood was so completely scattered and destroyed that it virtually ceased to exist, as a force to be taken into account in any future movement. This was the final blow which ended the war in the West, so that General Schofield, with his command, was transferred to the East, and sent by sea to join Sherman in North Carolina; while Grant held fast to Lee. All these movements were linked together, so that a check in one would have been a disaster to all. If Schofield had not "held the fort" at Franklin, Thomas might not have been able to hold it at Nashville, and Hood would have swept through Kentucky to the Ohio; so that all that was being done in Virginia and in the Carolinas, might have been neutralized by a great defeat in Tennessee. All portions of the country were comprised in that splendid strategy, which, manœuvring over half the Union in a vast circle winding round and round, and contracting towards a common centre, finally closed in and crushed the Rebellion within its mighty folds.

Those were heroic days that should never be forgotten. Since then twenty-five years have passed, and a new generation has come upon the stage that may forget the terrible cost at which the Union was restored, except as it is recalled by some memorable anniversary. But a few months since we looked out of our windows in New York upon the greatest pageant that ever swept through its streets, the celebration of the completion of a hundred years from the foundation of the Government. In that brilliant array the President of the United States was accompanied by all the high officers of State, and representatives of the army and navy. The enthusiasm for these heads of the nation was divided with that for the Southern Governors, some of whom—like Buckner of Kentucky and Gordon of Georgia—had been Generals in the

Confederate army, and now appeared leading the troops of their respective States—not as captives in a triumphal procession, but as equal partners in One Country : rejoicing as fully as the North in the immeasurable blessings of a restored Union.

At the head of this great procession rode General Schofield, the same who had fought the battle which I have attempted to describe, and who, after a long life of service, has succeeded Grant and Sherman and Sheridan as head of the army of the United States. How could one who had but lately come from the field of Franklin, help thinking with a shudder of what *might have been* if he had not planned so wisely and stood so firmly, while so many brave men died for their country, on that decisive day a quarter of a century ago!

In visiting a battlefield after the lapse of a few years, there is at least this satisfaction, that nature soon obliterates all traces of the passion and the violence of men. The earth drinks up their blood, and the grass grows green again over their graves. As we walked along the line of the intrenchments, I found every trace of them had been destroyed, as the ground has been many times ploughed over. But every Spring, as it is turned up anew, fresh relics are brought to light. My friends picked up a handful of bullets, which they turned over to me, to which I answered that I thought I would take them to General Schofield with the compliments of his Confederate friends, who, as they had not had the opportunity of presenting them when he visited the town on a certain memorable occasion, would make amends for this neglect by presenting them now. The gallant Major charged me especially to say how glad they were that they had *not* been presented on the appointed day! This duty I performed on my arrival in Washington. The General received them with a smile, and as he took them in his hand, pointed out the peculiar shape of each ball, which showed whether it had been fired by friend or foe, and kept specimens of each, as interesting and harmless souvenirs of a great event, not only in his own life, but in American history.

General Schofield said that after the war he had a great desire to see General Hood, and renew the acquaintance which they had in the old days, when they were four years side by side at West Point. Hood had settled down in New Orleans. Schofield wrote to him several times to come on to the meeting of his old classmates. But he never came. In his last letter he said: "To tell the truth, I have ten children to provide for, which takes all my time and care." The reason did honor to the soldier's heart. These were soon to be left without father or mother: for both died within a few days of each other, and the eldest daughter a few hours after her father. A blow so sudden and so terrible enlisted great sympathy at the South, where every heart and every home was open to those who were thus doubly orphaned. Nor was it in the South only, but in the North also, where more than one were taken into the closest relations, as if they were of the same blood. So is it that an unnatural alienation is sometimes followed by a reaction of feeling, which in its return causes an overflow of affection and kindness. Especially when the grave has closed over the heroic dead, old strifes give place to kindly memories, and flowers blossom out of the dust. Severed hearts yearn to be knit again, and hands long withdrawn are stretched out once more; and, though it may be only in the next generation, new affections spring up, and sweet household ties come in, to bind all together.

CHAPTER XVII.

VISIT TO THE HOME OF ANDREW JACKSON.

Next to the scene of the battle of Franklin, the one place in the neighborhood of Nashville which I desired to see, was the Hermitage, the home of Andrew Jackson. When I was a boy, I can just remember his election as the President of the United States. During the two terms of his administration, and for years after, he was the greatest political power in the country: indeed it is doubtful if any man from the time of Washington to the opening of the Civil War, filled a larger space in the public eye. He is a very picturesque figure in American history. He was not of the ordinary run of politicians—smooth-tongued and "all things to all men"; but a man original and unique, a product of nature rather than of education. A child of poverty, he came up in the backwoods, like some prodigious growth of the forest. Without the polish of society, he had a natural courage and force of will that put him at the head of the rough communities of the border, from which the force of circumstances pushed him on till he reached the highest position in national affairs. A man who has acted such a part in his generation, is a subject of interest to the student of history, and hence the desire which I felt to see the place where he lived and died.

The visit was made easy for me by the courtesy of Ex-Governor Marks, who offered to be my guide, and to whose company was added the attraction of that of his wife, and of Mr. Jno. W. Childress, a nephew of Mrs. Polk. Thus I was shut up in a carriage with three Confederates, and I do protest that I might have been in a worse place. Indeed I could not have been with more delightful companions. The very fact that their experience had been so entirely different from mine, put it in their power to tell me much which I could not know before, but was eager to hear. As a full-blooded Northerner, I like to tell of all the things done by the brave men, and brave women too, of the North. One of my heroes is General Bartlett of Massachusetts, that young student fresh from Harvard, so fair and delicate that it seemed as if he could hardly march in the ranks, but who proved a soldier "without fear and without reproach"; who at the siege of Port Hudson, being unable to walk, insisted on mounting a horse that he might take part in the battle, which exposed him the more to the fire of the enemy, who were so struck with his courage, that it is said the officers gave orders not to aim at him, which however did not save him, as he was shot in two places, and had in spite of his protests to be carried to the rear. He could not learn prudence by repeated wounds, but continued to expose himself till he was "shot all to pieces," when, like the brave soldier he was, he wrote to one who had pledged him her love, releasing her from her engagement to such a wreck as he felt himself to be, to which she replied, like the brave woman she was, that "she would marry him as long as there was body enough to contain his heroic soul"! As I told this story, I observed a flush in the lady at my side, which indicated that she had a similar story to tell; and to my inquiring look she answered that just before the war she had been engaged to one who was called to the field, whom she, with anxious and trembling heart, watched as he marched away to an uncertain fate. Then came the great battle of Murfreesboro. She heard that he was wounded: and for a few days was in an agony of suspense, an agony that grew more intense as night came on, and she sat alone in the moonlight, and imagined him lying on the cold ground! At length the storm of battle swept farther away, and the wounded were in reach of warm hearts and gentle hands, and she was able to take her place by the couch of the brave soldier whose name she was to bear, and soon after to enter on the life of perfect happiness that has continued to this day.

Mr. Childress, though much younger, was not too young to take part in the war at its close, and was in the battle of Franklin which I have described; and had the most vivid memory of that night march, when Schofield's army passed in full view of the camp fires of the enemy: and of the terrible scenes of the following day.

While thus engaged in conversation, we had been riding over a succession of hills, till we were ten miles from the city. The country around Nashville is not picturesque; there are no mountains on the horizon; but the land rises and falls gently, turning up a thousand slopes to the sun and rain, which bring forth abundantly so that the whole region is a garden of fertility.

At the top of one of these slopes, a gateway opens into a long avenue of trees, at the end of which stands a large house, built in the old Southern style, with a row of pillars in front, the chief architectural decoration of a planter's house in the old slavery days, as it stood in the centre of a great plantation—a sort of Feudal Castle around which gathered the mixed population that owed allegiance to the Lord of the Manor. This was the Hermitage, the home of Andrew Jackson.

On this spot he settled in the early part of the century, though not in the great house which we now see. The pioneers in the valley of the Cumberland, as in other parts of the West, lived in log cabins. Jackson's first home was not much better. It stood in the rear of the present Hermitage: you may still see the old chimney, up which huge fires flamed and roared long ago, round which sat the mighty hunters of that day (for it was not long after the time of Daniel Boone, whose exploits were the tradition of the border), and talked by the firelight of their contests with wild beasts and savage men. In this humble dwelling Jackson lived long after he became a famous man in the State of Tennessee; it was from under that roof that he went forth to fight his battles, and (as the servant told us) "done all his big things"! But in the course of years, as his military achievements gave him wide distinction, the cabin had to give place to something more stately, that was fit to be the abode of so much greatness. It was at the steps of this mansion we now drew up.

Ringing at the door, a figure appeared that was in keeping with the general aspect of the place, venerable indeed, but a good deal worn by the ravages of time. This was an old servant, over eighty years of age, who had been born on the place, and lived here all his life. He was now gray and grizzled, and his thin garments looked as if they had fluttered in the wind for many a year, making him altogether fit to be the keeper of an old baronial hall, that had long since seen its best days, and was now going to decay. Indeed he seemed like the very ghost of the olden time, but a gentle and kindly ghost, who was himself a part of the place, through which he moved like a shadow, and who (instead of rattling off a string of commonplaces, like a professional guide,) talked simply and naturally of his old master, the beloved dead. He now led the way into the interior of the house, which is divided by a broad hall, after the old fashion. On the left, as you enter, is the parlor, where the faded hangings and worn-out chairs and sofas are the fit mementoes of departed glory. Here is a collection of souvenirs of the old soldier: the chair in which he sat, and the couch on which he reclined; the sword that he wore in battle, and the pipe that he smoked in peace.

Some of the relics tell of the rough times in which he lived in the early days of Tennessee. Here is a bullet that he carried for years in his body, where it was planted, not by a foe on the field of battle, but in a bar-room fight in Nashville, in which he was shot by a man who was one day to fight on his side as fiercely as he now fought against him—Thomas H. Benton of Missouri, who, when Jackson was President, was his chief supporter and defender in the Senate of the United States. Some may think it a wrong to Jackson's memory to recall these personal encounters. On the contrary, I think it but just to paint him exactly as he was, and not to soften his features as if he were a saint. Let us tell the truth. He lived in rough times, in which he was a rough fighter. We need not hide this feature of the man, since we can go on to tell how, in his later career, his undaunted courage was devoted to the service of his country.

As the border was in those days, as in ours, the resort of many desperate characters, the quality most prized and most honored was personal courage. A coward could not live in such a community. A man must be ready to defend himself at all times and in all places. Nor was this courage needed only in personal combats, but in enforcing the law. Jackson had picked up a smattering of the law before he left his native State of North Carolina. His mother, a good Scotch-Irish woman, had intended him for the pulpit, and he had actually begun his studies for that holy calling (no doubt he would have been a rousing preacher, setting forth the terrors of the law with tremendous power!) when circumstances turned him aside to another vocation. As he crossed the mountains to what was afterwards to be the State of Tennessee, it was with an appointment as a "solicitor," in the duties of which he had often to deal with the invaders of public lands—a task which called for a good deal of courage. Not less was this required when he became a Judge. On one occasion he had ordered the sheriff to arrest a drunken brute who was noted for his strength and his ferocity. The sheriff attempted to execute the order, but returned, saying that the man was armed, and threatened to kill any one who should approach him. Jackson told him to go back and take the man dead or alive; and if he could not do it alone, to summon anybody whom he wished to help him, "even if it were the Judge on the bench," to which the officer quickly replied, " I summon your Honor "! Instantly he rose from his seat, and taking a loaded pistol in his hand, advanced upon the desperado, who, seeing that further resistance was vain, at once surrendered.

A man of such courage naturally took the lead in times of public danger. The settlements had to be in constant preparation against an attack of Indians. Jackson had had a training in the school of war, for he remembered the Revolution, when, a mere boy, he was taken prisoner, and struck by a British officer with a sword, inflicting a scar which he carried through life, while his brother received a wound from which he died (he had but one other brother who had already died in the war); and his mother too sank under the fatigues of marching after the pitiless soldiers, and nursing the wounded and the dying; so that, except himself, the family was literally exterminated, and he was left alone in the world. These were bitter memories, which inspired in the young orphan a hatred of oppression and cruelty; and to the latest hour of his life, nothing roused him to fury more than an act of injustice to helpless childhood or womanhood.

This is not the place to enter into the military career of General Jackson. That is a matter of history. Whether he was a great soldier, is a question for the military critics. Certainly he had the quickness in conception and promptness in action which are the first requisites of a leader. He had also a comradeship with his soldiers that gave him great power over them. He shared their hardships and privations, tramping by their side in the long marches through forest and swamp, in which he proved so incapable of fatigue, that the soldiers, who delight to give nicknames to their favorite commanders, dubbed him "Old Hickory." When the day was over, he was ready to lie down under the open sky, with no bed but the leaves of the forest. Often provisions ran low, and the whole camp was put on short rations. Not unfrequently many a brave man had not a biscuit in his knapsack. But "Old Hickory" made as light of starvation as "Old Eliott" did at the siege of Gibraltar. In his Indian campaign his men were reduced to the lowest point, but he said "if they could only get an ear of corn apiece," they would carry it through to the end. On one occasion a soldier came to him, saying that he was literally starving, perhaps prompted to make his wants known as he saw the General sitting at the foot of a tree, eating something with apparent relish. Instead of reproving him, Jackson replied that he was always ready to share what he had with his men, and thrusting his hand into his pocket, drew out a handful of acorns, saying that that was all he had to eat! When a commander was thus ready to suffer the extreme of privation, and even to give his last acorn to a hungry soldier, his men quickly learned the lesson taught by such an example. And when at last he was able to face the enemy, and there was nothing to do but the fighting, that was mere play; indeed he seemed really to enjoy it (perhaps this was the Irish blood that was in him); his ardor rose with danger, he pressed forward to the front, and seemed to be everywhere present, inspiring his soldiers with his own unconquerable spirit.

If it be the best proof of a great general that he wins victories, certainly Jackson proved his right to that distinction. In his campaign against the Indians in Florida, he broke their power as effectually as he afterwards stopped the English invasion at New Orleans. In the latter case he was pitted, not against savages, but against an army of fourteen thousand men, the veterans of the Peninsular War, with whom Wellington had marched from victory to victory. Against these Jackson had less than half the number, the greater part of whom were mere militia. True, they were the rifle-men of Kentucky and Tennessee, but they could hardly be expected to stand against a disciplined army, unless they had been inspired by a resolute commander. It was then he showed an energy almost superhuman. It is said that for four days and nights he did not close his eyes. To be sure, he carried things with a high hand; he declared martial law, he seized cotton bales wherever he could find them to make breastworks, and no doubt in many cases went beyond the limit of his authority, but his plea was the necessity of the case. Everything was to be sacrificed to self-preservation. He violated the law, but he saved the city!

HOME LIFE.

But this is not the place to fight his battles over again. Under the roof of the Hermitage, it is more in keeping with the domestic surroundings, to speak of the home-life of its former occupants. No life could be more in contrast with the rugged scenes of war. When the army disbanded, and its commander retired to his home, it was to enjoy tranquillity and peace. He had had enough of public life, civil and military; and now he had but two thoughts—his family and his farm. The latter had been a good deal neglected during his absence, and needed the care of its master. He was not rich; he could not be reckoned among the wealthy planters of the South. Nor was he a large slaveholder. Not that he had any scruples about holding slaves, but as he had no need of them, if they came into his hands, our old guide said that "he put 'em all out to traders and let 'em go." This reduced the number of his cares, and made his life more simple and easy. It was then he built his new house, and planted the long avenue of trees before the door; as his servant told us, his master "set 'em all out his-self."

If such was the growing beauty around the Hermitage, still greater was the beauty of the life within. Strange as it may seem in one of his violent temper, Jackson was a very affectionate husband. If he hated bitterly, he loved warmly, and the wife whom he had married in his early manhood, was to her last hour the object of his most ardent devotion. With such elements of happiness without and within, the life of the country gentleman flowed on as smoothly as the river that flowed by the Hermitage. In this happy retirement he remained till he was called to enter once more into the service of his country.

All readers of political history are familiar with the circumstances which led to his nomination for the Presidency; to his defeat in 1825, when, there being no election by the people, John Quincy Adams was chosen by the House of Representatives; and to the election of Jackson four years later. Then he had reached the height of his ambition; and yet at that very moment all the joy of it was taken away by the greatest blow that could befall him, in the death of his wife—a blow that dashed his triumph to the ground, and cast a shadow over his whole life. As our guide said, "He was never the same man again." It was just as he was about to leave the Hermitage for Washington—the carriages were already packed—that she was suddenly taken ill and died in three days. All this came back again as her old servant conducted us to the corner of the garden where she is buried. He remembered the day when his master stood beside the open grave, into which was let down the form of her whom he had loved so long and well. The old man said, "It cut him to the heart. You see," he added with his simple negro pathos, "it comes mighty hard for a man to lose his wife!" When all was over, "ashes to ashes, dust to dust," the old soldier, now alone in the world, walked to the carriage, which bore him away from the scene of so much happiness and so much sorrow. The journey to the Capital was a melancholy one. In all the honors that awaited him, there was a feeling of inexpressible sadness that she who had been his companion in earlier days, who had shared his humbler fortunes, was not with him to share his honors now; and in all the years of power, whenever he looked across the Potomac to where the sun was going down in the west, his heart was far away by that lonely grave on the banks of the Cumberland.

For eight years the Hermitage was empty, as its Master was transferred to other scenes. When Jackson came to Washington, there was great curiosity to see him, as he had been pictured in very different forms by friends and foes. Some who looked for a rough specimen of the border, a sort of untamed barbarian, were surprised to find "a gentleman of the old school," with a fine soldierly presence, a natural dignity, and courtly manners. It was soon discovered that he was to be President not merely in name; that he was not to be simply an ornamental personage, a mere figure-head of the ship of State, but an embodiment of power, that would be felt in every department of the Government. And how did he use this vast power? Wisely and well? or capriciously and to the injury of his country? There can be no doubt that the imperious temper which fitted him for military command, to some extent unfitted him for civil administration. Military power is not the best preparation for a more restricted authority. It has often been said of General Grant that he thought he could conduct a government as he commanded an army, simply by issuing his orders to his lieutenants. The same could have been said with more truth of Jackson, as he was of a temper more arbitrary. He was not a man to weigh public questions in the balance with slow and cautious judgment. He could not brook opposition. He had strong likes and dislikes: he loved his friends and hated his enemies; and viewing public questions in their personal relations, his administration ran into a personal government. That the powers and the emoluments of office should be enjoyed by those who were hostile to the head of the Government, seemed to him an injustice to himself and to his loyal supporters, though the saying which has been imputed to him, "To the victors belong the spoils," was in fact the utterance (such I believe is the truth of history) of Governor Marcy of New York, whom its people at least regard as being entitled as much as any man of his day, to the name of a statesman and a patriot. He may have spoken it in jest, but it was a most unfortunate phrase, and declares a vicious principle. While condemning it in the strongest terms, it is but simple justice to Jackson to say, that his faults grew to some extent out of his virtues; that they were the faults of a generous nature. If he had been a man with no hot blood in his veins, but cold and passionless, he might have been saved from mistakes into which he was led by his ardent temperament. If he had not loved his friends so well, he might have served his country better. But his friendships, like his hatreds, warped his judgment. So in his political views, whichever side he took, he took strongly; he was sure that he was right; and his fierce determination to do right often led him to do wrong.

In the glass case which contains the personal relics, is a pen which has a history, that makes it as interesting as a pen that has been used in the signature of a treaty of peace or a declaration of war. It is the pen with which he signed his veto of the bill that had passed Congress to renew the charter of the United States Bank! It is a plain quill pen, for, as the old darky said, "The Gineral allus wrote with a quill; he didn't use none o' them fine gold pens, like you 'uns." But though it was only a gray goose quill, it was enough to write a decision which shook the country. His enemies claimed that it caused a financial convulsion, which spread ruin and disaster far and wide. Certain it is, that it precipitated a fierce conflict; and when he followed it up by removing the deposits from the United States Bank, the bitterness of feeling was such as has rarely been known in the history of the country. The Senate recorded its disapproval in a Resolution offered by Mr. Clay, that "the President had assumed upon himself authority and power not conferred by the Constitution and laws, but in derogation of both"—a censure which stood upon its record till, after a long agita-

HE PUTS DOWN NULLIFICATION.   269

tion, it was formally "expunged!" This was effected chiefly by the efforts of Col. Benton, who atoned for the bullet he had once sent into the body of General Jackson by this determined and at last successful effort to remove a blot upon his name!

It was at such times as this that the old Whig Party vented its rage in wrathful imprecations upon the head of one whose purpose they could not change. But even they had to confess that there were times when the country was all the safer because of "Old Hickory's" fiery temper and tremendous will. It was in the year 1832 that nullification raised its head in South Carolina—a demonstration that, if unchecked, might have ended in civil war. For such a crisis Jackson was the man of all men, for he permitted no trifling. He did not meet it with soft phrases, but with a decision and energy that soon put an end to this incipient rebellion. His proclamation was one of the most masterly State papers ever issued in the history of the Government. It dealt with the argument of nullification in a calm, judicial manner, ending with this conclusion: "I consider the power to annul a law of the United States, assumed by one State, incompatible with the existence of the Union, contradicted expressly by the letter of the Constitution, unauthorized by its spirit, inconsistent with every principle on which it was founded, and destructive of the great objects for which it was formed." These were solemn words, and they were made more impressive by a knowledge of the personality which stood behind them, ready to enforce them with all the power of the Government; for Jackson had declared his purpose, if the movement of nullification were persisted in, to treat its leaders as "traitors," whom he "would hang as high as Haman"! This mild suggestion set the nullifiers a-thinking, and they soon concluded that it would be more prudent to wait for another time, when a weaker man should sit in the Presidential chair. That time was yet to come when the executive power was in the hands of one of infirm purpose, who saw the country drift to ruin, and felt himself impotent to stay its course. In the last days of Buchanan, when the Government was falling to pieces, because there was a weak old man in the White House, there were millions of voices that cried in despair, "Oh for one hour of Andrew Jackson!" The obligation of the country to him for his prompt action in a like crisis, cannot be measured. True, it did not prevent the reappearance of Secession after he was in his grave, but it staved it off for a whole generation, till the country was strong enough to deal with it.

When after these stormy years he came back to his quiet home, he was still interested in public affairs, and the Hermitage was a shrine to which politicians came from all parts of the country. But for him the work of life was over. He lived chiefly in memories of the past. He used to walk slowly through the long avenue of trees, his servant following with a chair for him when he chose to sit under the refreshing shade, where he could talk with the friends who came to see him, or muse in silence on the events of former years. It was then his mind took a turn of meditation on the great hereafter. Of Scotch-Irish descent, he had never forgotten the faith of his childhood. In all the wild passion of former years, he had never lost his reverence for sacred things. While he was President, it was said by one who was a frequent visitor at the White House, that he would not partake of a meal without a grateful recognition of the Giver of all good. If there was no clergyman present, or any one whom he could request to ask a blessing, he would ask it himself. And now, as he sat in the twilight of his years, the old man became a child again, and went back to the prayers and the hymns that he learned at his mother's knee. Near his house he erected a small Presbyterian church, that he might worship God according to the way of his fathers. In it he was wont to meet every Sabbath day, with a little congregation made up of his neighbors and their servants. It was proposed to make him a ruling elder, which he said he should consider the greatest honor of his life, but of which he thought himself unworthy. Looking to the future, it was natural that his anticipations should be connected with her who had been the light of his home and the joy of his existence. As often as he visited her grave, and bent over her dust, he thought, without pain, that he should soon be laid beside her. An American Commodore, who had been in the Mediterranean, had brought home a sarcophagus, said to have been that of the Emperor Severus, which he desired to present to General Jackson, as worthy to contain the remains of one so dear to his countrymen. To this he replied, acknowledging the courtesy, but declining the honor, saying, "I cannot consent that my body shall be laid in a sarcophagus made for an emperor or a king. I have prepared a humble depository beside that wherein lies my beloved wife, where, without any pomp or parade, I have requested, when God calls me to sleep with my fathers, to be laid, to remain until the trumpet sounds to call the dead to judgment, when we, I hope, shall rise together, clothed with that heavenly body promised to all who believe in our glorious Redeemer, who died for us that we might live, and by whose atonement I hope for a blessed immortality." The anticipation was soon to be realized. In a few weeks after this letter was penned, the end came. The old servant took us to the room in which his master breathed his last. It is a very modest room on the ground floor. All his surroundings were plain and simple in life and in death. Within these bare walls, on this very bed, the old warrior surrendered at last to a foe that was mightier than he.

With this description of our visit to the Hermitage, the home of Andrew Jackson, I leave it to my readers to form their judgment of a character so extraordinary. I have only to say that, whatever it may be, be it one of praise or of blame, of eulogy or condemnation, they will find abundant reasons to sustain it, for in him, as in all powerful natures, there was a mixture of good and evil that almost defies analysis and forbids classification. But with every drawback, no one can read the story of this life without confessing that Jackson was a great personality.

Among the treasures of the Hermitage is a chair that once belonged to the Father of his Country. To say that Jackson "filled" the chair of Washington, would be assuming too much. But with all his faults—and they were many and marked—no man, not even Washington, loved his country more. Like him, Jackson had fought for it, and was ready to die for it, and in the hour of danger to that Union which the Fathers of the Republic labored so long to establish, no successor of Washington—not even Lincoln—stood more firmly to maintain the country's integrity and honor.

CHAPTER XVIII.

STONEWALL JACKSON.

A few weeks before I left New York for the South, I drove out to Riverside avenue to the grave of General Grant. It was a beautiful autumn day. The leaves were falling from the trees; the woods were almost stripped and bare; and all things wore the sombre, funereal look which is the token of the change that comes alike on nature and on man. The spot is one of great natural beauty—a swelling mound, perhaps a hundred feet above the Hudson; commanding a view of great extent up and down the river; across to the Palisades and beyond to the mountains; and far down the bay to where the sheen of the waters fades into the distant gleam of the ocean. What a place for a warrior to rest after his stormy life! And yet, though it be so calm and still, it is within the limits of the great city in which he spent his last years; and thus he is recalled to us if it be only by his grave. As the Laureate of England says of Wellington, who sleeps in the very heart of London, under the dome of St. Paul's, so may we say of our honored dead:

> "Let the sound of those he wrought for,
> And the feet of those he fought for,
> Echo round his bones forevermore."

From the grave of our beloved soldier it is a natural transition to that of his great adversary, who sleeps far away among the hills of the old Commonwealth which he so much loved. The fact that he led the opposing armies, does not abate the interest with which we study his extraordinary career. The time has come when we can do justice to those who fought against us, and even claim their valor and self-devotion as a part of our national inheritance of glory. As I have somewhat of the instinct of an Old Mortality, I confess to a very great interest in visiting their homes and sepulchres. And so, as I returned from the South, I took my way across the mountains, that I might spend a day in the retired and most beautiful spot where General Lee spent his last years; where he died and is buried; and where his "right arm" (as he called "Stonewall" Jackson) was buried before him.

I came an entire stranger, knowing no one; but as I stepped from the car, a gentleman called me by name, and "took me to his own home." It was Professor J. J. White of the College, who received me with as much kindness as if I had been an old friend. Perhaps it gives color to all my impressions both of the College and the town, that they are associated with such kindly hospitality.

Lexington is situated in that part of the Old Dominion, which, being between the Blue Ridge and the Alleghanies, is known as the Great Valley of Virginia. This is at a considerable elevation above the sea—it is, in fact, a genuine table-land, or plateau—but being walled in by ranges on both sides, it has the aspect of a broad and open valley, lying in the lap of its guardian mountains. The region is both picturesque and historical. Settled at an early day by a sturdy race from the North of Ireland, sons of the men who fought at the siege of "Derry," it has always had a remarkable population. A place of such

WASHINGTON COLLEGE.

"sightliness," and in the centre of such a people, seemed fitted for an Institution of Learning, and here, more than a hundred years ago, was set up on the hill-top one of the best Academies of the times before the Revolution, whose name of "Liberty Hall" showed that even then the spirit of independence was abroad—a name which gave way, after a few years, when the Academy had grown into a College, to that of Washington, to which it had a just title, as it received its first endowment from the Father of his Country, in a property valued at fifty thousand dollars, given to him by the State of Virginia, which he accepted only on condition that he might devote it to this object. And here, half a century later, rose, as a fit accompaniment to the College, a Military Academy, modelled after that at West Point, to furnish defenders to the country. But intensely Southern in its associations and sympathies (or it might be more accurate to say, intensely *Virginian*), it followed its State in the movement of Secession, and among the first recruits that went into the Confederate army were students from Washington College, and cadets from the Military Academy.

Indeed they had hardly need to *go* to the war, for the war came to them. From the very beginning the Valley of Virginia was a scene of conflict. As it is a rich agricultural region, it was the nearest and most convenient source of supplies to the Confederates in the field, and was called "the backbone of the Confederacy," and hence its possession became an object of contest for both armies.

Among the earliest of those who volunteered for service, was a professor in the "Military Institute," Thomas Jonathan Jackson. A Virginian by birth (born in 1824), he was educated at West Point, where he was in no wise conspicuous. He did not rank high in his class. His mind was not a brilliant one, at least in acquiring knowledge, it was not dull, but it was slow; and whatever he learned came by the hardest. But he kept at it with a dogged persistency, so that each year he stood higher than before, particularly in mathematics, a study most necessary in war. Graduating in 1846, at the time of the Mexican War, he was immediately ordered to Mexico, where though but a lieutenant, he showed such courage and capacity, particularly at the storming of Chapultepec, that he was brevetted a Major. After his return to the United States, he became a Professor in the Military Institute at Lexington, a position in which he did fairly well; but he was not a great teacher, as he had not been a great scholar. In his class-room exercises, he was faithful and exact, and always showed that he had himself mastered the subject; but he had none of the personal magnetism which inspires young minds with enthusiasm. In short, there was nothing to indicate that this man was to prove himself one of the greatest soldiers of his time.

In external appearance there could not be a greater contrast than between this plain soldier and General Lee, who was the model of a military commander, graceful in person, and stately in manners, with a natural dignity that, while it did not repel, did not permit any familiarity. Jackson had not a particle of grace. Brave as a lion in battle, he was never at ease in society. One of his old friends here in Lexington, who met him often, tells me that his manner was so wanting in ease, that when he entered a room, he greeted the company with an awkward military salute, and sat down on the edge of a chair, bolt upright, as if eager to be off, asking a few abrupt questions, and answering "Yes" or "No"; and then, rising as abruptly as he came, with a bob of his head, and a short "Good morning," jerked himself out of the room!

But Professor White, who knew him equally well,

thinks this does not do him justice, and says, "There has been some disposition even among Southern writers to caricature Jackson as a man, in the effort to place Jackson the soldier in bolder relief"; and then he draws such a loving picture, that I cannot refrain from letting my readers enjoy it with me:

"A certain blunt, curt, and reticent habit, which marked the soldier, has been thought to characterize him in social intercourse. Such was not the case. I met him very often in society, and do not hesitate to say that he was modest, genial, courteous, and notably polite to every one. He was not graceful in *figure* or in *movement*, but in *spirit* was highly so. He had a peculiarly gentle expression of countenance, and moved easily in a social scene, making it a point to speak, at least for a few minutes, to every lady present, with no appearance of constraint or embarrassment, and had a smile and pleasant word for every acquaintance. His whole manner was so gentle and unobtrusive, his punctilious regard for the feelings of others so invariable, his unselfishness so striking, that if his reputation in the Mexican war had not been known, I do not think that the rough soldier would have been thought of in connection with him. My friends of both sexes concur with me in these views."

This is exquisite. Here are two pictures very unlike, and yet not incompatible: for they are the pendants of each other. The same man, who was shy even to bashfulness in general society and among strangers, might among his intimate friends lay aside all constraint and reserve, and be as simple and natural and delightful as he was in his own home.

But whatever lack of grace of manner there might be in him, one thing was always conspicuous—his prompt response to any call of duty. For his pastor, the late Dr. White (the father of my friend and host), he had a respect amounting to reverence, looking up to him as a superior, to whom he was to "report," and from whom he was to receive "orders." Once, when this faithful shepherd of the flock had dwelt on the duty of taking part in prayer-meetings, Jackson called to ask if the obligation rested upon *him*, alleging his own great diffidence; but being answered in the affirmative, soon made known that he was "ready for duty." But when it came to the point, he was so hesitating and confused as to produce the utmost embarrassment in all present; and from that time forth the pastor would gladly have excused him; but the intrepid soldier would not be excused: he was determined "to fight it out on that line," and by the grace of perseverance finally acquired a degree of freedom in prayer, that, if not very eloquent, was deeply impressive, as the utterance of a great, manly, Christian heart.

Crystal streams issue out of the hardest rocks, and so under this rugged exterior there was a vein of tender feeling, half poetical and half religious. In writing to his wife he said: "I love to stroll abroad after the labors of the day are over, and indulge feelings of gratitude to God for all the sources of natural beauty with which He has adorned the earth. Some time since my morning walks were rendered very delightful by the singing of the birds. The morning carolling of the birds, and their notes in the evening, awaken in me devotional feelings of praise and gratitude, though very different in their nature. In the morning all animated nature appears to join in expressions of gratitude to God. In the evening, all is hushed into silent slumber, and thus disposes the mind to meditation. How delightful it is to associate every pleasure and enjoyment with God the giver!"

It may seem a little in disaccord with this deeply religious feeling, that Jackson often fell asleep under the most faithful preaching. Perhaps it was because he had such unbounded confidence in his pastor: he "knew that it was all right." Or the explanation might be the same as that of another celebrated man, Horace Greeley, who once told me that it was impossible for him to keep awake during a sermon: and knowing him as well as I did, I could understand the reason. He was always overworked, and though his vitality was prodigious, and would keep him up so long as there was anything to be done, yet the vital force was going out of him at such a rate that it left him exhausted; and the moment the pressure ceased, there came a reaction; and "as soon as he began to hear the droning from the pulpit" (these were his words, though he listened to one of the most eloquent preachers in New York, the late Dr. Chapin), he could not resist the drowsiness that came over him; indeed he did not try to resist it, for the feeling was delicious to his tired frame, and he sank into blissful unconsciousness. Jackson, therefore, had good company. Yet out of this "sleepy head," as some might call it, was to come the thunderbolt of war!

The first indication that he gave of what was in him, except that in Mexico, was at Bull Run, where his command, though they had never been in battle before, stood firm as a rock, or in the phrase of the camp, "as a stone wall," from which it was thenceforth known as the Stonewall Brigade, and its commander as Stonewall Jackson.

Here begins a tale which it would take long to tell of the military career that commenced at Bull Run and ended at Chancellorsville. It was all comprised in less than two years, but they were years of incessant activity. If I had the intimate personal knowledge of my friend, Major Jed. Hotchkiss of Staunton, Va., who was with him almost daily during these two years, I could tell a story that would be worth the hearing. He was as near to Jackson as any man could be. Not only was he on his staff, but in the very responsible position of topographical engineer, whose duty it was to keep his chief informed of the whole field of operations, mapping out the country—not only giving its great features, its mountains and valleys and rivers, but the minutest details, to every country road and every gap in the mountains, by which perchance he might execute a flank movement, and by a rapid night march appear in the morning in the rear of the enemy. Thus the engineer sometimes virtually designated the field in which the general was to fight his battles.

This old companion of the great Confederate leader, gave up a day to accompany me down the Shenandoah Valley, part of the Valley of Virginia. The object of our excursion was to visit the wonderful Grottoes of the Shenandoah, but in our way we passed over the ground, which was the scene of all those campaigns in "The Valley," of which we heard so constantly in the war—events which were now described by one who was an actor in them. Indeed, I hope my readers will appreciate *my* opportunities as second only to those of an eye-witness, for if the Major rode by the side of Stonewall Jackson, *I rode by the side of the Major*, and listened to the marvellous story. True, between his ride and mine twenty-five years had come and gone, but as the memory was fresh in his mind, and he fought the battles over again, some faint reflection of his own vivid impressions fell upon me, and I felt that to hear him describe Stonewall Jackson, was next to seeing the old hero himself.

From the outbreak of the war, Jackson had attached supreme importance to keeping possession of the Valley, as a barrier against invasion from the North. He said, "If the Valley is lost, Virginia is lost." But how to hold it against much greater forces, was the problem. With his quick military eye, he saw that it could only be done by what is known in war as an offensive-defensive campaign, in which the weaker side makes the attack, in order to prevent being closed in upon and crushed by overwhelming numbers.

"The Valley Campaign" of 1862, which was entirely Jackson's own, the Major looks upon as the most brilliant of the whole war. As we were riding in the carriage, he took out a pad, and drew a sketch of the country, showing the position of the several armies (for there were two or three operating at once against Jackson), in order to illustrate the latter's moves in this great game of war. Jackson had made a study of the campaigns of Napoleon, whose secret of victory he found to be in his marvellous combinations, and in *a rapidity of movement* of which there had been no example before. This was carrying into war the simple rule in mechanics, that the momentum of a ball depends on its weight *and its velocity;* and sometimes what is wanting in weight can be made up by increased velocity. Reasoning from this principle, Jackson was sure that what the French had done, Americans could do. He believed that an army could be marched twenty-five miles a day, and still retain strength to fight a battle : indeed he once marched his Stonewall Brigade forty miles! To do this, he must needs make the day a long one, by starting with the first streak of light in the east. This was his habit, so that the boys used to say, "He always marches at early dawn, *except when he starts the night before.*"

It is a study in war to see how he carried out this principle in the famous Valley Campaign. His principal antagonist in the field was General Banks at the head of a large army,* whose chief business seemed to be to watch Jackson, and keep him from crossing the Potomac and threatening Washington. At the same time Fremont was

---

* On the 6th of April, 1862, Banks reported 23,093 men present for duty. Ten weeks later (June 16th) he reported nearly ten thousand less, or 13,631.

menacing his left at the head of a force on the west, with which he might advance into the Valley and put himself in Jackson's rear. With these two enemies to look after, Jackson suddenly disappeared from the one in front (leaving Banks still "watching" his abandoned camp), and literally hurled his small force across half a dozen mountains and as many valleys, and struck Fremont a blow which sent him reeling down the valley of the South Branch of the Potomac; and then, before he could recover from it, he turned upon Banks, who, as soon as he had heard of Fremont's defeat, had fallen back in haste to Strasburg, where he was overtaken by Jackson, who gave him a similar "love-tap" that sent him on sixty miles farther, clear across the Potomac. The moral effect of these two defeats was not limited to those immediately engaged: it stopped McDowell, who was on the march with 40,000 men, to take part in the campaign against Richmond—a movement which was immediately arrested, that he might be held in a position to cover Washington. Having thus defeated two armies and paralyzed a third, Jackson obeyed the injunction to "gather up the fragments that nothing be lost." At Winchester the Government had accumulated enormous stores—the waggon train that took them up the Valley was fourteen miles long!—all of which fell into Jackson's hands, and was removed to Staunton to furnish supplies for the Confederate army. No wonder that they nicknamed Banks their Commissary General! But Jackson's work was not over, for other forces were gathering against him. McDowell was preparing to cross the mountains; while Fremont, who had been reinforced, was returning to the attack, so that Jackson was confronted by sixty thousand men approaching from opposite quarters. In the advance of such forces he fell back till he could place himself between the two; and then, facing about at Cross Keys, he gave Fremont a second blow as stunning as the first; and *the very next day* fought an equally decisive battle with McDowell's advance, under Shields, at Port Republic. This was the famous "Valley Campaign," and I leave it to the students of both to say, if there was anything more brilliant in the Italian campaigns of the First Napoleon.*

* For the reader who wishes to study this wonderful Campaign more minutely, Major Hotchkiss has kindly prepared a Map of the country, with lines indicating the direction of Jackson's movements, showing how he zigzagged all over the Valley, crossing rivers and mountains, to the widely separated points at which he fought his battles. The following note, written to accompany the Map, gives these rapid movements more in detail than they could be given in the text:

Jackson spent the Winter of 1861-2 at Winchester, holding the line of the Potomac, on the north bank of which, at Frederick City, Maryland, lay the Federal Army, under command of Gen. Banks, which began a forward movement Feb. 22d; crossing the Potomac at Harper's Ferry on the 24th, and appearing March 11th in the vicinity of Winchester, Jackson falling back towards Woodstock. Banks followed to the neighborhood of Strasburg, and then fell back and established his headquarters at Winchester. Learning that Banks was about to send part of his force to McClellan, Jackson advanced towards Winchester, and fought the battle of Kernstown, March 23. He then fell slowly back, reaching the vicinity of New Market on the 2d of April, Banks following to near Mount Jackson. On the 17th Banks advanced, and Jackson fell back to Harrisonburg, and then marching around the southwestern end of the Massanutton Mountains, and across the Shenandoah River, established himself at Conrad's Store on the 19th. Banks's next move was to Harrisonburg. On the last day of the month, April 30th, Jackson moved to near the southwestern end of the Massanutton Mountains, and offered battle. While absent from his camp that day, Ewell's Division of the Confederate Army came across the Blue Ridge at Swift Run Gap, and occupied Jackson's camp. Jackson returned to Conrad's Store, and then turned up the river towards Port Republic, struggling through quicksands and mud for two days to reach the vicinity of that village. On the 3d of May, Jackson crossed the Blue Ridge at Brown's Gap, apparently abandoning the Valley, and marched to Mecumk's River Station of the Virginia Central Railroad (now Chesapeake and Ohio), where his troops took the cars to Staunton. On the 6th he advanced to the top of the Big North Mountain, on the way to McDowell, and the next day attacked the advance of Fremont's army at Shenandoah Mountain, and the day after that fought the battle of McDowell, defeating Fremont, who retreated to Franklin, Jackson following in pursuit till the 11th. The next day, leaving Fremont at Franklin, Jackson turned back, and reaching McDowell on the 14th, marched to the vicinity of Bridgewater by the 17th, and on the 19th marched down the valley by way of Harrisonburg (Banks having in the meantime fallen back to Strasburg), reaching New Market on the 21st, where he turned across the Massanutton Mountains to the vicinity of Luray, where Ewell's Division joined him. Continuing down the South Fork Valley, he fell on Banks's right at Front Royal on the 23d, routing it, and crossing the rivers on the way to Middletown and Winchester. The next day he attacked Banks's retreating army at Middletown, following it all night to Winchester, where the battle of Winchester was fought on the morning of May 25th, and Banks's army defeated, and driven across the Potomac by way of Martinsburg. Jackson's advance marched to the vicinity of Harper's Ferry, where it remained until the 30th of May. Threatened by the concentration of Fremont's and McDowell's armies at Strasburg, Jackson collected his army southwest of that place, June 1st, in a strong position. As the Federal Army did not attack him, he fell back slowly up the Valley, reaching Harrisonburg June 5th, Fremont's army following, and McDowell's marching up the valley of the South Fork by way of Luray. Jackson fell back to Cross Keys, and awaited Fremont's advance, which attacked him June 8th, and was repulsed. That night Jackson crossed the river at Port Republic, and the next day (June 9th) fought the battle of Port Republic with McDowell's advance, at Lewiston, four miles below Port Republic, routing it completely. Jackson then encamped between the rivers, southwest of Port Republic, near the famous Weyer's Cave, where he remained until June 17th, when he marched for Richmond to form the left of General Lee's army in his attack on McClellan.

With almost any other leader, this incessant motion would only have brought on a speedy catastrophe : for it would have set his brain in such a whirl, that he would strike at random—uncertainly, and therefore unsuccessfully. But in these rapid marches and countermarches, with constant fighting, he never lost his head. Instead of his mind being confused by the incidents of battle, it was quickened to the utmost intensity of action. As long before as the Mexican war, when conversing with his brother officers as to the effect of the danger of battle upon their spirits, he said that to him "it was always exalting, and that he was conscious of a more perfect command of his faculties, and of their more clear and rapid action, when under fire, than at any other time."

One who had frequent occasion to see Jackson in all the vicissitudes of war, speaks thus of his "stoicism":

"Victory and defeat were received with the same degree of stolidity and unconcern. He never seemed elated by the one, nor depressed by the other. I saw him at the battle of Antietam, in the midst of the carnage, when the air was filled with flying shot and bursting shells; and he sat upon his horse as unmoved as if he were on dress parade. As the Confederate losses were very great, Lee ordered a retreat across the Potomac—a movement which was a very critical one, as a swollen river was behind us, and the Federal forces, directed by McClellan in person, were pressing us in front. Every moment added to the confusion. But during the whole scene Jackson maintained the same stoical demeanor. I watched his face and the expression of his eye. He gave his orders just as if all was going well, betraying no despondency, nor even any undue excitement. Again I have seen him where, as in his last effort at Chancellorsville, he swept everything before him. But he showed no more elation in the hour of victory than of depression in the hour of defeat. He contemplated both with the complacency of a Moslem, as if he were a child of destiny, or rather simply an instrument in the hand of the Almighty to execute His will."

Some who are disposed to be critical of great military achievements, ascribe this marvellous success, not to the genius of Jackson, so much as to the weakness of those opposed to him; and indeed it is hardly probable that he would have "careered" up and down the Valley so triumphantly, if instead of Banks and Fremont, he had struck Sheridan. But with all abatements, it must be confessed that he showed a wonderful capacity and vigor.

Of course, his success could not have been obtained without rigid military discipline. While kind to his men, he would tolerate no disobedience. Once on a march, fearing lest his men might stray from the ranks and commit acts of pillage, he had issued an order that the soldiers should not enter private dwellings. Disregarding the order, a soldier entered a house, and even used insulting language to the women of the family. This was reported to Jackson, who had the man arrested, tried by drum-head court-martial, and shot in twenty minutes!

Again, three men had deserted, and were retaken and sentenced to death. Their old companions made every effort to save them, but Jackson was inexorable. To an officer who petitioned for their pardon, he answered sharply, "You ought to be ashamed of yourself! Here are my brave men exposing their lives, and these cowards run away, and leave their comrades to fight the battle alone." Then the chaplain tried a religious appeal, telling the General that "if those men were shot, they would certainly go to hell!" "That is my business," said Jackson as he turned upon him with disgust, and seizing him by the shoulders, literally whirled him out of his presence. The men were shot the next morning.

Indeed Jackson was perhaps a little too ready in these matters, presenting in this respect a contrast to Lee, who was always disposed to leniency. Once they were riding together, when some cases of trespass were reported, at which Lee said, "We shall have to shoot some of these fellows yet." Instantly Jackson caught at the word, and said, "I will have them shot to-morrow," to which his commander answered in a way that showed that he did not mean to be taken in such grim earnest as to order his soldiers to immediate execution.

But the most remarkable thing in this extraordinary man, was the union of the soldier and the saint. It was no ordinary faith that had possession of his mind: he lived and moved and had his being in God. No Roundhead of Cromwell, no ancient Crusader, had more absolute assurance that he was simply an agent of the Divine will. One who knew him well, says that "he was always praying when he was not fighting," two things which seem not to go together, yet that have been combined in some who were at once great soldiers and religious fanatics. Macaulay records the fanatical enthusiasm of one of Cromwell's Roundheads as, bursting out in a kind of holy frenzy, he exclaimed "Oh how good it is to pray and fight!" So was it with Stonewall Jackson. In his view, a human being could no more stand in the way of a Divine decree than in the path of one of his own cannon balls. Sufficient for him was it that he could be the humble agent of executing the Almighty will. If one had broken in upon his tent before he went into battle, he might have found him on his knees in an agony of prayer that God would give him the victory; those who rode beside him on the march, often observed that his lips were moving in silent prayer; and when the battle was won, he always recognized it as not by his own wisdom or valor, but by the favor of that Almighty Ruler to whom he bowed again in humble thanksgiving.

As he was so strict in his own religious habits, this

modern Roundhead kept Sunday in the camp as if he had been at home. To be sure, he had sometimes to fight a battle on that day, but in that case he made it up by keeping another day in its stead. "Sometimes," said the Major, "he would keep two or three Sundays running, to make up for lost time, so as to balance the account!"

In the afternoon of the day we were riding up the Valley, we passed a beautiful grove which recalled some reminiscences to my companion. "In this very grove," he said, "we spent a Sabbath in the Summer of 1862. We had divine service, and all was as still as in any Sabbath-keeping village of New England. The tents were pitched under the trees; and the soldiers were stretched on the ground, resting after the fatigues of their long marches and hard battles. The next day the General sat apart, brooding over something in his mind, but what it was he communicated to no one: for he never told his plans to anybody. Not a word did he whisper to me, though I shared his confidence as much as any one, and we often slept under the same blanket. Towards evening he sent for me, and asked to see the maps of the country towards Staunton, which I brought, and he pored over them a good while, and then said carelessly, 'By the way, they are having some fighting towards Richmond: have you any maps of the country there?' I brought them, and he looked at them, but without any sign of eagerness or mark of peculiar interest. About ten that night he called me and said, 'Please mount your horse and ride to such a point in the Valley, and tell Colonel M—— to go ahead!' It was pitch dark: but I picked my way over the blind roads, till about midnight I reached the place, and delivered the order. I did not return until the next morning. About nine o'clock I reached the grove in which we had been encamped the day before, but not a soldier was to be

AT CHANCELLORSVILLE

seen! Every tent had been struck; there was not an army-waggon, not a single piece of artillery, not a man, nor a gun. An army of 20,000 men had vanished as completely as the host of Sennacherib when

> "The might of the Gentile, unsmote by the sword,
> Had melted like snow in the glance of the Lord."

It was all a riddle and a mystery, till, when it was explained, it was seen to be a marvel of military genius and execution. The errand of my friend was to carry an order to the Colonel who was left in command in the Valley, to make a demonstration towards Winchester, to keep up the impression that the Valley was still to be the scene of important military operations, while Jackson executed one of his astonishing marches, through a gap in the mountains, and when next heard from was striking the right wing of McClellan's army advancing towards Richmond! That flank attack was the blow that decided the fate of the Peninsula Campaign.

But it would be too long a story to follow him in all his marches and battles. The Major was with him to his last and greatest victory at Chancellorsville: indeed as topographical engineer he had studied the position, and pointed out the opportunity which it presented for a great flank movement. That movement decided the day, the glory of which Lee justly ascribed to the "skill and energy" of Jackson. When the sun set on that day, it seemed as if the Confederates had gained a victory that might end the war. But Jackson never left a success incomplete, and even when night came on, and one could hardly distinguish friend from foe, he was still pressing to the front, and even beyond his own lines, to find the position of the enemy, which he no sooner discovered than he ordered a new line of battle of fresh troops to be formed for immediate action; and then riding back with his staff

THE FLANK MOVEMENT.

and escort at full speed, the rush of horses was mistaken by the "new line of battle" that had been thrown across the road after he had ridden forward, for a charge of cavalry, and was fired upon by his own men.* It was an accident

* An officer who took part in this flank movement, gives the following account of what passed under his own eyes, and of the circumstances of Jackson's death:

"On Saturday morning General Lee and Stonewall Jackson came and sat down under a tree near where I was, with a map spread out between them. [The Major was one of that group, and adds yet more minute details of the scene. He says: "Lee and Jackson were seated on two empty cracker boxes, that had been left from the camp of the Federals, which had been pitched there the day before; while on a third I had spread out a map that I had prepared, showing the whole position, with the direction of every road."] General Lee, with a pencil in hand, explained the position, and Jackson from time to time nodded assent, at the close of which Jackson called his chief-of-staff, Major Pendleton. A few moments later the troops were moving off at double-quick in an entirely unlooked-for direction. As each regiment passed, Jackson said a few hurried words to the commanding officer. To me he said: 'Detail a strong guard, and keep your own position with them behind your men. Bayonet any stragglers, and keep the ranks closed up.' In addition to this precaution, he kept a squadron of cavalry in the rear, to keep the men up in the march. Thus urged on, the column moved forward silently but rapidly for nine miles, with only three halts to catch breath.

"The first intimation that I had that we were in the presence of the enemy, was the sight of deserted camp-fires, dressed beeves, coffee-pots, and steaks still broiling on the gridiron. This was a tempting sight to our men, who were always poorly fed and very hungry, but they could not stop, and each man grabbed what he could and kept on. One man attempted to dispose of the whole of a beefsteak as he ran, and others drank at double-quick from the spouts of steaming coffee-pots.

"The next sight which greeted us, was a long line of knapsacks stacked up in piles behind the Federal rifle-pits, in front of which had that might have happened on either side in the gathering gloom. He fell from his horse into the arms of one of his staff, and was found to be wounded in two places, in his right hand and in his left arm. Both were at once tied up to stop the flow of blood; but such was the confusion that it was some time before a stretcher could be brought to carry him to the rear, where he could receive proper attention. At length it came, and the bearers raised up their beloved chief, but had gone only a few steps when one of them was killed by a shot of cannister from a Federal battery, and he was thrown to the ground with a violence that caused him intense agony. Again he was lifted up and started on his way. Meanwhile the Major had gone for the surgeon, Dr. McGuire, who took him in an ambulance to the rear, where he found the arm so shattered that it must be amputated immediately, to which the General submitted with his usual fortitude.

But the wound was considered by no means fatal. Nothing was needed but care and rest. That he might

been left a line of Confederate skirmishers and sharp-shooters, to deceive the enemy with a show of attack *in front*, who were only apprised of the change of base, as Jackson's ubiquitous and irresistible 'Stonewall Brigade' came charging down upon them *from the rear!*

"Towards evening I had deployed my regiment as skirmishers, when a squadron of Federal cavalry rode right into our midst, and we bagged them to the last man. Just then Jackson rode up with a few staff officers, and said, '*Colonel, fire at anything that comes from that direction!*' This order, which it was my fortune to receive, was the last Stonewall Jackson ever gave. He then rode on to reconnoitre the position of the enemy. Later my regiment was relieved by one of the North Carolina infantry, to whose Colonel I repeated Jackson's order. In a few moments Jackson and his staff and escort came riding back rapidly, and the men of this regiment mistook them, as it was then dark, for another squadron of Federal cavalry, and fired!"

be away from the noise of the camp, and in a place of safety, he was carried a few miles across the country to a private house west of Fredericksburg, near Guiney's Station, which was pointed out to me as we came up from Richmond. Here for a few days he seemed to be on the road to recovery. The Major, who accompanied him thither, found him the following day cheerful and hopeful. Indeed, with his strong religious faith, he felt that he *could not die*, for he was sure that "the Lord had more for him to do," and he fully expected to get well, and to take part in the campaign. But even then he would not let those around him pray for his recovery, *except in entire submission to the Divine will*, and that will had decreed otherwise. The shock had been very great from his double wound, with the loss of blood, the fall from the litter, and the amputation; and when, after all this, pneumonia set in, the end was inevitable.

It was on the Sabbath day that he saw the light for the last time. He said "I have always desired to die on Sunday," and his wish was granted. The sun rose brightly that morning—the tenth of May, 1863—and though he had been told that this day would be his last, he would not keep his chaplain at his bedside, but insisted that he should go to headquarters, and preach as usual. It was a sorrowful service, for all hearts were bowed with a sense of the great loss that was impending. When it closed, General Lee inquired eagerly for the latest news, and when told that Jackson could not live through the day, he turned away, unable to control his emotion. Even then he was passing through the valley of the shadow of death. He still breathed, but his mind was wandering. Perhaps a gleam from the river of life caught his dying eye, as he murmured faintly, "Let us cross over the river, and rest under the trees," and the strong, brave heart stood still.

BURIED AT LEXINGTON.

The death of Jackson caused universal mourning throughout the Confederacy, where he was regarded as the greatest of the Southern leaders, with the exception only of General Lee. It took away all the exultation of Chancellorsville. As the Commander-in-chief himself said, "Any victory would be too dear at such a price." It was but a melancholy consolation to pay the highest honors to his memory. The body was borne to Richmond and laid in state in the Capitol, where tens of thousands thronged to look for the last time on the face that they had seen so often amid the smoke and thunder of battle; and then they carried him away to his last resting-place among the hills which he so much loved. Spending Sunday in Lexington, I went to the church where Jackson had worshipped for ten years, after which two of the Professors who had been associated with him, took me to the spot where he rests. It is on a hill-top, looking down into the peaceful valley, beyond which rise the everlasting hills. "As the mountains are round about Jerusalem," so are they round about Lexington, and no saint or soldier could desire a better spot in which to lie down and sleep till the heavens be no more.

In the opinion of many the death of Jackson was a fatal blow to the Confederacy. No one felt the loss so much as General Lee, when two months later, he fought the battle of Gettysburg, the result of which might have been victory if his "right arm" had not been taken from him. But that was not to be. The Ruler of Nations had ordained a different issue—a fact which we have to recognize, even if we cannot explain. It is not necessary to go quite so far as a good priest of New Orleans, an ardent Confederate, a chaplain of one of Jackson's Louisiana regiments, who felt called upon, in a prayer at the unveiling of a monument to Jackson, to offer an excuse for the Almighty, which he did in this remarkable address to the Throne of grace : " When *in Thine inscrutable decree* it was ordained that the Confederacy should not succeed, *it became necessary for Thee to remove Stonewall Jackson!*" But we need not inquire into the purposes of Him with whom are the issues of life and death. Without attempting what does not belong to us, we can recognize the great qualities of the heroic dead, and on this day of peace, beautiful as the Sabbath on which he died, I would place a flower on the grave of Stonewall Jackson.

Six months passed, and I visited Lexington again, and once more turned aside to stop at the gate of the old Cemetery, and walked along the path trodden by so many feet, to the well known spot which attracts so many pilgrims. I found beside it a new made grave, which had been opened but a few days before to receive the only daughter of Stonewall Jackson, who was but a babe when her father died, and was brought to him in his last moments to be laid upon his bed to receive a last fond caress. Little seemed it then that she would be with him again so soon. But with gentle footsteps she, like the true daughter that she was, has followed him till she too has "passed over the river"; and now the warrior and his child, forgetting all the sorrows of this troubled life, "rest together under the trees" in the Paradise of God.

CHAPTER XIX.

THE LAST YEARS OF GENERAL LEE.

"The last hope of the Confederacy was dead when Stonewall Jackson was laid in his grave at Lexington!" So said the Major after he had taken the greater part of a day in detailing to me, to my intense interest, the marvellous career of that great soldier. But not so reasoned all those who had fought by Jackson's side. Not so Jackson himself: for when, on hearing of his wound, Lee wrote to him, "Could I have directed events, I should have chosen, for the good of the country, to have been disabled in your stead," he answered, "No, no! Better that ten Jacksons should fall than one Lee!" And now, though Jackson was dead, Lee still lived, and hope lived with him; victory was still possible; and in that faith, and under that leadership, the Confederates fought on for two years more. (Jackson died on the 10th of May, 1863; but Lee did not surrender till the 9th of April, 1865.) How well they fought is matter of history. They fought as they could *not* have fought, had they not been led by a great Commander. From the very beginning of his military career, all around him recognized his extraordinary capacity. General Scott, with whom he served in Mexico, pronounced him "*the very* *best soldier that he ever saw in the field.*" But the greatest proof of his ability was when he did not serve under anybody, but planned his own campaigns. Some military critics I know assume to criticize him even here. To such I have only to say that it is a very poor compliment to *our* leaders and our armies, to question the ability of one who, with less than half the numbers,* kept back for two years the tremendous forces of the North that were pressing in on every side. Whatever others may say of General Lee, the great soldiers who fought against him, fully concede his splendid military genius.

But it is not my purpose to speak of his military career. That belongs to history. "The world knows it by heart." But there is a chapter in that life which the world does not know so well, which ought to be told, to the greater honor of the illustrious dead.

The war was over. The Northern armies had returned victorious, while the veterans of the South, defeated but not dishonored, took their way back to their desolate homes. The army disbanded and dispersed, what should its leader do? His old ancestral home, standing on that noble height which looks down on the Potomac, and across to the dome of the Capitol, was in the hands of those against whom he had been fighting for four years, and had even been turned into a national cemetery, in which slept thousands of the Union dead, whose very ghosts might rise up against his return. But if he was an exile from his own home, there were thousands of others

---

* When the surrender took place, almost the first question which General Meade asked General Lee, was "How many men had you at Petersburg and in your lines, when they were broken?" "Forty thousand," was the reply. "I am amazed," said Meade, "and could not believe it, if it were not you that said it."

open to him all over the South, and across the sea, where his fame had gone before him, and would have made him a welcome guest in princely halls. But such a flight from his country (for so he would have regarded it) was impossible to one of his chivalrous spirit. He had cast in his lot with his people : they had believed in him and followed him, as they thought, to certain triumph ; he would not desert them in the day of their adversity.

Of course, had he been willing to listen to them, he could have received any number of "business" proposals. Rich moneyed corporations would have been glad to "retain" him at any price as President or Director, so that they could have the benefit of his great name. One, it is said, offered him $50,000 a year. But he was not to be allured by such temptations. The very fact that they were coupled with offers of money, was reason enough why he should reject them all, as he did without a moment's hesitation. Nor could he be lured by any military proposals. Maximilian offered to place him at the head of his army if he would go to Mexico, thinking that his genius might save the fortunes of the falling empire. But he would not accept any exile, however splendid. His answer was "I love the mountains of Virginia still." His work must be at home, for work he must have. After his active life he could not sink down into idleness. With his military career ended, he must find a new career in civil life. Besides, he had a proud spirit of independence, which would not permit him to live on the bounty of the rich at home, or the titled abroad. He would "work for a living," like the poorest of his soldiers.

At length came a proposal that seemed most alien to his former pursuits : that the Commander of the Southern Armies should become the President of a College! And yet this change from a military to an academic career, was not so violent as it might seem. He had been for three years Superintendent of the Military Academy at West Point, where he was associated with young men, an intimacy which was continued during the whole period that he was in the army. He was at home among students, for he had been a student, and gone through all the stages of scholarly discipline. Besides, the position of the College to which he was invited, in Lexington, Virginia, was attractive to him. It was remote from cities, among the mountains, and yet within the limits of that Old Dominion which he looked upon as his mother.

When it was known that he had accepted the position, his coming was looked for with great eagerness by the people of Lexington; but he did not fix the time, as he wished to avoid any public demonstration. But it had been arranged that *when* he came, he should spend a few days in the hospitable dwelling in which I was so fortunate as to be a guest. While thus in expectancy, the Professor was one day taking a walk, when he saw riding up the street a figure that he instantly recognized as the same that had been so often seen at the head of the army; and to make the picture perfect, he was mounted on his old war-horse—a magnificent iron-gray called "Traveller"— that had so often borne his master through the smoke of battle. He wore no military uniform, nor sign of rank, but a light Summer dress, while a broad Panama hat shaded a face that no one could mistake. Advancing towards him, the Professor told of the arrangements for his entertainment till he could be established in a house for himself, and led the way to his home.

Naturally my friend's family were at first somewhat awed by the presence of their illustrious guest. But this was soon dissipated by his simple and unaffected manner. What "broke the ice" most completely was his manner with the children. He was always very fond of the little people,* and as soon as they appeared, "Uncle Robert," as he was affectionately called in the army, had them in his arms and on his knees, till they soon felt perfectly at home with him. They "captured" him at once, and he "captured" them, and in this captured their parents also. From that moment all constraint disappeared, though nothing could ever take from the profound respect and veneration with which they looked up to "General Lee."

This was in September, 1865, and on the 2d of October, after solemn prayer by the venerable Dr. White, he took the oath of office, as required by the laws of the College, and thus became its President. Naturally his name drew great numbers of students, not only from Virginia, but from all parts of the South, who were eager to "serve" under such a leader, and the number of undergraduates rose from a hundred and fifty to over four hundred.

From this some may imagine that he was expected to be, and that he was, a mere figure-head to the Institution. No mistake could be greater. From the moment that he took the office, he applied himself to its duties with conscientious fidelity. He did not teach in the classes, though he *might* have taught in any department, for he was an excellent scholar, both in classics and in mathematics; but like a good soldier, he wished to take his place where he could be the most useful, and clearly his office was that of general superintendence. He visited all the class-rooms, not in regular course, but coming when not expected, and followed each professor in his lecture, generally asking

---

* This love of children, and other domestic traits, are very beautifully depicted in an article in the Century Magazine for June, 1889, by Mrs. Margaret J. Preston, a personal friend as well as neighbor of General Lee during all the time of his residence in Lexington.

some questions at the close. He informed himself of the standing of each student, and the rules of study were as rigid as military discipline, the alternative being "study or the plough"! If any college boy was idle, or disposed to shirk his books, he was summoned to the President's office for a gentle admonition—so gentle indeed, that when he came away, his fellow students were apt to say, "Who said 'Good-morning' first?"—that is, "Did you know when General Lee was done with you?"

One gift he had which stood him in good stead at the head of a College as at the head of an army: he understood in perfection the art of administering rebuke in a way to be effective, and yet not to leave too deep a sting. In this there could be no greater difference between two men than there was between Lee and Jackson, which had frequent illustration in the army in the way they showed their displeasure at one particular form of rudeness. I hope it will not be set down as a mark of disloyalty to their native State, that they did not pay tribute to its chief staple, *tobacco*, which neither of them took, or could tolerate, in any form. Both had a positive dislike to it, which they did not hesitate to express, though each in a characteristic way. If an officer came into Jackson's presence, puffing the smoke of a cigar in his face, he was very likely to get a rough salutation, which sent him to the right about in double quick time, and taught him better manners in the future. But General Lee could not administer a rebuke except in a courtly way. If an officer rode up to deliver a message, or in military phrase, to make a report, and the General perceived that he had a cigar in his mouth, or even in his hand, he would not mortify him by a sharp thrust, but turn the point of his own rapier by a compliment. If, on a glance at the shoulder-straps of the new comer, he perceived that he was a Major, he would address him as "Colonel," thus putting him a peg higher in military rank, and then add in his blandest manner, as if to relieve him from embarrassment, "I will excuse you till you have finished your cigar," a gentle reminder that he had forgotten the courtesy due to his superior, which, while it did not wound his pride so openly, touched his sense of propriety not less than the blunt and somewhat scornful reprimand of Stonewall Jackson.

In one respect his influence was immeasurable. Every man in the South looked up to General Lee as the highest type of manhood, and his very presence was an inspiration. This is the influence which young men feel more than any other—that inspired by intense admiration—an influence that would have been very potent for evil if the object of their admiration had been merely a great soldier, dazzling them by his genius, but destitute of high principle. Had that been the case, his influence would have been as demoralizing as now it was elevating, since his superiority in all other respects was united with a character that was so gentle and so good.

That he might reach the young men in College, he sought their acquaintance, instead of standing apart in icy dignity. Prof. White tells me that, if they were walking together in the grounds, and a student was seen approaching, he would ask who he was, and when he came up, instead of passing him with a stiff and stately bow, would stop and call him by name, and ask about his family and his studies, and speak a few words of encouragement, which the young man would not forget to his dying day. To be under the authority and influence of such a man, was an education in manliness. There was not a student who did not feel it, and to whom it was not the highest ambition to be guided by such a leader, to be infused with his spirit, and to follow his example.

From the first he attached great importance in any system of education to Religion. He was himself a devout member of the Episcopal Church, and no one was more regular in attendance on its services. No one knelt with more humility in the house of God, or responded more fervently to the prayers. But it was not merely because he found his own personal comfort in this faith or worship that he desired it for others. He believed that Religion lies at the foundation of all that is worthy to be called character. In his long military life, which was of necessity a public one, he had seen a great deal of men of the world—men of society, men of fashion—and he knew how all this outward grace might cover the meanest selfishness and the blackest heart. He had come to feel more and more that one could not be truly great who was not truly good; that life was not given for pleasure only, but that it had grave responsibilities; and he wished his young men to recognize that they had duties to others as well as to themselves, and that the truest heroism was in self-forgetfulness and self-denial. This type of character, he knew, could not be formed on mere sentiment: it could be inspired only by a profound religious faith; and so he esteemed it as above all science to "know God." If he had been the College pastor, he could not have been more earnest that his large household should be infused with spiritual life; and hence he often expressed to the pastors of the churches around him his desire for "a revival" in the College; that the young men should go out, not only thoroughly educated, but having in them the elements of a strong religious character.

Soon after he came to Lexington a house was built for him in the row of the College buildings. It is a very plain brick house, with nothing pretentious without or within. Here he lived the life of a modest country gentleman,

HIS CAUTION IN SPEAKING OF OTHERS. 303

seldom going away from home, and then only to the White Sulphur Springs, or some other quiet resting place. Now and then he paid a visit to his old home in Richmond, and once or twice to Baltimore. Once he was called to Washington to give testimony before a Committee of Congress, when he was received by General Grant, who was then President, with the distinction which belonged to him. But he never went North, and indeed with these exceptions, scarcely went beyond the bounds of his own beloved Virginia. Accustomed in the field to the saddle, he still loved the exercise, and was often seen riding over the hills around Lexington, either alone, or accompanied by one of his daughters. He was fond of plain country people, and delighted to rein up by the roadside, and talk with the farmers about their farms and their crops; and no painter or poet could enjoy more intensely the beauties of nature, the hills and valleys, the woods and waters, the sun-risings and sun-settings.

Of course, wherever he went he was an object of curiosity, and sometimes it required all his tact to parry the advances of those who intruded upon him. Some with more eagerness than politeness, asked him questions about his battles, even his opinion of the officers who served under him, or those who fought against him. To such questions he always made a courteous reply, even while avoiding a direct answer, for while he was too modest to speak of himself and what he had done, he was very reticent in speaking of other military men in either army. He knew that whatever fell from his lips would be repeated, and not always as he said it, but with a change of words, or in a different tone of voice, that might give it quite another meaning. Indeed with all his caution, he was often quoted as saying what he did not say. As an illustration, Prof. White told me that a story had gone the rounds of the papers to the effect that in a conversation Gen. Lee had brought his clenched hand down on the table, to give emphasis to his utterance, as he said, "If I had had Stonewall Jackson with me I should have won the battle of Gettysburg and established the Southern Confederacy!" "Now," said the Professor, "without ever asking him, I *know* that such an occurrence never took place, for in the first place General Lee never 'brought his hand down on the table'—he was not that sort of man—it is impossible to conceive of him as using any violence of gesture or of language. And as to Stonewall Jackson, while he did feel keenly the absence of that great corps-commander, he was not the man to indulge in sweeping and positive statements; he never spoke with such absolute assurance of anything, but always with a degree of reserve, as once, when we were riding together, he said in his usual guarded and cautious manner: 'If I had had Stonewall Jackson with me—*so far as man can see*—I should have won the battle of Gettysburg.' So careful was he to put in this qualification: for he always recognized an overruling Power that may disappoint the wisest calculations, and defeat the most careful combinations of courage and skill."

To the same habit of reserve we must ascribe it, at least in part, that he never wrote anything in regard to his own military career. The friend to whom I have referred so often, Major Jed. Hotchkiss, writes me that "it was the intention of General Lee to write his 'Memoirs,' following the example of his father, 'Light Horse Harry' of the Revolution; but that his private papers were all burned by a foolish guard, who was left in charge of his waggon, and who, when it was about to be captured, set fire to it, thus destroying the records which would furnish the most accurate information. Still he did not relinquish his purpose, but began collecting materials for it, and asked me to prepare the maps to illustrate his campaigns. I went to Washington for him to get copies of his reports from the captured archives, but they would not let him have them then; and afterwards, when they were more willing, his health had given way, and it was too late." This is a great loss to history. Of course whatever papers were captured at Richmond, and transferred to Washington, may still be preserved to furnish the materials of history. But it is not the same thing to have these materials "worked up" by some future historian, as to have them used by the very man who dictated these orders and despatches. There is a fascination in the story of a great war told by one who was a chief actor in it. Cæsar wrote his own Commentaries: and the conversations of Napoleon at St. Helena furnish invaluable materials for the history of that great soldier. So with our General Grant. No man was more modest, or more reserved and shy, and it was only the pressure of sudden disaster overwhelming his household that forced our Ulysses the Silent to break through his accustomed reserve, and tell a story that, though told with a soldier-like simplicity, is of marvellous interest. So it would have been a priceless contribution to history if we could have had the other side of our civil war told by the pen of General Lee. Had he but opened his lips, the whole world would have listened to the thrilling story. But he may well have been reluctant, not alone because of want of materials or failing health, but also because it would bring back too many painful memories. Even a soldier's courage might hesitate to renew the anguish that was being softened by time; to call up again the hopes and fears that belonged to what was irrevocably past. And if he had written, he would have had to pass judgment on his old companions-in-arms, the living and the dead—an ungrateful task, from which he, with his extreme reluctance to give pain, might well shrink. And so he died and made no sign.

With all this in mind, I went to the house where he lived and died. It is occupied by his son, General Custis Lee, who succeeded him as President of the College—a man of such extreme modesty that only those who know him intimately know his real worth : how much there is in him of his illustrious father. I had a letter to him from the Hon. John Randolph Tucker, and he received me with great kindness, and showed me the house, which, plain as it is, has its treasures. As he is the great-grandson of Mrs. Custis, who after the death of her first husband became the wife of Washington, he has inherited many household articles which belonged to the Father of his Country— the old family plate on the side-board, and the old family pictures hanging on the wall. But of even more interest is whatever is connected with General Lee — the home in which he lived for five years—the chamber in which he slept; the library in which he received his friends ; the books around him ; the table at which he wrote ; and the dining-room in which he died ; for it was here, while standing at the head of his table, in the very act of asking a blessing, that he received the fatal stroke. As he sank into his chair, those around him caught him and raised him up, and brought a bed and placed him upon it, but did not attempt to carry him to his room. Here he lay for two weeks, between life and death, saying but little, though conscious apparently that the end was approaching. One who watched with him, Colonel Preston Johnston, has described the scene, as he "lay in the darkened room, with the lamp and the hearth-fire casting shadows upon his noble face," so calm and peaceful with the greater shadow that now rested upon it. "Once in the solemn watches of the night," he says, "when I handed him the prescribed nourishment, he turned upon me with a look of friendly recognition, and then cast down his eyes with such a sadness in them as I can never forget. But he spoke not a word: not because he was unable—for at times he did speak brief sentences with distinct enunciation*— but because he saw (before the family or friends or physician) the portals of death opening to him, and chose to wrap himself in an unbroken silence as he went down to enter them." Thus he lingered till on the morning of the 12th of October, 1870, the tolling bells announced to the sorrowing community that he had breathed his last.

From the house it is but a few rods across the College grounds to the chapel, in the rear of which is a recess, where lies a recumbent statue of the great leader. It is in marble, and represents the soldier at full length, as we have seen in old cathedrals the bronze effigies of those whose crossed limbs tell how they took up arms for the Cross, and fought for the recovery of the Holy Sepulchre at Jerusalem. But it is no mailed Crusader that is stretched upon the tomb: for the hand that once grasped the sword, is folded on the breast, and the whole impression is one of profound repose. It is a heroic figure, full of strength, as of a warrior taking his rest, and yet over all there is an expression of calm, as of one with whom the battle of life is over; who hears no more the morning drum-beat or the trumpet's call:

"He sleeps his last sleep; he has fought his last battle;
No sound shall awake him to glory again."

* This was probably in the earlier part of his illness, or if later, could only have been at intervals, for General Custis Lee, who was constantly at his father's bedside, says that he "made repeated efforts to speak to him, but could not from utter exhaustion and weakness." So it was that the wave of life kept moving to and fro, sometimes being strong enough for utterance, and then ebbing too fast for the lips to move.

While standing here, in the very presence of death, I am moved to say a few words in regard to the life that ended in this tomb, and the character of the man whose name it bears. As I read history, and compare the men who have figured in the events that make history —in wars and revolutions—it seems to me that General Lee was not only a great soldier, but a great man, one of the greatest that our country has produced. After his death, the College which had hitherto borne the name of Washington, by whom it was endowed, was re christened "Washington *and Lee* University"—a combination which suggests a comparison of the two men whose names are here brought together. Can we trace any likeness between them? At first it seems as if no characters, as well as no careers, could be more alien to each other, than those of the two great leaders, one of whom was the Founder of the Government which the other did his utmost to destroy. But nature brings forth her children in strange couples, with resemblances in some cases as marked, and yet as unexpected, as are contrasts in others. Washington and Lee, though born in different centuries, were children of the same mother, Old Virginia, and had her best blood in their veins. Descended from the stock of the English Cavaliers, both were born gentlemen, and never could be anything else. Both were trained in the school of war, and as leaders of armies it would not be a violent assumption to rank Lee as the equal of Washington. But it is not in the two soldiers, but in the two men, that the future historian will find points of resemblance.

Washington was not a brilliant man; not a man of genius, such as now and then appears to dazzle mankind; but he had what was far better than genius—a combination of all the qualities that win human trust; in which intelligence is so balanced by judgment, and exalted by character, as to constitute a natural superiority; indicating one who is born to command, and to whom all men turn, when their hearts are "failing them for fear," as a leader. He was great not only in action, but in repose: great in his very calm—in the fortitude with which he bore himself through all changes of fortune, through dangers and disasters, neither elated by victory nor depressed by defeat—mental habitudes which many will recognize as reappearing in one who seems to have formed himself upon that great model.

Washington was distinguished for his magnanimity, a virtue in which no one more closely followed him than Lee. Men in public station are apt to be sensitive to whatever concerns their standing before the world; and so, while taking to themselves the credit of success, they are strongly tempted to throw upon others the blame of failure. Soldiers especially are jealous of their reputation; and if a commander loses a battle, his first impulse is to cast the odium of defeat upon some unfortunate officer. Somebody blundered; this or that subordinate did not do his duty. Military annals are filled with these recriminations. If Napoleon met with a check in his mighty plans, he had no scruple in laying it to the misconduct of some lieutenant, unless as in Russia, he could throw it upon the elements, the wintry snows and the frozen rivers—anything to relieve himself from the imputation of the want of foresight, or provision for unexpected danger. At Waterloo it was not *he* that failed in his strategy, but Marshal Ney that failed in the execution. In this respect, General Lee was exactly his opposite. If he suffered a disaster, he never sought to evade responsibility by placing it upon others. Even in the greatest reverse of his life, the defeat at Gettysburg, when he saw the famous charge of Pickett melt away under the terrible fire that swept the field, till the ranks were literally torn in pieces by shot and shell, he did not vent his despair in rage and reproaches, but rushing to the front, took the blame upon himself, saying, "*It is all my fault.*" Perhaps no incident of his life showed more the nobility of his nature.

When the war was over, General Lee had left to him at Lexington about the same number of years that Napoleon had at St. Helena; and if he had had the same desire to pose for posterity in the part of the illustrious exile, his mountain home would have furnished as picturesque a background as the rocky Island in the South Atlantic, from which he could have dictated "Conversations" that should furnish the materials of history. He need not have written or published a single line, if he had only been willing to let others do it for him. By their pens he had opportunity to tell of the great part he had acted in the war, in a way to make the whole chain of events contribute to his fame. But he seemed to care little for fame, and indeed was unmoved when others claimed the credit of his victories. If it be, as Pascal says, "the truest mark of a great mind to be born without envy," few men in history have shown more of this greatness than he. And when, as was sometimes the case, old companions-in-arms reflected upon him to excuse their own mistakes, he had only to lift the veil from the secrets of history to confound them. But under all such temptations, he was dumb. Nothing that he *did* or *said* was more truly grand than the *silence* with which he bore the misrepresentations of friend and foe. This required a self-command such as Washington had not to exercise at the end of his military career: for he retired from the scene crowned with victory, with a whole nation at his feet ready to do him honor; while Lee had to bear the reproach of the final disaster—a reproach in which friends sometimes joined with foes. Yet to both he answered only with the same majestic calm, the outward sign of his inward self-control. Such magnanimity belongs to the very highest order of moral qualities, and shows a character rare in any country or in any age.

This impression of the man does not grow less with closer observation. With the larger number of "historical characters," the greatness is magnified by distance and separation. As we come nearer they dwindle in stature, till, when we are in their very presence, and look them squarely in the face, they are found to be but men like ourselves, and sometimes very ordinary men—with some special ability perhaps, which gives them success in the world, but who for all that are full of the selfishness which is the very essence of meanness, and puffed up with a paltry conceit and vanity that stamps them as little rather than great.

Far different was the impression made by General Lee upon those who saw him in the freedom of private intercourse. It might be expected that the soldiers who fought under him, should speak with admiration and pride of their old Commander; but how did he appear to his neighbors? Here in Lexington everybody knew him, at least by sight; they saw his manner of life from day to day, in his going out and his coming in; and to all the impression was the same: the nearer he came to them the greater he seemed. Every one has some anecdote to tell of him, and it is always of something that was noble and lovable. Those who knew him best, loved him most and revered him most. This was not a greatness that was put on, like a military cloak: it was in the man, and could not be put on or put off; it was the greatness which comes from the very absence of pretension.

And those who came the closest to him, give us a still further insight into his nature, by telling us that what struck them most, was the extent of his sympathy. Soldiers are commonly supposed to be cold and hard—a temper of mind to which they are inured by their very profession. Those whose business is the shedding of blood, are thought to delight in human suffering. It is hard to believe that a soldier can have a very tender heart. Yet few men were more sensitive to others' pain than General Lee. All who came near him perceived that with his manly strength, there was united an almost womanly sweetness. It was this gentleness which made him great, and which has enshrined him forever in the hearts of his people.

This sympathy for the suffering showed itself, not in any public act so much as a more private and delicate office which imposed upon him a very heavy burden—one that he might have declined, but the taking of which showed the man. He had an unlimited correspondence. Letters poured in upon him by the hundred and the thousand. They came from all parts of the South, not only from his old companions-in-arms, but from those he had never seen or heard of. Every mother that had lost a son in the war, felt that she had the right to pour her sorrow into the ear of one who was not insensible to her grief. Families left in utter poverty appealed to him for aid. Most men would have shrunk from a labor so great as that of answering these letters. Not so General Lee. He read them, not only patiently, as a man performs a disagreeable duty, but with a tender interest, and so far as was possible, returned the kindest answers. If he had little money to give, he could at least give sympathy, and to his old soldiers and their wives and children it was more than money to know that they had a place in that great heart.

While thus ministering to his stricken people, there is

HIS SERVICE TO THE WHOLE COUNTRY.

one public benefit which he rendered that ought never to be forgotten. Though the war was over, he still stood in public relations in which he could render an immeasurable service to the whole country. There are no crises in a nation's life more perilous than those following civil war. The peace that comes after it is peace only in name, if the passions of the war still live. After our great struggle, the South was full of inflammable materials. The fires were but smouldering in ashes, and might break out at any moment, and rage with destructive fury. If the spirit of some had had full swing, the passions of the war would have been not only perpetuated, but increased, and have gone down as an inheritance of bitterness from generation to generation. This stormy sea of passion but one man could control. He had no official position, civil or military. But he was the representative of the Lost Cause. He had led the Southern armies to battle, and he still had the unbounded confidence of millions; and it was his attitude and his words of conciliation that did more than anything else to still the angry tempest that the war had left behind. A soldier in every drop of his blood, he accepted the result, not with muttered imprecations on his lips, but frankly and honestly, like the brave man that he was; and from the hour of surrender, acknowledged it to be his place to be henceforth a true and loyal citizen of the Republic. As the war had been ended in the field, he held that it should be ended everywhere. And nothing roused his spirit, usually so calm and self-controlled, to anger so much as to hear the hisses and curses that found vent in the more violent papers of the South. On one occasion, after reading such ill-timed words, he said, "I condemn such bitterness wholly. Is it any wonder the Northern journals should retort upon us as they do, when we allow ourselves to use such language?" Even if it had not been from a sense of the injustice of this violence of speech, and the impolicy of reviving passion and hatred, he had too much respect for himself and for his own people to indulge in such recriminations. The whole South felt the force of his example. Even the old soldiers of the Confederacy could accept what had been accepted by their Leader; the sight of their great Chieftain, so calm in defeat, soothed their anger and their pride ; and as he had set the example, they deemed it no unworthy sacrifice for them to become loyal supporters of the restored American Union. It is therefore not too much to say that it is owing in great measure to General Lee that the Civil War has not left a lasting division between the North and the South, and that they form to-day One United Country.

These are grateful memories to be recalled now that he who was so mighty in war, and so gentle in peace, has passed beyond the reach of praise or blame. Do you tell me he was "an enemy," and that by as much as we love our country, we ought to hate its "enemies"? But there are no enemies among the dead. When the grave closes over those with whom we have been at strife, we can drop our hatreds, and judge of them without passion, and even kindly, as we wish those who come after us to judge of us. In a few years all the contemporaries of General Lee will be dead and gone; the great soldiers that fought with him and that fought against him, will alike have passed to the grave; and then perhaps there will be a nearer approach of feeling between friend and foe.

"Ah, yes," say some who admit his greatness as a soldier and leader, "if it were not for his ambition, that stopped not at the ruin of his country!" Such is the fatal accusation :

"Cæsar was ambitious:
If it were so, it was a grievous fault,
And grievously hath Cæsar answered it."

But was that ambition in him which was patriotism in us? How is it that *we* who were upborne for four years by a passion for our country, that stopped at no sacrifices, connot understand that other men, of the same race and blood, could be inspired by the same passion for what they looked upon as *their* country, and fight for it with the same heroic devotion that we fought for ours? They as well as we were fighting for an idea: we for union, and they for independence—a cause which was as sacred to them as ours to us. Is it that what was patriotism on the one side, was only ambition on the other? No: it was not disappointed ambition that cut short that life; it was not the humiliation of pride; but a wound that struck far deeper. One who watched by him in those long night hours, tells me that he died of a broken heart! This is the most touching aspect of the great warrior's death: that he did not fall on the field of battle, either in the hour of defeat or of victory; but in silent grief for sufferings which he could not relieve. There is something infinitely pathetic in the way that he entered into the condition of a whole people, and gave his last strength to comfort those who were fallen and cast down. It was this constant strain of hand and brain and heart that finally snapped the strings of life; so that the last view of him as he passes out of our sight, is one of unspeakable sadness. The dignity is preserved, but it is the dignity of woe. It is the same tall and stately form, yet not wearing the robes of a conqueror, but bowed with sorrows not his own. In this mournful majesty, silent with a grief beyond words, this great figure passes into history.

There we leave him to the judgment of another generation, that "standing afar off" may see some things more clearly than we. When the historian of future ages comes to write the History of the Great Republic, he will give the first place to that War of the Revolution by which our country gained its independence, and took its place among the nations of the earth ; and the second to the late Civil War, which, begun for separation, ended in a closer and consolidated Union. That was the last act in the great drama of our nation's life, in which history cannot forget the part that was borne by him whose silent form lies within this sepulchre.

Only a name! As I took a last look at the recumbent statue, I observed that its marble base bore no epitaph ; no words of praise were carved upon the stone : only above it on the wall was the name,

ROBERT EDWARD LEE,

with the two dates,

BORN JANUARY 19, 1807;
DIED OCTOBER 12, 1870.

That is all: but it is enough ; any eulogy would but detract from the spell of that single name:

"One of the few, the immortal names,
That were not born to die."